Imagination and
Meaning in
Calvin and Hobbes

T0105980

EDITED BY JAMEY HEIT

Vader, Voldemort and Other Villains:
Essays on Evil in Popular Media
(McFarland, 2011)

Imagination and Meaning in *Calvin and Hobbes*

Jamey Heit

McFarland & Company, Inc., Publishers
Jefferson, North Carolina, and London

LIBRARY OF CONGRESS CATALOGUING-IN-PUBLICATION DATA

Heit, Jamey.
    Imagination and meaning in Calvin and Hobbes / Jamey Heit.
      p.   cm.
    Includes bibliographical references and index.

    ISBN 978-0-7864-6354-1
    softcover : acid free paper ∞

    1. Watterson, Bill. Calvin and Hobbes.   2. Comic books,
strips, etc.— United States.   I. Title.
PN6728.C34H45 2012
741.5'973 — dc23   2012001141

BRITISH LIBRARY CATALOGUING DATA ARE AVAILABLE

Cover art © 2012 Brenda Carson

Manufactured in the United States of America

*McFarland & Company, Inc., Publishers
  Box 611, Jefferson, North Carolina 28640
    www.mcfarlandpub.com*

For Jon,
a gifted explorer and better friend

Acknowledgments

This book would not exist without the help of a great many people. First and foremost, I offer my thanks to Bill Watterson for giving the world such an imaginative gift. I think people really are better off having spent time with Calvin and Hobbes. I am also deeply grateful to Universal UClick for the permission to quote from Watterson's text.

There are any number of intellectual imprints on this work from my family, friends, and colleagues. Specific thanks are due to Dr. A.K.M. Adam at Glasgow University for his patience in helping me brush up on my Greek; to Dr. Will Williams for sharing his recent dissertation on irony; Professor David Jasper for providing the right tools when I needed them, and Professor George Newlands for his continued encouragement.

As always, my wife continues to be a bedrock of support, no matter how crazy my adventures may seem. My infant daughter was infinitely patient in the early hours of the morning in listening to me work through some of the more difficult ideas in this book. Finally, I extend my infinite gratitude to my brother for knowing exactly what strip I needed when I called for help.

Table of Contents

Introduction

Graham Allen introduces *Intertextuality (The New Critical Idiom)* with a basic point about what a reader expects from a text. He writes: "[When] we read a work of literature we are seeking to find a meaning which lies inside the work."[1] This "commonsensical"[2] anticipation follows from a basic logic: "Literary texts possess meaning; readers extract that meaning from them."[3] Despite the simplicity that this equation brings to questions about what a text means, as readers search for this meaning they quickly find that their goal is a rather elusive target. Meaning is a composite of the various factors that gather in and around the text. Authorial intent, a reader's associations, the text's latent properties, and many other factors coalesce to provide a context wherein the reader must decipher the text's aggregate significance. Not surprisingly, this comingling can produce unexpected results. Thus, texts are really intertextual spaces characterized by a plurality of meanings. The result is that the reader's simple task of unearthing meaning turns out to be a more complex undertaking. Rather than shutting a book and positing a definite sense of what the text means, the reader must continually retrace[4] its constituent parts, a task that inevitably generates new meanings.

When confronting the text's refusal to grant a definitive reading, there is a common tendency to respond by retreating to tidy summaries that refuse the always present multiple possible readings. In response to the frustration that can result when the text will not fit into the category that a reader determines, there is often a stronger claim that the reading in question is the "right" one. Allen echoes this point in cautioning against a single definition of intertextuality, a term coined to contain the intertextual spillover that frustrates the search for meaning.[5]

Intertextuality is, then, a concept that complicates hermeneutics,[6] yet in its disruption it ensures that a text is given room to breathe deeply. Allen's introductory remarks lift out from a wide, deep, and often dense

1

critical discussion several important textual features I intend to highlight at the outset of this book. First and foremost, he emphasizes that a text cannot (and indeed should not) be reduced to simple formulae. Texts are expansive in their ability to bring into conversation a variety of experiences. In *Calvin and Hobbes*, this complexity is a crucial asset insofar as it permits the text to accommodate critical analysis and leisure reading. Though it is a comic strip, it is an intertextual space just like any other text. The various influences — verbal, visual, allusive, to name a few — give rise to a particular space that in turn leads to numerous readings. One can interact with *Calvin and Hobbes* as "just" a comic strip, but to do so cuts off access to the unpredictable meanings that are, at times, buried deeply.

The desire to explore the textual space that *Calvin and Hobbes* establishes grows out of this point. When read as an intertextual space, Calvin's world reveals a vast reservoir of meanings. As a result, a boy's adventures with his stuffed tiger speak to some of life's deepest questions. Calvin's tense relationship with Susie Derkins, for example, opens an ordinary schoolyard occurrence into a reflection on how to find meaning amidst life experiences that appear overly burdensome. This is a simple point from a much larger dynamic at work in *Calvin and Hobbes* — namely, the freedom the text grants to imagine different meanings in response to the circumstances, often unexpected, that constitute life's journey.

The second point to highlight from Allen's introduction is the reader's task in tracing the text's constituent influences. A distinction within this broad point is helpful. In tracing the text, the reader can follow any number of presences. As will become apparent in the analysis that follows, in *Calvin and Hobbes* there are frequent nods to significant concepts in the West's intellectual tradition. These allusions enrich the particular contexts in which they appear, and, moreover, when read collectively they provide a more nuanced appreciation of who Calvin is and, therefore, why he might do some of the things he does. Other considerations bring about similarly expansive readings. The visual elements of a particular strip often mirror the verbal exchange and thus advance a narrative. At other times the visual components can undermine the meaning that appears at first glance. When engaging an intertextual space, one must be mindful of these numerous influences — many of which remain unseen — that complicate meaning. The flip side of this intricacy is that as these references surface they support further readings, which in turn lead to more meanings.

A further derivative that follows from Allen's emphasis on tracing the relationships within text is that the reader who traces them is, in essence, another text. The various biases and expectations a reader brings to the text inevitably mold particular readings to produce certain meanings. On the one hand, this is an entirely legitimate way of engaging the text. At the same time, it places a specific burden of responsibility on the reader to identify the limits of one's own engagement with the text. I highlight this point at the outset of this book to address up front the notion that I offer readings that are my own in their understandings, associations, and meanings. While I hope the readings I offer are interesting and perhaps enhance other readers' experiences with *Calvin and Hobbes*, it is important to state outright that what is discussed throughout this book in no way constitutes a normative understanding of the text.

In claiming these readings as my own, I indicate a further point that must be voiced. Discussing the thematic parallels I see between *Calvin and Hobbes* and other texts does not mean that Bill Watterson meant for me (or any other reader) to associate a particular strip with a particular idea. For example, just because I see a common denominator between Calvin's behavior at the dinner table and Blaise Pascal's Wager does not mean that Watterson had this idea in mind when he wrote a particular strip (though I similarly will not claim that he did not have this idea in mind). A reader who is aware of his assumptions must acknowledge the gap between the author and the reader if he is to enjoy the freedom to find meaning in *Calvin and Hobbes*. This book, then, is not about discovering Watterson's motivations in a given strip (though I am sure there are many such treasures buried in unexpected places). This book is about a particular approach to the text and a personalized search for meaning. As is the case when engaging all intertextual spaces, this is a legitimate undertaking, yet the results constitute only a single thread in the web of meaning that characterizes *Calvin and Hobbes*.

While this book is decidedly an academic exercise, it is worth noting a non-scholarly assumption: *Calvin and Hobbes* is an engaging text. I say this to emphasize that I find reading *Calvin and Hobbes* to be an intellectual exercise of some depth, whether one is reading a single strip or the entire collection. There are multiple opportunities to explore the kinds of analogous readings I offer, which ultimately provide a broader search for meaning. On a related note, I state another assumption: I appreciate *Calvin and Hobbes* on an academic and personal level. While I bracket the latter consideration for the vast majority of what follows — with a handful of asides when the meaning I find in the strip is too good to pass up — I argue that a critical engagement with Calvin's adventures adds significantly to a pleasurable reading. There is thus another intertextual layer at work in my analysis. This admission serves to highlight the indefinite number of considerations that inform a reading of any text and, I believe, enhance the arguments I offer.

I have tried, then, to strike a balance in constructing my overall argument. On the one hand, it is important to offer a close textual analysis in order to trace (some of) the various meanings that function within the examples I have chosen to analyze. On the other hand, there are frequent tangents that refine the point at hand. In order to maintain a certain cadence in how I bring *Calvin and Hobbes* into conversation with the figures and ideas that I read alongside the strip, I have placed some of the denser points that arise in the endnotes. While there is often the (intertextual) temptation to skip over the notes, they are expansive in order to provide further side streets to explore should the reader feel inclined to trace what I am tracing in a bit more detail. There are frequent references to strips from *Calvin and Hobbes* that I do not discuss in detail, yet in providing these signposts the hope is that readers will find some measure of value in venturing further into Calvin's world. Though I offer what I take to be good examples of a point at hand, there are often other strips that could similarly be discussed. Of course, even those I list in the endnotes are not exhaustive in scope; with each re-reading of the entire collection, another example to support a point frequently emerges.

Having articulated these introductory points, I can state the overarching thesis in this book: *Calvin and Hobbes* enables an imaginative search for meaning that is unique to the space it occupies. Calvin embodies many of life's challenges, and the capacity in which he seeks to understand these occurrences provides a space wherein readers can similarly reflect upon how particular experiences from their lives — or, perhaps, life in general — clarify, enhance, or frustrate meaning. The underlying ability to consider specific circumstances in different ways is a direct result of the imagination's privileged role in Calvin's world. Consequently, the title of this book captures the structuring concern throughout the discussion below: The imagination opens the text into new meanings, which release the individual from the often paralyzing frustration that accompanies the human condition. This argument assumes a certain conception of what defines humanity.

While I discuss these presuppositions in more depth throughout this book, at the outset I will highlight a common theme in *Calvin and Hobbes*: Life is difficult because it often unfolds in a way contrary to what we expect.

A key factor that causes this disruption is the long reach of the question about what we consider to be valuable in life. Because human life is ultimately fragile, questions about the self and whether or not there is some divine reality relevant to human life become harder to answer. The moments when Calvin shows vulnerability in response to the potential for loss are symptomatic of why the imagination plays an important role in finding meaning. There are times when reason fails to reconcile what Calvin thinks with what goes on around him. In such circumstances his imagination provides meaning in a capacity he cannot find otherwise.

This book is separated into two sections. The first four chapters examine issues of meaning as they relate to specific textual features. In the first chapter I discuss how reading *Calvin and Hobbes* alongside major thinkers associated with Critical Theory helps to understand the openness that characterizes the strip. Through his deconstructive reading strategies, Jacques Derrida indicates how a text's necessary absence of meaning is the first step towards a discovery of multiple meanings. Thus, the impossibility of "fixing" a meaning enables the text to resist closure, which in turn allows it to accommodate an infinite number of readings. As a result, there exists always the possibility to re-read that which has already been read. The end of a single strip, a narrative arc, or indeed the entire collection remains an invitation for the reader to examine again how the imagination opens into new possible meanings.

Chapter Two expands on the themes I have discussed in this Introduction. By elaborating on how the imagination functions, I strengthen the deconstructive points made in Chapter One. By holding the text open, these elements give rise to specific kinds of textual spaces, which I demarcate in order to highlight the tension that occurs when Calvin's imagination takes over. Because the text straddles multiple viewpoints in this capacity, it is able to manifest meanings that speak in more varied ways. The implication of this complex relationship between the imagination and reason thus serves to highlight the ability of the former to generate meanings the latter cannot conceptualize.

In Chapter Three I discuss in more detail how to conceptualize *Calvin and Hobbes* as a text. There are two distinct discourses that give rise to

Calvin's world: the verbal and the visual. By examining how these elements interact, the relationship between Calvin's real life (i.e. the life he experiences when interacting with others besides Hobbes) and his imaginative departures from that context come into focus. By finding an outlet from life's stresses in his imagination, Calvin is able to recalibrate his experiences in the real world as meaningful in a more fulfilling capacity. This oscillation relies on the dynamics that the two discourses enable, which is the stepping off point for the entire strip. These textual issues make clear that the strip functions because the imagination can cross over the boundary between the real and the imaginary. This foundational dynamic speaks, in turn, to the central role imagination plays in generating meaning within *Calvin and Hobbes*.

Chapter Four discusses how irony affects the dynamics outlined in the two previous chapters. As a frequent pivot between the real world and the imaginary contexts to which Calvin flees, irony thus announces how a particular understanding will unfold and, moreover, affects the subsequent experiences (often in surprising ways). Paradoxically, the consequence of irony's enriching presence is its ability to undermine the very meaning it permits, a fact that frequently brings different — and often combative — meanings into close proximity. Calvin's viewpoint often clashes with the secondary characters that appear repeatedly, and in such cases irony's presence allows these different characters to interact in a way that extends the imagination's reach.

Having discussed these different textual issues, the book then moves into the second section wherein I discuss three specific areas of meaning. In Chapter Five I focus specifically on the concept of the self and how this individualism affects the kinds of meanings Calvin entertains. More specifically, his attempts to navigate life rest upon a certain conception of value that is decidedly self-oriented. By drawing on the Danish philosopher Søren Kierkegaard's notion of the aesthete, I identify specific tendencies in Calvin's value system that constrain where he finds meaning when seeking the kinds of immediate gratification that Kierkegaard associates with the aesthete. I then bring three examples from Plato's dialogues alongside Kierkegaard in order to further my discussion on how these limits usually prove unsatisfactory in Calvin's search for meaning.

After discussing how an individual can define value in wholly self-interested terms, I then discuss in Chapter Six how the individual looks to others to find a more sustainable meaning. The bond of friendship is, of course, a central theme in *Calvin and Hobbes,* and thus I examine this specific relationship between the individual and the other as the groundswell of a more lasting kind of meaning. In the context of this discussion I draw on Aristotle and Plato's conception of friendship to indicate how the relationship between Calvin and Hobbes reflects long-held values concerning the role of the other in overcoming some of the anxieties that the self cannot outrun on its own. A specific concern is the different capacities in which friendship can function, which in turn articulates the different ways Calvin and Hobbes engage in a relationship that is at times uneven yet ultimately an enduring source of meaning.

In Chapter Seven I turn to the search for meaning in categories that transcend life. In discussing the various contexts in which Calvin struggles to understand his experiences as part of a larger narrative, I highlight how *Calvin and Hobbes* engages with some of life's "big questions." In reflecting on these, I then examine how the various answers that emerge in the text influence subsequent questions about what is good in life and the important corollary to this value structure: how one should behave. In the end, these different issues return to the question of whether or not some divine agent/presence/god exists, and, therefore, if there is a connection between the values Calvin embraces in life and the possibility that these values might affect his afterlife. Throughout this discussion there emerges a tendency for Calvin to realize that answers are hard to come by, a realization that emphasizes the fragility of life and the difficulty of finding meaning that helps to make sense of life.

To conclude this book I return to the initial concern: how the imagination generates meaning. The Conclusion specifies that this question demands certain considerations — such as life's fragility — that in turn warrant gestures towards something/someone beyond the world. The implication is that meaning may not be wholly available in life, but there exists other possibilities in which the individual can account for the human condition. As a result of this point, the Conclusion considers again the dichotomy between reason and the imagination in order to explain how the latter is able to extend into spaces reason cannot reach.

CHAPTER ONE

One Final Sledride

The Imagination's Endless Freedom

On December 31, 1995, *Calvin and Hobbes* rode their sled for the final time. By then, more than 2,400 newspapers were carrying the strip, a presence that generated a fan base numbering in the millions.[1] The result of this last adventure, according to Lucy Caswell, the former curator of the Billy Ireland Cartoon Library and Museum at Ohio State University, was palpable; among fans of the strip, there was "true emptiness."[2]

Despite the closure the final strip establishes, a closer look at the text reveals a regeneration that Bill Watterson's work achieves even as it ends, an openness that is the specific result of the imaginative construct that governs the strip. The first panel in the December 31, 1995, strip shows Calvin trudging eagerly across a field, waist-deep in snow, his familiar smile indicating he is anxious to experience the "fresh, clean start"[3] that awaits. Hobbes echoes the excitement Calvin feels: "It's like having a big white sheet of paper to draw on!"[4] In this context, there is only one thing to do, which Calvin announces as the sled rushes down the hill towards the strip's border: "Let's go exploring!"[5]

Though Watterson's fans were sad to see the strip end, this final adventure captures the breadth and depth of what he accomplished in his ten years of work. The strip's imaginative framework opens continually into a world of interpretive possibilities. Though some read this openness in hope that the strip might someday return,[6] the note that sounds during this final adventure engenders a different kind of expectation. An erasure occurs, one that announces the end of the strip by sledding into re-readings of Watterson's work. The blank canvas is both the emptiness of further storyboards, as well as the freedom to revisit the adventures that preceded Calvin and Hobbes' final departure.

Importantly, in this final strip Calvin and Hobbes' final journey is never complete. They remain just inside the final border; their smiles contain a lingering trace of their previous adventures. This image calls to mind a salient feature of Deconstruction: the impossibility of fixing meaning that results from a constant textual play. The border reiterates the freedom the reader has in following Calvin and Hobbes through their final sled ride. This interpretive openness is a hallmark of the strip and, according to Derrida, an inbuilt reminder of how meaning emerges. Derrida writes, "No one inflection enjoys any absolute privilege, no meaning can be fixed or decided upon. No border is guaranteed, inside or out."[7] The final strip bears out this caution; there exists throughout *Calvin and Hobbes* a resistance to simple readings. As a result, attempts to ascribe a definitive meaning to the strip falter. As Derrida explains, such hermeneutical instability is a hallmark of the text: "The self-identity of the signified conceals itself unceasingly and is always on the move."[8] Within the literal border that contains the strip, meaning oscillates and, therefore, permits the reader to import her/his own meanings. Derrida recognizes in this textual movement the freedom to engage the text on its own terms, which in turn requires that no one meaning can be set forth as definitive.[9]

Despite the text's constant play, there exists a trace as it unfolds. The reader can follow a pathway as s/he traverses the text because, Derrida explains, "That pathway must leave a track in the text."[10] The trace indicates this pathway, which, paradoxically, both anchors the text and disperses possible meanings. Derrida continues: "The trace is not only the disappearance of origin — within the discourse that we sustain according to the path that we follow it means that the origin did not even disappear, that it was never constituted except reciprocally by a nonorigin, the trace, which thus becomes the origin of the origin."[11] In the final strip of *Calvin and Hobbes*, one can see how the trace accents the text in order to erase meaning. The sled leaves the slightest track in the snow as a mark of the unfolding adventure, which simultaneously establishes the strip's closure and its openness to further adventures in the reader's imagination. For Calvin and Hobbes, this is both the final and first sled ride because the adventure begins anew with every re-reading. Furthermore, this duality holds the text open in order to accommodate new readings, each of which depart from an origin that is not present. The adventure cannot be anchored to a specific meaning, and, as such, the text resists the final reading implied within the context of the last strip Watterson published.

As a mark of the text's play, the trace reminds the reader that the text remains subject to the variations that its own play generates. According to Derrida, "It is in the specific zone of this imprint and this trace, in the temporalization of a *lived experience* which is neither *in* the world nor in 'another world,' which is not more sonorous than luminous, not more *in* time than *in* space that ... make them emerge as such and constitute the *texts.*"[12] The trace, then, "*is the difference* which opens appearance [*l'apparaitre*] and signification."[13] Derrida outlines a dense textual process, but when reading *Calvin and Hobbes* through this critical lens, the effect Derrida describes becomes clear; in *Calvin and Hobbes* this dynamic produces obvious effects. For example, when faced with the need to write a story for school, Calvin expresses frustration in not being able to constitute a text. He laments: "This is the worst assignment ever! I'm supposed to think up a story, write it, and illustrate it by tomorrow! Do I look like a novelist? This is impossible! I can't tell stories!"[14] Hobbes, however, disagrees and offers a helpful suggestion: "What about your explanation of the noodle incident?"[15] Calvin offers a spirited defense in response: "That wasn't a story! That was the unvarnished truth!"[16]

The noodle incident affords an excellent example of the dynamic Derrida articulates. The reader encounters an event within the text that exists within the zone that the question of truth opens. Watterson explains that the noodle incident's purpose is to encourage readers to imagine the context to which this exchange (and others) refers.[17] The effect is the sonorous invitation to the reader to occupy the textual space that coalesces around the disjunction between Hobbes' suggestion and Calvin's response. More broadly, Watterson introduces an idea that is a trace of some previous incident. No one knows what, exactly, occurred; this conversation about the noodle incident is a trace of some unwritten event. Calvin lived the noodle incident, and the text is constituted through the textual play that refuses a clear account of what actually happened. The imaginative possibilities thus open through the difference between what the reader encounters and the nonorigin that Hobbes recalls in bringing up the noodle incident.

This dynamic can be seen in a different, anticipatory capacity frequently found in *Calvin and Hobbes*. The trace not only invites the reader's imaginative involvement with the strip through a constructed memory, it also projects the reader into possible readings. Julian Wolfreys summarizes well how Derrida approaches a text:

> The notion of "reading" is one that implies a comprehensive commentary on ... [a text] in its entirety, an achievement that is impossible. One can

never *finally* read or claim to have read a text in its entirety. One must continue carefully to read and re-read, because the act of reading is always marked by a continually receding horizon.[18]

Those who posit a final reading attempt to fix what Derrida argues against: a textual anchor that resists the text's necessary and continual play. In such cases, Derrida explains, positing a center serves "not only to orient, balance, and organize ... but above all to limit what we might call the play of the structure."[19] The noodle incident clarifies yet again the concept at hand. It is precisely because Watterson never reveals what occurred that the text invites the reader to imagine what might have happened. A definitive account remains forever outside the text, erased in and through the act of reading. The incident disorganizes the text in the sense that it forever leaves the reader moving toward the specific horizon of meaning with which the noodle incident frames the text.

What remains undefined thus encourages the act of reading insofar as it demands the necessary re-readings that Derrida identifies. According to Wolfreys, "What remains unread therefore is not which the future holds as the final promise of the closure of reading. It is that which is always to come, always coming at any given moment of reading.... This is the secret of literature."[20] Watterson's ability to pique his readers captures the importance of denying a final reading. Watterson's secret, so to speak, lies in the always unspoken origin to which the trace speaks; the noodle incident structures the text precisely because the reader can never know what happened. This impossibility enables multiple contexts in which the elusive trace of the noodle incident advances specific contexts in which the noodle incident arises.

In her helpful guide to Derrida's *Writing and Difference*, Sarah Wood calibrates the point at hand in a way that strengthens the reading of *Calvin and Hobbes* alongside Derrida. She writes, "Derrida keeps beginning, he is the absolute beginner par excellence and this is why it's so important to read him in a spirit of beginning and re-beginning, with a kind of second-order naivety."[21] The circularity that appears to cast the text into an endless pursuit of an impossible clarification is precisely the magic that Watterson generates by withholding whatever actually happened during the noodle incident. When the noodle incident reappears in the text after a lull, the specific context allows the reader to re-imagine the events to which the trace refers. The different ways in which Calvin not only denies responsibility for whatever happened but also affirms that his explanations are objective[22] capture the endless beginnings that the noodle incident creates. Because there is no textual anchor — when, where, and why the incident happened will forever remain unspoken — the imagination can wander. This spirit is the freedom that Derrida's deconstructive readings allow. By resisting the notion of textual closure, Derrida ensures that the text always accommodates the interpretations that anticipate and follow on from the point in the text when the noodle incident surfaces. In other words, Derrida happily encourages readers to go exploring in the text's endless possible meanings.

The result of Derrida's analysis is a text that permits multiple interpretive possibilities and therefore refuses a closing off of the text. There must always be space to re-read, and this is a distinct characteristic of *Calvin and Hobbes*. An example from later in the strip's run captures the need to leave the text open. Hobbes walks over as Calvin looks up from his activity. Excitedly, he invites Hobbes into the context of what he is doing: "Look Hobbes. I got a paint-by-numbers kit! It's really fun!"[23] Hobbes then points out an obvious departure from what the paint-by-numbers kit implies: "But you're not painting in the lines and you're not using the colors that correspond to the numbers."[24] After looking down at his work as he considers Hobbes' comment, Calvin offers a response that conveys the salient issue at hand: "If I did *that*, I'd get the picture they show on the box!"[25] Calvin's explanation captures the elusive characteristic that allows *Calvin and Hobbes* to be an enduring text. He announces that the text is open to interpretation through his refusal to paint by numbers. The activity of painting by numbers is, by definition, restrictive, yet in transcending the guidelines that frame the activity, Calvin engages in a meaningful, enjoyable activity. Hobbes' response emphasizes the point. Rather than expressing surprise, he offers a simple "Ah."[26] Hobbes indicates that a literal crossing of boundaries signals the broader thematic implications of Calvin's refusal. Watterson offers a rare insight into this element of his work in his preface to *The Complete Calvin and Hobbes*. He states, "As flattering as it is to have a lavish book like this, it can be a little disturbing to see one's own career embalmed in a box."[27] Just as Calvin resists instructions that prescribe what his efforts will produce, Watterson voices a similar distrust of efforts to contain the text in a tidy way. This refusal is, in the end, the constant imaginative departure from a controlled textual environment.

Calvin, then, makes clear (a point evident in Watterson's initial remark) that meaning derives from this release. Following instructions or reading only within a prescribed way produces an experience that offers no surprise. The instructions that accompany his paint-by-numbers kit convey an antecedent conclusion, which circumscribes the freedom of imagination that Calvin prefers. Similarly, Calvin's decision not to follow these guidelines offers the reader a similar interpretive opportunity to imagine what Calvin might be painting (as with the noodle incident, the reader will never know based on what the text offers). This strip thus refuses to engage in the kind of definitive reading that Derrida cautions against. Yet again one finds the necessary disjunction that engenders meaning. Derrida's notion of *différance* clarifies the significance of resisting the "reading" that a painting by numbers would provide. Derrida writes: "One can expose only that which at a certain moment can become *present*, manifest, that which can be shown, presented as something present, as being present in its truth."[28] *Différance*, then, reveals the continually possible reading that emerges in the moment wherein the reader mirrors Calvin's willingness to discard an antecedent "meaning." As a result, one can recognize with Calvin that not painting by the numbers is the best possible way to engage the text imaginatively.

The text, then, is *différance*. In this conception, one realizes that "[the text's] *Différance* is not only irreducible to any ontological or theological — ontotheological — reappropriation, but as the very opening of space in which ontotheology — philosophy — produces its system and its history, it includes ontotheology, inscribing it and exceeding it without return."[29] Calvin offers a self-reflexive example of how *Calvin and Hobbes* enables readings that exhibit significant depth. Several salient issues for the argument below warrant mention, given the entire strip avoids following the instructions, so to speak. The invitation to explore Calvin's world is predicated on the exclusions that Derrida identifies. There is no final reduction of the text; the strip does not offer a fixed hermeneutical baseline against which to measure Calvin's adventures. There are, as will be discussed below, significant moral threads that develop during the course of the strip, but no one example can be pegged as directly correlating with a specific conclusion. Meaning emerges as the strip traverses any given context because at its core meaning is irreducible. Paradoxically, the lack of a definitive reading is the source of an endless number of possible readings.

In articulating the notion of *différance*, Derrida echoes the adventurous tenor that characterizes *Calvin and Hobbes*. When meaning is inscribed as the text unfolds, the reader can embrace the journey across the text as meaningful in its process. According to Derrida, approaching the text in this capacity is "adventurous because this strategy is not a simple strategy in the sense that strategy orients tactics towards a final goal, a *telos* or theme of domination, a mastery and ultimate reappropriation of the development of the field. Finally, a strategy without finality, what might be called blind tactics, or empirical wandering."[30] This wandering is the basis for the individual to interact with the text without antecedent expectations. As Valentine Cunningham argues, this deconstructive approach opens the text towards every individual's exploration: "But still there is evidently much to be gained in the strong personal encounter, in intimate self-reflections and self-satisfactions in the reading encounter, and not only if they're what entice readers into texts and keep them enticed by reading."[31] In emphasizing the individual's personal encounter with the text, Cunningham recalls the final strip of *Calvin and Hobbes*. The reader shares the intimate moment wherein Calvin and Hobbes sled down the hill for a final (and initial) adventure. The delicacy with which Watterson handled the strip's conclusion thus becomes apparent. Millions of readers share the moment on their own terms because the text does not demand a specific acquiescence to a particular reading. The result, Cunningham suggests, is to follow Calvin's lead in not painting by numbers: "reading as it were by numbers, by algorithm, a kind of automated, mechanistic hermeneutics."[32] To bring a rigid framework to the text when reading is to limit the opportunity for the text's openness to accommodate multiple readings.

There exists, then, a strong need to avoid reading the text in a capacity that denies its elusive, elastic nature. According to Cunningham, there exists a simple caution to keep in mind when bringing a critical analysis to bear on a particular text. Quite simply, "Theory is, all too often, bad for texts."[33] There is an uncomfortable irony[34] in this claim that is nonetheless true. A reading that precludes further readings fails to uphold the text's integrity. This is not to discount Theory's ability to bring to light significant concerns within a text; as Derrida makes clear, an incisive reading can, through its deconstructive effects, provide fresh meanings. The problem occurs when Theory prescribes "models of their [the text's] being, their ontology, their essence, their nature, are driven by a huge negativity and despair, but because of how it promotes a view of text and so of readings of texts which plays fast and loose with the idea and then also the praxis of a demanding textual thereness."[35] When reading a text becomes a kind of calculus, the text's essential magic is lost. The things Cunningham identifies as symptomatic of bad reading are the things that prohibit the text's freedom to prick the reader's imagination, and, moreover, the reader's freedom to interact with the text in her/his own way.[36]

One of Calvin's signature activities reflects clearly the need to heed Cunningham's advice. Calvinball appears in response to a prescriptive set of rules that for Calvin makes baseball less than enjoyable. After spending a recess on the playground with Susie, Calvin has to sign up to play baseball because other boys tease him endlessly. After doing so, he explains to Hobbes the root of his dislike: "I signed up to play baseball every recess, and I don't even *like* baseball that much."[37] This is precisely the reason not to be playing if one follows Cunningham's argument. When the joy of the activity (be it playing baseball or reading about Calvin playing baseball) is lost, the activity loses its ability to provide meaning to those involved. Unfortunately for Calvin in this particular circumstance, those involved with the baseball game are the source of the problem, and therefore there is no way to play the game in a way that is enjoyable for him. Calvin explains to Hobbes: "I mean, it's fun playing baseball with just *you*, because we both get to pitch, bat, run and catch all at once. We get to do everything.... But this will be with *teams* and assigned positions and an umpire! It's *boring* playing it the *real* way."[38] The activities and instruments for baseball are not the problem; the issue is how these things are structured. The game as it will be played at his school requires adherence to a set of predetermined rules. This is fine in some contexts, but Cunningham's point is clear how such restrictions smother the freedom to explore the context in question on one's own terms. The fact that Calvin mentions the umpire (who never actually appears in the strip) amplifies this point. The umpire's presence will enforce the rules, which, as Calvin makes clear, he finds restrictive and therefore reason enough not to enjoy the game.

A few strips later, within the same narrative thread, Calvin's fears are manifest. He is in deep left field, and the lack of activity — a clear opposite to the openness his version of the game permits — leads to an exploratory monologue: "I think baseball is the most boring game in the world. I've been standing out here in deep left field all this time, and not a single ball has come out here!"[39] The opportunity to reflect more deeply on his dislike of baseball when playing in an organized context reverses the immediately prior appearance of baseball in *Calvin and Hobbes*. In the Sunday strip from August 6, 1989, the reader can follow the kind of baseball that both Calvin and Hobbes prefer.[40] With no dialogue, Watterson shows Hobbes winding up and sending a pitch well over Calvin's head. Calvin, of course, watches the pitch that is out of the strike zone, but Hobbes calls him out on strike three (the obvious conflict of interest of the pitcher serving as the umpire does not register). Calvin argues his case by gesturing that the pitch was far too high, but Hobbes retorts by signaling what for him is the real problem: Calvin is too short. A dust-kicking argument ensues, which, as many disagreements between the two friends tend to do, turns into a wrestling match. Both friends finally collapse out of exhaustion before Calvin says something to Hobbes, who listens intently. The final panel indicates the solution Calvin suggests; he stands on a ladder to continue the game, a compromise that affirms both players' sides of the initial disagreement.

A different conflict emerges out of the organized version of baseball that Calvin plays at school. When he does catch a fly ball to left field, it turns out that his team was batting, so the out he makes is against his own team.[41] Calvin's teammates berate him for his mistake, an experience he endures with an uncharacteristically crestfallen face. Whereas he exerts his side of the argument with Hobbes, here Calvin reveals how deeply the encounter affects him negatively. In the next frame, Calvin responds in a way that echoes Cunningham's caution against prescribed reading: "C'mon guys, it's just a *game*! This is supposed to be fun!"[42] The point is the activity, the freedom of playing a game (or, for Calvin, imagining the game as another one of Spaceman Spiff's adventures[43]). The other kids' antecedent expectations reduce the game to a zero-sum experience; a nameless teammate responds angrily that "Games are only fun when you *win*."[44] The activity is good only because it results in victory, which necessarily means that it is not fun for the other team. This understanding the game is one of the many points that Calvin expresses in reminding the other kids what the purpose of playing is in the first place. Games should be enjoyable for all involved.

Importantly, this exchange undermines the very argument that Calvin's teammates make. The confrontation thus occurs in a way that strengthens the disconnect between the rules and what is enjoyable. Despite their emphasis on rules, the players who are mad at Calvin ignore the fact that the umpire would not have let the pitcher commence if a player on the batting team were still in the field. The rules, then, are helpful only when they provide a specific benefit at Calvin's expense. A broader point thus emerges when considering Cunningham's warning. Clinging to rules often limits the experiential opportunities that the situation in question would otherwise provide. Additionally, this restriction is often upheld at the cost of the argument's legitimacy. The kids on Calvin's team require a scapegoat for the threat to their victory, but they are wholly unaware that any such victory is pyrrhic given the way they approach the game itself. With regards to the text, this example emphasizes the need not to preclude other readings in order to support one's own understanding of a given text.

The organized nature of the team sport thus limits Calvin's ability to experience the specific context of baseball, which in turn provides a clear example of how the freedom to explore is a crucial element of *Calvin and Hobbes*. To emphasize this point, following Calvin's unsuccessful foray into organized sports, Watterson introduces an alternative. In the spirit of the strip, this game is unhinged from all of the factors that make Calvin's experience with playground baseball an ordeal. That weekend, away from school, Hobbes asks Calvin what he wants to do. Calvin answers that he would like to do "Anything but play an organized sport."[45] Hobbes' suggestion to play Calvinball immediately changes Calvin's expression from reserved to elated. The final panel captures the essence of imaginative freedom from restrictive preconditions. Hobbes states the underlying point in this particular discussion: "No sport is less organized than Calvinball!"[46] Calvin's response punctuates the claim; he makes up a rule on the spot that "if you don't touch the 30-yard base wicket with the flag, you have to hop on one foot!"[47] The absence of rules allows Calvin to condense baseball, football, and capture the flag into a game that ceases to resemble any of these recognizable — and now unorganized — constituent parts.

The next appearance of Calvinball nearly a month later summarizes what is at stake in Calvinball as an imaginative alternative to rules. In the midst of a good game, Calvin comments: "The only permanent rule in Calvinball is that you can't play it the same way twice!"[48] This is precisely the kind of enticement that brings readers back to the strip and continues to offer new possibilities for exploration. Calvin and Hobbes imagine a game that is essentially not a game by virtue of its complete lack of structure. Paradoxically, the single rule is that no rule can contain what unfolds next. Derrida explains the implications of this paradox: "That which gives us to think beyond the closure cannot simply be absent. Absent, either it would give us nothing to think or it still would be a negative mode of presence."[49] Consequently, Derrida calibrates the text's absence (of rules, in the example concerning Calvinball) in a way that permits endless play: "Presence, then, far from being, as is commonly thought, *what* the sign signifies, what a trace refers to, presence, then, is the trace of the trace, the trace of the erasure of the trace."[50] As this indefinite series of erasures spills through the text, the reader thus finds that a definitive structure will "evade us forever."[51] For some, the text's elusive nature is confusing at best and to be avoided at worst, but in Derrida's conception the impossibility of fixing meaning is precisely the text's invitation. Stated differently, for those who want to play Calvinball but require an explanation of the rules to proceed, the game will prove frustrating. For others, however, the very lack of rules is the endless beginning that Calvinball offers. This is one of the strip's defining legacies. As will become apparent in the argument throughout this book, the ability to deconstruct the circumstances that act as rules is how *Calvin and Hobbes* generates meaning. The world Watterson constructs is one that resists the mindset that Calvin's classmates exhibit about what it means to play a game. The text, like Calvinball, should be explored without constraints, a hermeneutical freedom that enables the endless re-readings that make *Calvin and Hobbes* a welcoming text.

Given this emphasis on textual openness, a fundamental disjunction that gives rise to meaning is crucial to the textual world of *Calvin and Hobbes*. The central conceit is similarly open to endless interpretation: Is Hobbes "real?" In the first two strips the reader encounters the Hobbes that occurs the vast majority of the time. He is alive, active, and participatory in whatever Calvin is doing. The reader meets Hobbes in this guise. When Calvin goes to check his tiger trap in the first-ever strip, the final panel shows Hobbes, hanging upside down, eating the tuna sandwich that Calvin uses as bait. His first words mirror Calvin's expectations; in Calvin's world, tigers are "kind of stupid in that way."[52] From Calvin's perspective, Hobbes is not only real, but the imagination does not even consider this a relevant point. Calvin is clearly using his imagination because presumably there are few tigers roaming about in whatever suburban neighborhood Calvin lives (to say nothing of what these tigers like to eat). What matters from the outset is that Calvin and Hobbes act in a way that is not constrained by the reality of the world that Calvin occupies. The text unfolds on its own terms, which in turn permits the imaginative freedom that prompts Calvin to set his tiger trap and causes Hobbes to take the bait.

The second-ever strip extends the notion that Hobbes functions in the same capacity as Calvin. Tiger in hand, Calvin asks his dad what to do next. His dad answers in a way that parallels how the first strip introduces Hobbes. The thing to do is to feed Hobbes, which Calvin does emphatically in the final segment of the strip. It is only in the third strip that the reader encounters Hobbes' other side. When Calvin's dad tells Calvin to be quiet, Hobbes is no longer active. Rather, he appears as a stuffed animal, inanimate and certainly unable to "do" things that Calvin says he was doing. Hobbes calls attention to the disjunction at work by defending himself against Calvin's explanation for all the noise: "Well, *you* were the one playing the cymbals."[53] These few words establish the duality that governs the rest of *Calvin and Hobbes*. To one set of eyes, Hobbes is merely Calvin's stuffed tiger, while in Calvin's world — which the reader must enter imaginatively to recognize the depth of the world that Watterson creates — Hobbes is able to function not just as a living tiger but also as an anthropomorphic tiger.[54]

As the basis for the world in which *Calvin and Hobbes* exists, Hobbes provides the crucial textual fulcrum for generating meaning. Like the openness that encourages re-readings, examining this disjunction with Derrida's critical scaffolding offers insight into the capacity in which meaning emerges throughout the strip. In *Margins of Philosophy*, Derrida locates in a text's (non-) origin the ability to accommodate the kind of paradox that characterizes Hobbes. Derrida writes, "Because the metaphoric is plural from the outset that is does not escape syntax; and that it gives rise, in philosophy too, to a *text* which is not exhausted in the history of its meaning (signified concept or metaphoric tenor: *thesis*), in the visible or invisible presence of its theme."[55] Hobbes' paradoxical identity enables the text; if he were just a stuffed tiger or just a figment of Calvin's imagination, the strip would not function. Watterson affirms the ability of Hobbes to slide between realities as crucial to the world in which Calvin and Hobbes go exploring:

> When Hobbes is a stuffed toy in one panel and alive in the next, I'm juxtaposing the "grown-up" version of reality with Calvin's version, and inviting the reader to decide which is truer. Most of the time, the strip is drawn simply from Calvin's perspective, and Hobbes is as real as anyone. So when Calvin is careening down the hillside, I don't feel compelled to insert reminders that Hobbes is a stuffed toy. I try to get the reader completely swept up into Calvin's world by ignoring adult perspective.

Hobbes, therefore, isn't just a cute gimmick. I'm not making the strip revolve around the transformation. The viewpoint of the strip fluctuates, and this allows Hobbes to be a "real" character.[56]

Hobbes' reality is an entry point into the text, which in turn enables the text to be explored as a groundswell of imaginative meaning. The decision to accept this basic conceit is, for the reader, not a simple suspension of disbelief. The dual nature that characterizes Hobbes requires an acquiescence that is hardly simple. Traversing *Calvin and Hobbes* is, as will be discussed in more detail in the following chapters, a reading that exhibits the distinct willingness to confront a reading of the human condition that is far from simple. On this point David Jasper offers a helpful reminder: "There is no privileged 'innocent' point of access to a text."[57] In applying the term metaphor, then, one does not discount the complexity of Hobbes' function in the strip.[58]

Hobbes, then, emphasizes the importance of context for reading *Calvin and Hobbes* imaginatively. His dual role calls attention to an important textual property: Context is "never absolutely determinable ... never certain or saturated."[59] By eliding reality, Hobbes dislocates a simplistic understanding of Calvin's world, which plays a crucial role in accommodating explorative re-readings. As a result, Derrida highlights the role that absence plays in determining the contextual parameters of a text such as *Calvin and Hobbes*. The first is the ability to do exactly what Hobbes does: be present and absent simultaneously. Derrida clarifies this effect: "This operation of supplementation ... is not exhibited as a break in presence, but rather as a reparation and a continuous, homogenous modification of presence in representation."[60] The reparation is, in effect, the play that contains the secret of literature. The simultaneity of Hobbes' presence to Calvin and absence (as a non-presence in Calvin's terms) is, in Derrida's words, "born at the same time as imagination and memory, at the moment when it is demanded by the absence of the object for present perception."[61] The tension that this duality generates provides the basis for Calvin and Hobbes' adventures and, moreover, the events that follow.

As discussed above, the imaginative construct at work in *Calvin and Hobbes* holds the text open in order to allow imaginative readings to emerge. In the case of the noodle incident, the effects are clear for the reader. At other times the result of Hobbes' ability to be both present to Calvin and absent from others is to extend the narrative context at hand by juggling various viewpoints. When Calvin secedes from the family, he and Hobbes do not get very far before they descend into a fight. Calvin decides to return home in hopes that his parents have neither moved nor rented out his room.[62] He frantically rushes home and tells his mom that he still wants to be in the family, and then proceeds to spend the rest of the day as he normally would. It is only when his mom tells him that it is bedtime that Calvin realizes Hobbes is still out in the woods.[63] With the same urgency that he ran home to make sure his parents still wanted him to be their kid, he runs out the door, flashlight in hand, to look for Hobbes.

From Calvin's perspective, Hobbes is still lost in the woods and unable to find his way home. The interesting aspect of this particular narrative arc is how Calvin's parents respond to the situation. They deserve credit for their willingness to search in the dark for Hobbes, who from their perspective will remain wherever the fight occurred because he is a stuffed tiger. For both parties, Hobbes is lost, but the urgency to find him is decidedly different, which in turn continues the narrative as two distinct stories (though Calvin's mom does call out to Hobbes, which causes the two perspectives to intersect momentarily[64]). His textual presence, to recall Derrida, follows from his absence, which in turn generates two contexts for perceiving Hobbes. This duality manifests continually a present representation of Hobbes' narrative absence in the actions of the two parties. Within the strip's structure, then, Hobbes' absence extends both the storyline and the imaginative anxiety that this experience generates. The ability to accommodate simultaneously each of these viewpoints indicates how the context that Derrida mentions remains in flux. This dynamic ultimately keeps the text open to different readings and, therefore, different meanings.

Even after Calvin's dad returns Hobbes safely, the two ways of reading Hobbes' absence continues to generate different perspectives. How Hobbes got back ignites a further disagreement between the two friends. He tells Calvin that he "got so bored I hiked back."[65] Accepting this explanation requires a significant imaginative leap for Calvin because, speaking literally, this cannot have happened. Still, from Calvin's imaginative perspective, Hobbes' explanation makes perfect sense and, therefore, brings the narrative towards resolution. Thus relieved that his friend managed to find his way home, Calvin rushes to tell his mom that everything is o.k., which again brings the two perspectives into conflict. She tells a different story to explain Hobbes' return: "Your dad found him last night and brought him in."[66] Upon hearing this, Calvin confronts Hobbes angrily, which speaks to his understanding that Hobbes lied in claiming he walked home on his own. The disjunction is obvious, as Calvin is speaking angrily to Hobbes, who is depicted as a stuffed tiger. This disjunction illustrates how Hobbes' identity can juggle the multiple perspectives that drive the strip. Importantly, there is no resolution to this meeting of viewpoints. Calvin's mom continues what she is doing, and Calvin's accusation hangs in the air, but the text never addresses how Calvin and Hobbes sort out the competing explanations about what happened. The result is that the reader can imagine what comes next based on the events that lead to this point, which in turn generates continued narrative meanings.

The invitation to return to the space that Calvin and Hobbes traverse one final time is the critical entry point for the exploration that follows. In reading *Calvin and Hobbes* alongside Derrida's deconstructing analysis, one can recognize the implicit invitation Watterson extends in Calvin's exhortation to explore the strip's world. Timothy Clark discusses the specific possibility that books afford their readers in such circumstances:

> A book seems to lack in its very material solidity the separation which, for instance, sets off at once a work of architecture or painting. Reading, freeing the work from its author and opening it to an anonymous horizon of public readability, grants the work this necessary separation: "to read is not to write the book again, but to allow the book to *be*."[67]

For Watterson, this point is a crucial part of Calvin's world; the space to be entered is one that accommodates multiple adventures, but the expectation is that readers will engage Calvin's world on its own terms.[68] An important point of clarification is helpful at this point with respect to the argument that follows. First, the decision to enter the world of *Calvin and Hobbes* rests with the reader, and the critical insights to follow cannot be ascribed to Watterson. Attempts to bend what occurs in the text back to a particular motivation Watterson might have had in developing the strip cannot be substantiated. As such, the readings that occur throughout this book affirm a disjunctive relationship between Watterson and his readers.

The need to bracket Watterson from the text may sound problematic, yet the gap between the author and the reader is an important consideration when examining *Calvin and Hobbes*. As such, it is a point that warrants a brief excursus that should clarify the need to keep separate Watterson's authorship from the analysis at hand. Making claims about how *Calvin and Hobbes* reflects anything beyond an imaginative strip is a dangerous thing to do. From a critical perspective, such arguments would run directly afoul of Cunningham's guidelines for not limiting a text's potential meanings. A particular instance of trying to decode Watterson's motivations can be seen in attempts to prove the claim that Calvin is an autobiographical composite of Watterson's life. Again, such presuppositions limit the text's openness. It is important to note, then, the distance that Watterson establishes between his life and Calvin's adventures: "One of the reasons that Calvin's character is fun to write is that I often don't agree with him."[69] While Watterson does admit that he shares with Calvin an interest in the topics that emerge in the strip,[70] there is little to be gained either from trying to pry Watterson's life out of *Calvin and Hobbes* or, similarly, from injecting Watterson into the strip's textual dynamics.

At the same time that Watterson is clear in his desire to project the integrity of his intellectual work, he is equally straightforward in releasing *Calvin and Hobbes* to be read as an open space to be explored. On this point Watterson is clear:

> The only part I understand is what went into the creation of the strip. What readers take away from it is up to them. Once the strip is published, readers bring their own experiences to it, and the work takes on a life of its own. Everyone responds differently to different parts.[71]

Watterson's explanation echoes the responsibility that any reader has for engaging the text on the text's terms. Cunningham offers a helpful summary of these demands: "Theory's maps may help, but its maps, like any map, will always need supplementing, supplementing by the reading equivalent of walking down the street for yourself."[72] In positing the readings below, it is important to highlight the extent to which this chapter (and, indeed, this project) draw on theoretical/critical sources. Reading *Calvin and Hobbes* through Deconstruction's lens reveals the intellectual ballast that the strip contains. Derrida's critical apparatus identifies how the text, in its refusal to accommodate a closed reading, yields the multiple possible readings that enrich the text's identity.[73] At the same time, the reader cannot rely solely on the scaffolding that critical resources such as Derrida's analysis erect around the text. This chapter's remarks, then, are meant both as a recognition of how others can enrich a reading of *Calvin and Hobbes* while simultaneously outlining the results of the particular explorations that follow. This dual nature reflects, in the end, how Calvin's and Hobbes' relationship defines the strip, and, moreover, the implications of that relationship for the capacity of their adventures to engage the reader.

The corollary to this point is that when engaging (and entering) the world that Calvin and Hobbes explore, one must resist the temptation to bend the text back to Watterson's supposed motivations. The main characters' names offer a helpful look at the risk of mis-handling the invitation to wander the strip in a way that makes too much out of Watterson's intentions. In the case of Hobbes, the name is a stated nod to Thomas Hobbes. Watterson explains that the name indicates "a dim view of human nature."[74] Given Watterson's background in philosophy as an undergraduate,[75] there exists a strong risk of plunging too deeply into a textual feature that does not support a definitive, correlative reading.[76] Hobbes certainly views humans with a measure of suspicion, but beyond a handful of instances, the need to make sure that he fits this profile ultimately limits Hobbes' character within the text. When one assumes that Hobbes is a direct embodiment of a philosopher's ideas, the result is a narrow reading.

This point of caution crystallizes when one considers Calvin's namesake: John Calvin, one of the key figures of the Protestant Reformation. On the one hand, Watterson is clear that there is a link between Calvin the boy and Calvin the reformer: "Calvin is named for a sixteenth-century theologian who believed in predestination."[77] Though there are clear examples in *Calvin and Hobbes* that examine the theme of predestination, any thematic link between Calvin and his namesake ranges from implicit to coincidental, as the strips that examine issues similar to predestination are broad in scope.[78] Even when a particular strip picks up this idea, the context does not make any clear reference to Calvin the reformer's theology. Moreover, the examples in which Calvin invokes this point do not cohere with the reformer's understanding of predestination.[79] More broadly, there is very little in Calvin's world that suggests a specific faith tradition, though there are occasional echoes of specific Judeo-Christian texts that could be intentional.

One of the more interesting examples of a (possible) reference to a specific Christian text occurs in the poem "A Nauseous Nocturne" that Watterson wrote specifically for *The Complete Calvin and Hobbes*. As Calvin is about to meet his end at the hands of a monster in his bedroom, he implores Hobbes to wake up.[80] The specific language and narrative arc echo strongly the scene in the Garden of Gethsemane wherein Jesus laments that his disciples cannot stay awake during his final hours. Jesus' rebuke to Peter is essentially the same as Calvin's rebuke to Hobbes: "So, you could not stay awake with me one hour?"[81] In raising this similarity for consideration, it is important to note that these connotations are thematically linked by virtue of a related narrative context. In both cases the protagonist is about to meet his end and longs for the support of his friends. Each then suffers the disappointment of realizing that these close friends were unable to meet the urgency that the unfolding events demanded. That being said, however, one will notice in drawing out the similarities that there is no specific mention of any theological points. The parallels are there, but they should not be taken to suggest anything beyond the imaginative possibilities that an analogous reading enables.

In addition to this specific distinction between Calvin and his namesake, there is very little in Calvin's personality that suggests a coherence with the strict moral life that the reformer led, much less with the motivations for living this life. A simple example should make this point clear enough. A particularly troubling thread begins when Calvin rips his pants as he leaves the swings at the end of recess.[82] Unfortunately, this is the day he is wearing underwear with little rocketships — and when everyone has to do a problem on the chalkboard.[83] The potential embarrassment is enough to prompt Calvin to reach out to some higher power to prevent the disaster the reader knows is coming. In all earnestness, Calvin pleads, "Please, don't let the teacher call on me! Don't make me go to the board in my ripped pants!"[84] A few points deserve mention in response to Calvin's thoughts. First, this is one of the few examples wherein the reader has access to Calvin's thoughts as opposed to something spoken. This particular insight, in combination with the embarrassment he wants to avoid, speaks to the strength of his anxiety. The second salient point to mention is that this plea is to a nondescript listener. Though there are implicit religious overtones at the beginning of this strip — which become explicit by the strip's final panel — Calvin's request is unfocused with respect to the assumed listener. This, in turn, frames his anxiety not in any kind of denominational terms, but, rather, as a distinctly personal interest.[85] In combination with the fact that this plea is thought and not spoken, the motivation is clearly to avoid an immediately relevant experience.[86]

In the final panel of this strip, what Calvin is thinking becomes thematically clear, which in turn establishes a particular disjunction between Calvin and the reformer for whom he is named. When Ms. Wormwood asks Calvin to do a problem on the board despite his gritted teeth, clasped hands, and profuse sweat, a look of cynical frustration crosses his face. He mutters his disappointment: "So much for my joining the clergy."[87] This final panel reveals that Calvin's initial pleas are actually prayers, which connote the listener is God (though, again, there is no specific reference to who/what this God might be). For such a strong prayer, Calvin shows remarkably little faith in the sense that his desires are wholly separate from any kind of institutional religious context. While he is praying, the content in question ultimately reflects a desire to avoid embarrassment. This example distances Calvin from his namesake because there is no specific link between showing the class his rocketship underpants and a nascent Reformed Theology. The professed desire not to join the clergy can be seen as a punch line, which, given the immediately prior detail, would be a viable analysis. There is, however, an important kernel of truth in Calvin's comment; the reason he will not join the clergy is that his specific manifestation of "faith" does not pay dividends. Stated differently, there is very little depth to the prayer he utters, which indicates a religious identity that is decidedly different than Calvin's (i.e. the reformer) commitment to his faith.

Some might argue that this is stretching a point, but Watterson provides helpful ballast in defending the argument. He describes how when he writes he allows his characters to experience the events at hand from their own perspective.[88] Calvin's immediate recourse to prayer thus reveals a bit of truth about his willingness to adopt a religious identity. He is, then, completely honest in his response to Ms. Wormwood. This faith — however convenient — is one that reflects an understanding of the world from Calvin's perspective, which in this particular instance conceptualizes God in a way that really cannot be reconciled with Calvin the reformer's understanding of God and prayer. Calvin writes in the *Institutes*: "We see nothing that is set before us as an object of expectation from the Lord which we are not enjoined to ask of him in prayer."[89] The motivation for seeking God's help in prayer should be a response to God's character as manifest in the Bible. While there is no specific mention of praying to avoid math problems at the chalkboard, one can assume safely that John Calvin would not count Calvin's specific prayer as something God enjoins. The motivation for prayer is crucial for John Calvin, as it reflects the specific character of the one who prays. Thus, when Calvin says he will not join the clergy, he really is distancing himself from his namesake, even if this claim requires an analogous reading. In the end, there exists an irreconcilable difference of character between Calvin the boy and Calvin the reformer, and this lack of congruence should limit comparative readings that attempt to associate them too closely.

Despite these cautions, there are still more than a few attempts to posit a meaning in *Calvin and Hobbes* than the text strains to accommodate. A good example can be found in Richard Beck's essay "The Theology of Calvin and Hobbes' Part I, Chapter I: '*Virtue needs some cheaper thrills.*'" Beck takes into account Calvin's name in a particular reading of how the strip explores whether human nature is good or evil.[90] Drawing on the link between Calvin the boy and Calvin the reformer,[91] Beck offers the following reading of how Watterson presents the question of whether humans are good or evil:

> For readers new to *Calvin and Hobbes* it is difficult to overstate just how much this question dominates the strip. This should not be surprising given the names of the two lead characters. Calvin is named after John Calvin, the 16th Century theologian who strongly endorsed St. Augustine's notion of *Peccatum Originale*, what Christians refer to as "original sin." Notoriously for some, Calvin preached a doctrine of the "total depravity" of man. The Protestant Reformer Martin Luther framed this doctrine in an interesting way, stating that "every good work is a sin." That is, human self-interest contaminates all human endeavors, nothing we ever touch can be "clean." We are all stained.[92]

On the one hand, the point of entry into this analysis is well-taken; in *Calvin and Hobbes* there are clear and frequent examinations of human nature with respect to questions of good versus evil (one of the most obvious examples of this question is the extended narrative wherein Calvin adds an ethicator to his duplicator and is thus about to create a duplicate that is a manifestation of his good side).[93] The fact that Beck does not cite this example when offering his take on how Watterson examines human nature in *Calvin and Hobbes* is a single example among many that indicates the danger of insisting on a direct correlation between the text and a specific reading of that text. Ultimately, Beck's analysis exposes the danger of projecting Watterson's textual nod too forcefully into the entire strip's world. Calvin's ruminations on good and evil do not reflect a sustained theological characterization of an important theme throughout the strip. Beck's own analysis undoes this suggested reading in another essay that makes the claim that "Calvin is self-indulgent."[94] Calvin the reformer was a complex man, but one would be hard-pressed to portray him as self-indulgent in the same capacity that Calvin the boy is.

What Beck makes clear in reading is the importance of striking a balance when examining *Calvin and Hobbes*, as this project has done and will do. Watterson offers a world that frequently alludes to a thinker, a concept, or a narrative that is part of the West's intellectual story (which is yet another example of the intertextuality that characterizes *Calvin and Hobbes*). At times this reference is obvious. Such examples enrich possible readings insofar as they open the strip towards further readings of what can be perceived as inconsequential, or constructed in the interest of a particular strip's punch line. What does not occur in such instances, however, is the setting of a particular reading. Just because Calvin shares his name with a Protestant reformer does not mean that one should filter every instance wherein the strip reflects on human nature as a theological statement on original sin.

Given the context in which this point is made, the following disclaimer is important. The analysis throughout this book engages in reflections that are similar to what Beck offers. The crucial difference, however, is the conclusion that such readings offer. Whereas Beck attempts to support an overarching claim, the ideas presented in this project identify thematic parallels. Such readings are meant to offer further ways to interact with the world Watterson has created. In so doing, there is no normative claim for either Watterson's intentions or for subsequent readings. In recognizing how consonant themes enrich the strip, there is no attempt to claim a structuring element. Even a clear tip of the hat to a particular idea does not necessitate that the reader understand the text *only* through this filter. The text remains open, always, for further exploration.

A specific example will help to clarify the methodological point at hand. The strip dated March 6, 1994, brings together two discordant worlds. In the first frame Calvin sticks out his tongue in disgust in response to the mound of green food in front of him. After poking the food with his fork in the second frame, the food comes alive in the third frame. An imaginative reframing or departure from what is on the dinner table is a conceit that Watterson uses frequently. In this instance a pointed interaction unfolds when the food begins to recite some of Western literature's most recognizable passages: Hamlet's "To be or not to be" soliloquy.[95] One could offer an analysis of this literary condensation that follows in Beck's footsteps. For example, the fact a nondescript pile of food opens into a serious ontological reflection demands attention. Hamlet's ultimate conclusion about life remains a significant critical question; Shakespeare leaves plenty of textual ambiguity about whether Hamlet thinks he should live or die. Watterson, however, implies a particular reading of the passage by having the dinner stick a fork in its own head. This decisive act punctuates the final words that the dinner speaks: "For in that sleep of death, what dreams may come when we have shuffled of this mortal coil must give us pause."[96] The frame that follows shows Calvin reflecting on this point, which extends the ontological tension about whether life is worth living.

The point, of course, is that Watterson undercuts the link between Calvin's meal and Hamlet in what follows the end of the soliloquy. As Calvin scratches his head in a bewildered manner, the meal breaks into song: "Feeheelinggs. Wo, wo, wo."[97] The punch line comes when Calvin does what he often will not do when it comes to dinner; he finishes his plate. The disjunctive serves to undermine the suggestive link between Calvin's world and *Hamlet*. As a result, this strip reveals not how deeply Watterson embeds his intellectual allusions into the text, but rather how he expands the range of meanings the text supports. Richard Kearney offers a helpful analysis of this dynamic: "The 'perhaps' thus solicits a 'yes' to what is still to come, beyond all plans, programs, and predictions. It keeps the ontological question of 'to be or not to be' constantly in question, on its toes, *deferring* any last word on the matter."[98] The text refuses hermeneutical closure, and, consequently, one finds another example of the dynamic that Watterson captures so well in the final strip of *Calvin and Hobbes*. The point of his allusions to western figures is to encourage imaginative readings, just as Calvin resorts to his imagination to frame his experiences.

Calvin's encounter with the Hamlet-like meal reiterates the textual demands that Derrida identifies. The reader cannot settle on a final reading, and therefore s/he must avoid the rushed conclusions that Beck reaches. Derrida emphasizes that when reading, one must not be "in a hurry to be determined."[99] As a result, Sarah Wood explains while discussing Derrida's caution, is the need to discard tidy readings like the one Beck offers: "Derrida [finds] effects of detour, delay, delegation, division, inequality and spacing at work in the effects he analysed, so that they no longer have the simplicity and predictability that make concepts indispensible to the concept of philosophical systems."[100] The March 6, 1994, strip makes clear why readers must unhinge some associations from Calvin's world. Even when a clear textual echo frames the text, the result is, as Watterson makes clear when the food starts to sing, the emergence of an unexpected experience. For readers of *Calvin and Hobbes*, this lesson is helpful. Calvin inhabits a world that is always unpredictable by virtue of the imaginative release that *Calvin and Hobbes* allows.

The connective thread in this opening discussion is the imagination's ability to transform the text into a space that allows the reader to seek meaning alongside Calvin and Hobbes. Just as Calvin's imagination underwrites his adventures, this faculty enables a departure in response to the context that one seeks to understand. In *On Paul Ricoeur: The Owl of Minerva*, Richard Kearney highlights the imagination's role as the conduit between the reader, the text, and what meaning is possible: "As one moves from description to interpretation ... the imagination is considered less in terms of 'vision' than in terms of 'language.' Or, to put it more exactly, imagination is assessed as an indispensable agent in the creation of meaning in and through language."[101] Contrary to an understanding of what the term implies, the imagination is, in Kearney's conception, a specific derivative of the text. While it does constitute a departure from the actual circumstances that an individual experiences, it retains elements of the context that gives rise to the kinds of wanderings Calvin frequently undertakes. When he imagines that his food becomes Hamlet, the point of departure is the experience of sitting at the table and having to eat food he does not like. More broadly, Kearney suggests that the imagination is both a part of and a consequence of language. In the discussion that follows throughout the rest of this book, this point is crucial. The imagination cannot be bracketed fully in examining how Calvin searches for meaning (just as the reader cannot jettison her/his imagination if s/he is to engage the text as it stands). It filters through the particular narratives that range from the mundane to the fantastic. Meaning arises precisely because this adaptability molds the text's language in order to demarcate a space wherein the reader can join Calvin in the journey through life.

Chapter Two

When Dinosaurs Fly

Creative Spaces in Calvin and Hobbes

The topic of the imagination is admittedly broad. Current philosophical discussions center on the connection between the imagination and emotion. In the abstract of their chapter "Imagination and Emotion," Timothy Schroeder and Carl Matheson summarize well this current trajectory: "The particular topic is the power of imaginative acts to move us emotionally. How imaginative acts have this power has been an ongoing topic of discussion within the philosophy of art under the heading 'the paradox of fiction,' and has also been taken up by recent work on the imagination more broadly."[1] As a result, Schroeder and Matheson explain, "over time, the view has emerged that these acts have their power to move us through their activation of special cognitive attitudes, akin to beliefs in structure and in some of their effects, but distinguished from beliefs in others."[2] In light of this overview, Schroeder and Matheson frame their argument as follows: "While the emotional power of fictions has been a special topic of study in the philosophy of art, the emotional power of the imagination more generally has not received the same scrutiny from the philosophy of psychology."[3] While the subsequent analysis is helpful in taking the pulse of how philosophers are exploring the imagination, the intricate nature of this chapter warrants a clear demarcation with respect to the analysis that follows and, more broadly, in the scope of this book. Cognitive issues within philosophy and psychology are important to understanding an ability that emerges from the latter and speaks to the former, but to dwell on the kinds of abstractions that Schroeder and Matheson present would be to divert attention from the point at hand — namely, to interact with an imaginative text. This point is worth mentioning at the outset to indicate in broad terms some of the salient issues that are relevant to a discussion of the imagination, but, as a textually based analysis, what follows in this chapter will generally stay clear of technical philosophical language. As a general rule, then, the analysis at hand will not wade too deeply into cognitive territory. In establishing this from the outset, the goal is to stay as close to the text as possible in order to highlight how specific manifestations of the imagination enable (and affect) the search for meaning in *Calvin and Hobbes.*

Calvin and Hobbes establishes a textual space through an imaginative construct. To understand the relationship at the heart of the strip is to accept how Calvin's world intersects and layers over the "real" world in which his relationship unfolds. The tension between these worlds appears frequently throughout the strip; a symptomatic example, then, will calibrate this chapter's discussion. The Sunday strip from January 24, 1993, tells a story through dinosaurs, a framework that immediately signals Calvin's imagination. This particular narrative thread begins with a herbivore munching away on some leaves. A carnivore then approaches — presumably to eat the herbivore — and the following panels convey the encounter that ensues. In the sixth frame, the imaginative framework slides into what is happening in the "real" world: Calvin throws a snowball and knocks over Susie Derkins. As she lies in the snow, angry, Calvin stops to think. The strip then returns to the dinosaur world, but with a different narrative tenor. The predatory carnivore (Calvin) runs away from the angry herbivore (Susie). Once safe in his home, Calvin marches up the stairs in disgust. The final panel shows several dinosaur books in Calvin's trashcan as he walks away.

Through the medium of dinosaurs, this strip transforms Calvin's real-life experience into an imaginative journey. While the events that unfold in the context of dinosaurs are, of course, fictitious, its events do not suggest anything beyond the kinds of things that happen throughout *Calvin and Hobbes.* The imagination welcomes the reader into a space wherein reality can be bent to explore how Calvin understands the events that unfold in real life. Two crucial features emerge out of this basic point, which in turn warrant extensive analysis. The first is the imagination's ability to transcend the limits of reality in order to wrestle with questions of value, identity, and life's big questions. The importance of the imagination to Calvin informs the parameters that inform how readers interact with Calvin's explorations on the page. The imagination is, in short, the connective tissue that permits readers to enter a world that is, at its core, a constructed space. In its ability to move between life's experiences and the texts that process such moments, the imagination invites skepticism insofar as it relates to both but can be contained in neither.[4]

Though issues within the broad heading of religion will be discussed in more length in Chapter Seven, an introductory point is helpful at the outset of the current thread. As Mark Knight and Louise Lee note in a recent volume of essays on literature and the imagination, religion is a particularly charged environment in which this critical issue emerges. For example, they cite both Freud and Marx as examples of thinkers who conclude that "Religion is little more than an 'elsewhere' to the here and now; a 'nowhere' for tomorrow."[5] The problem with this suspicion, Knight and Lee note, is that the very thing these figures seek to invalidate becomes the vehicle through which they articulate the reason why religion can be distilled into the imagination's fancy. The root issue in this specific context in which the imagination functions is a broader question about how the imagination fits with a normative Western conception of the individual. When reason provides the cornerstone for constructing a notion of the self, faculties that are seen as departures from this objective basis — the imagination or the emotions come to mind as constituent parts of the individual that a rationality-based system will look askance at — become unwelcome complications as opposed to valuable components of the self.

Even Immanuel Kant, who anchors the modern stress on reason, admits that the imagination escapes thorough categorization. Despite (or perhaps because of) the imagination's elusive nature, however, Kant exhibits an obvious suspicion when summarizing the imagination's character: "[The imagination] is a blind but indispensable faculty of the soul without which we would have no knowledge whatsoever."[6] The contrast with reason and its derivative, truth, is important to identify in order to argue against establishing the imagination as a feature of the human condition. Paradoxically, the distance from reason risks tying the imagination to this very faculty. Kearney posits that "there is increasing evidence to suggest that the death of the imagination also implies the death of a philosophy of *truth* (along with the corresponding notions of interpretation, meaning, reference, narrative, history and value)."[7] Without imagination, the argument goes, reason will lack the ability to respond to deconstruction's fracturing of experience. When analyzing a text, the consequences of this inability call into question the decision to relegate the imagination to a secondary (or tertiary) consideration in discussions of human nature. As will be discussed throughout this book, Kearney's words of caution ring true by affirming the imagination's ability to release the individual who suffers under the weight of reason's failure to endure the unstable condition that a postmodern analysis exposes.

Stated differently, the imagination's role in *Calvin and Hobbes*, as the aforementioned strip makes clear, requires the ability to navigate a space that is deconstructive. For Calvin, the imagination provides an outlet for a reality that often must be endured rather than enjoyed. Calvin's ability to conceptualize his dislike for Susie as something that could have occurred in the world of dinosaurs gathers the text in a way that engages the reader specifically through the disjunction between text and reality. The effect recalls Samuel Taylor Coleridge's reflections on the imagination.[8] In *Biographia Literaria*, Coleridge explains the faculty that "diffuses a tone and spirit of unity, that blends, and (as it were) fuses, each into each, by that synthetic and magical power, to which I would exclusively appropriate the name of imagination."[9] In its ability to fuse divergent elements, the imagination is, as Calvin makes clear, the gateway into transcendent worlds. Coleridge continues:

> This power, first put in action by the will and understanding, and retained under their irremissive, though gentle and unnoticed, control, laxis effertur habenis, reveals itself in the balance or reconcilement of opposite or "discordant" qualities: of sameness, with difference; of the general with the concrete; the idea with the image; the individual with the representative; the sense of novelty and freshness with old and familiar objects; a more than usual state of emotion with more than usual order; judgment ever awake and steady self-possession with enthusiasm and feeling profound or vehement.[10]

Textually, the imagination coordinates elements that otherwise could not be held in appropriate tension. Dinosaurs, Susie, and snowballs are disparate things that exist in the actual world, but in the imagination's freedom to fashion new meanings independently of what is reasonable, they make little sense as a cohesive unit. Through the imagination, then, these elements blur such boundaries and produce a fresh world that offers new insights into questions of meaning.

The fusion of different worlds risks a strong response, and in Calvin's case this response is not limited to the restrictions that the real world eventually imposes. The unexpected behavior of Susie the supposed herbivore lingers as this particular strip concludes. Her unexpected aggression does not cohere with what herbivores should do, but Calvin's response ultimately privileges the imaginative events that contain this unexpected turn of events. He does not find solace in the fact that his imagination undercuts reality. Rather, he extends the imaginative space by tossing the factual basis for the initial imaginative context. Stated differently, this overlap between a specific context and an imaginative release from such circumstances indicates that in the world of *Calvin and Hobbes*, the imagination trumps reality. Calvin could have dismissed the fact that a predator became prey as factually impossible, but he opts to retain the imagination's framework. The strip's final panel does not return the strip to the real context that precedes the opening panel. The result is a sustained emphasis on the altered state of emotion that Coleridge recognizes as an outgrowth of the imagination's function. Calvin's anger rejects the factual basis for his imaginative departure, which, despite his obvious frustration at how events unfolded, affirms the profound feelings at work in his encounter with Susie.

In the strip from March 19, 1989, one finds a mirror example of this dynamic that reiterates the point at hand. Bored at school, Calvin imagines that his desk turns into a triceratops, which then bursts through the school wall and releases him from the boredom he experiences in the classroom. Miss Wormwood interrupts this journey by reasserting the reality from which Calvin wants to escape. She slams her ruler across his desk, an act that yanks Calvin back into the reality that prompts his initial, imaginative departure. The disruption threatens to smother the imagination, but the desire to transcend boredom ensures that Calvin's imagination will begin again. Thus, Ms. Wormwood's act within the real world quickly gives way to another iteration of Calvin's dinosaur-themed daydream. A few panels later, Calvin's boredom morphs into a similar escape; he soars through the air — free once again from school — on the back of a pterodactyl. Like his imagined encounter with Susie, Calvin's dinosaur-related escape from reality ultimately resists the order that his actual experiences impose. The final word is a ride (without borders) that boredom cannot contain.

Another strong example of the imagination's freedom comes in one of the more unexpected twists in the dinosaur corpus from *Calvin and Hobbes*. A large panel foregrounds a group of triceratopses that warily munch on some leaves. Their uneasiness results from more than the usual evolutionary need to avoid the predators that hunt them. A close-up look at a triceratops' face gives way to this new danger: "Tyrannosaurs in F-14s!"[11] The lower panel stretches across the page, and in place of the worried triceratops the reader encounters a tyrannosaur pilot at the controls of its fighter jet. Another jet in the middle frame expands this imagined scenario; the second jet has two triceratops icons stamped on its side to indicate past successful hunts. Within the imagined context, these details strengthen the reason that the triceratopses are "jittery."[12] At the end of the strip the reader finally understands what leads to this strange combination of ideas: Calvin and Hobbes are playing with toy dinosaurs and toy fighter jets. Calvin exclaims: "This is *so* cool!" to which Hobbes responds, "This is *so* stupid."[13]

In *The Poetics of Space: The Classic Look at How We Experience Intimate Places*, Gaston Bachelard suggests what is at stake in Hobbes' decision to continue the game despite its stupidity. On one level the conjunction of dinosaurs and F-14s invites Hobbes' response. Bachelard explains: "It is easy for a rhetorician to criticize a text like this. Indeed, the critical mind has every reason to reject such images, such idle musings."[14] Framed in terms of what is reasonable — however one defines the term — the game will be subject to ridicule because it smashes together two ideas that are just not congruent by a reasonable standard. However, just because an image is absurd does not mean that it does not contain meaning. The problem, according to Bachelard, is: "because an exaggerated image is bound to seem ridiculous to a philosopher who seeks to concentrate being in its center."[15] If one predetermines what is an acceptable format in which to look for meaning, dinosaurs flying fighter jets will likely fall outside the boundaries in question.[16]

In a related narrative thread, Calvin gets in trouble at school for drawing a series of pictures that show dinosaurs flying rocketships. Though Ms. Wormwood does not understand, Hobbes gets the point right away.[17] Hobbes' receptivity here suggests that he understands what is at stake in combining incongruent things and therefore indicates why he is willing to play the T-Rex/F-14 game with Calvin: the imagination cannot be bound by reasonable standards. Bachelard summarizes that the imagination's freedom trumps the complaint that it cannot generate viable meaning: "Even when the criticisms of reason, the scorn of philosophy and poetic traditions unite to turn us from the poet's labyrinthine dreams, it remains nonetheless true that he has made a trap for dreamers out of his poem."[18] Herein lies the point that Hobbes' reaction makes. Even though the game is stupid, it still offers an allure that transcends the question of what is reasonable. This is the essential freedom that underwrites *Calvin and Hobbes* and highlights, therefore, the important role that the imagination plays in finding meaning.

Coleridge offers a further explanation of how imagination is at work in this strip. Quite simply, the rules of the imagined world outweigh the real context that gives rise to the imagination.[19] Any limits the real world imposes dissolve, and the freshness that Coleridge ascribes to the imagination becomes the text's focal point. Hobbes' response makes sense in the context of playing with toys; the idea is so implausible that it is stupid. The point, however, is not what makes sense in the real context out of which the idea of dinosaur pilots emerges. While absurd in some respects, this junction captures the power of the imagination to create contexts in which stupid things can be normative. Coleridge summarizes the point well: "The rules of imagination are themselves the very powers of growth and production."[20] Despite the skepticism it contains, Hobbes' comment ultimately yields to the idea that the imagination produces. No matter how ridiculous the idea might be in the context out of which Calvin combines dinosaurs and fighter jets, Hobbes does not stop playing. As Timothy Clark explains, the text demands this continued participation, even if this occurs in a context that stretches the imagination: "[It] is necessarily uncomfortable, even unsafe, and usually fleeting: for a space in which new norms may be established is itself necessarily outside the claim of given laws, a realm of uneasy trust."[21] Consequently, one finds again that the real world's limits do not override the freedom that characterizes the imagination. The process of growth that Coleridge mentions cannot be pruned; the rules that constricts what is or is not stupid in the actual world that Calvin occupies pale in comparison to the imagination's generative lack of rules. Thus, Coleridge explains, the imagination can overcome any contextual restrictions that frame a text: "It dissolves, diffuses, dissipates, in order to recreate: or where this process is rendered impossible, yet still at all events it struggles to idealize and to unify. It is essentially vital, even as all objects (as objects) are essentially fixed and dead."[22] In this capacity the imagination's freedom functions because of the text's disjunctive character. The lack of unity is not, then, a victim of the stupidity at hand. Rather, the stupidity becomes the mark of its continued invitation to engage with an imaginative release that transcends reason's limits.

Just as Calvin's ability to reconfigure life circumstances through his imagination releases the text into multiple interpretive possibilities, the occasional emphasis on reason produces the opposite effect. Too much reality can halt narrative momentum. A good example arises when Calvin stands in a field and sees a cloud that looks just like him (appropriately, perhaps, the cloud sticks out its tongue). After the image dissipates, the final panel offers Calvin's response: "Boy, there's nothing worse than an inscrutable omen."[23] In conceptualizing the cloud as part of some supernatural process, Calvin projects the experience into imaginative possibilities. His words leave the reader to envision what, exactly, the cloud might portend. The effect is to extend a single strip beyond its immediate context. The strip from the following day picks up on this effect. Hobbes walks over, and Calvin recounts what happened: "I saw a cloud that looked just like me!"[24] Hobbes' familiar caution does not engage the report immediately; he simply asks, "Really?"[25] It is important to note that Hobbes' lack of enthusiasm does not collapse the narrative arc at work. Just as his comments that the tyrannosaurs in F-14s are stupid does not lead him to stop participating, his remark similarly provides a foil that allows the imaginative context to swell, which in turn further accommodates the reader's interpretive options.

Calvin echoes this point when he elaborates on what, exactly, he saw in the cloud. He continues: "There was my head, huge and white, floating in the ethereal blue! Obviously it's a *sign!*"[26] At this point Hobbes engages the disconnect between the cloud and Calvin's understanding of what the cloud means. He asks for more information, and Calvin explains that the cloud is a sign of "very peculiar high altitude winds, I guess."[27] Given Calvin's ability to imagine entirely new worlds, on the heels of the energy that precedes this explanation one might expect a bit more. Instead, the reader encounters the dampening effect that a return to reality brings to bear on the text. The sign turns out to be meteorological activity. As a result, the possibility that lingers at the end of the July 6, 1992, strip fizzles; when reason intercedes for imagination, the imagination's powers of growth are stunted. Hobbes emphasizes the point: "Science kind of takes the fun out of the portent business."[28] He may as well be talking about the effect of Ms. Wormwood on Calvin's dinosaur daydreams, or Susie's inversion of Calvin's expectations. The subtext in each of these examples is that the imagination underwrites the strip's invitation to readers to explore Calvin's world.

The text's emergence into an imaginative space often occurs in unexpected ways. For example, Hobbes asks for clarity about one of Calvin's snowmen, which seems like a simple question based on the abstract nature of Calvin's snowmaking endeavors. In one particular instance the snowman is holding a snowball, which he examines with a deeply thoughtful expression.[29] When Hobbes asks what the snowman is doing, Calvin responds "He's contemplating snowman evolution. Obviously, if he evolved from a snowball, it raises tough theological questions for him."[30] Hobbes gets the point, and after pondering Calvin's explanation he suggests the kind of difficult theological question this snowman might ask: "Like the morality of throwing one's precursors at someone?"[31] Calvin concurs by adding a further difficult question the snowman might think about: "Sure, and what about shoveling one's genetic material off the walk?"[32] The imagination's reach in this encounter is apparent in a variety of ways. First, of course, is the fact that Calvin thought up this specific way to transform a simple snowman into a probing theological statement. The subsequent queries are certainly funny as follow-up questions to the initial point the strip makes, but they also reflect the capacity of an imaginative act to extend into a context that affords significant meaning.

The tough theological questions this snowman addresses suggest a casual tone in some ways. Hobbes' immediate association of throwing one's ancestors suggests a levity that Calvin echoes when he mentions shoveling one's genetic material off of the sidewalk. However, there is a significant subtext to this brief exchange between Calvin and Hobbes, which captures the ability of a simple imaginative act to provide a foothold for examining life. The first clue to this particular strip's complexity occurs in the language Calvin uses to describe what is going on in this snowman's head. This is one of two instances in *Calvin and Hobbes* wherein the word theology or its derivative occurs.[33] The presence of this term thus emphasizes the depth of the idea that the snowman conveys. The question of whether to shovel his genetic material off the sidewalk (which in itself is a suggestive contrast between science and religion) exhibits the depth to which theological inquiry reaches. The specific question, then, is not as important as the implications that follow on from that question. Carl Raschke explains that theological questioning exhibits a willingness to engage the deepest of possible meanings: "*Inquiry* means a searching and a questing/questioning that does not glide and ramble across the surface of things, but *dives into their very depths*."[34] Following on from Raschke's point, there are two specific characteristics that define the snowman's reflection, which in turn suggest how *Calvin and Hobbes* engages in the type of thinking that Raschke describes. The first important feature is one that is part of Calvin's identity: He embraces fully the search for meaning, often to the point of suffering consequences. There exists in Calvin's imaginative journeys a confidence that allows him to probe the depths that Raschke ascribes to theological inquiry. A corollary to this confidence is a willingness to be vulnerable, as theological inquiry almost invariably leads to questions of mortality.[35]

The second salient feature to mention is the importance of choice for undertaking theological inquiry.[36] Raschke summarizes the concept of theological inquiry in a way that grants the option of not traveling down life's deep tunnels of meaning. One can read this strip as another clever example of Calvin's snow-fashioning abilities; there is still plenty of meaning to be had in this capacity. The point that Raschke raises, however, speaks to the risk and reward that come with a willingness to continue beyond the meaning that floats on the text's surface. Martin Heidegger offers a dense but illuminating analysis of how theological thinking can speak to the unstable nature of the human condition: "Vanishing can also be an inconspicuous passing away into what is coming, into a decisive belonging to whatever is coming. Such vanishing into what is coming does not turn its back on what has been. Rather, such vanishing is intimately entrusted with what has been from out of the fullness of its own proper essence."[37] A theological examining from this snowman's perspective can speak to the human experience insofar as the transient nature of this snowman's existence forces him to consider that his time as a snowman is short-lived.[38] In one sense, this snowman will literally vanish by virtue of who he is; snow will melt and thus return both his complex nature and the snowball he considers back into water. He presumably recognizes in his theological inquiry that he, like the snowball, is fleeting. This reality echoes Genesis 3:19, which establishes this cyclical nature of the human condition: "You are dust, and to dust you shall return."[39] In Heidegger's conception, however, this melting away is a kind of renewal insofar as the water this snowman will become will again transform into snow once the cycle of precipitation completes its revolution. The essential fragility that characterizes the snowman mirrors the instability of life's journey. This, in turn, echoes the textual properties that Derrida associates with endless possible readings. In questioning theological matters, then, this snowman provides a measure of hope in the face of a condition that is essentially hopeless in its mortal (as far as snowmen go) nature.

When examining the role imagination plays in structuring *Calvin and Hobbes* in this capacity, a related point must be mentioned. The strip is the product of Watterson's specific imagination. As discussed in the Introduction, there is little to gain in this study from positing what Watterson's intentions were when writing and drawing *Calvin and Hobbes*; the point in revisiting this issue is to highlight how imagination binds together the author, the text, and the reader. Cunningham summarizes well the importance of this triad: "The whole history of criticism, of theorizing, is merely a history of the varying, shifting preoccupation across the ages with these three zones."[40] With respect to the reader, it is important to note that Watterson makes no claim on what s/he might bring to or get from the text: "Readers will always decide if the work is meaningful and relevant to them, and I can live with whatever conclusion they come to. Again, my part in all this largely ended as the ink dried."[41] Specific textual examples have been discussed which speak to the imagination's role within Calvin's world. What remains, therefore, is to discuss how the author's imagination affects the text. On the one hand, Derrida makes it clear that some intention lies behind writing's communicative act.[42] However, as Roland Barthes argues, the author's gesture indicates simultaneously the text's severance: "The [author's] hand, cut off from any voice, borne by a pure gesture of inscription (and not of expression), traces a field without origin — or which, at least, has no other origin than language itself, language which ceaselessly calls into question all origins."[43] This death, Barthes explains, opens the text by virtue of establishing a gap — the text — between author and reader: "Once the Author is removed, the claim to decipher a text becomes quite futile."[44] Reading must therefore be an engagement with the text as a space between the author and the reader. Consequently, Barthes is clear that the text cannot accommodate rigid analyses: "[To] give a text an Author is to impose a limit on that text, to furnish it with a final signified, to close the writing. Such a conception suits criticism very well ... when the Author has been found, the text is 'explained'— victory to the critic."[45] Barthes is clear that such victories are pyrrhic insofar as they smother the reader in claiming to pinpoint the authorial presence that fades as the text comes into being.

Barthes, then, offers a strong word of caution in attempting to categorize how Watterson's imagination manifests particular features in *Calvin and Hobbes*. As mentioned above, Watterson recognizes what is at stakes in writing and drawing the strip, and therefore, grants Calvin's world the freedom to unfold without antecedent restrictions. This willingness echoes

Barthes, who states, "We are now beginning to let ourselves be fooled no longer by the arrogant antiphrastical recriminations of good society in favor of the very thing it sets aside, ignores, smothers, or destroys; we know that to give writing its future, it is necessary to overthrow the myth: the birth of the reader must be at the cost of the death of the Author."[46] This point is helpful in response to those who read *Calvin and Hobbes* (or indeed any text) as a closed space. Watterson's absent gesture — the world that Calvin occupies — provides a space wherein the imagination is free to look for meaning on its own terms. According to Clark, the text thus remains "in a realm of discomfort, [with a] lack of assurance and uncertainty, but also ... [kept] open [to] the possibility of a non-violent, non-appropriative relation to being."[47] Even when the strip is no longer written, it continues to lie between the author and the reader, and therefore encourages the process whereby the reader's imagination mirrors Calvin's exploration. The reader, then, must follow in Calvin's footsteps and cease any attempt to find in those footsteps a specific imprint from Watterson's own imagination.

Perhaps not coincidentally, Watterson offers a strip that echoes this point. Towards the end of *Calvin and Hobbes*, the Sunday strip from May 28, 1995, addresses the issue of the subconscious. The first panel shows two Calvinesque workers descending into a sewer-like space. A worker who climbs down a ladder comments, "Ugh. I hate going to the subconscious."[48] Another worker, wading in sludge up to his waste, substantiates the point: "Me too! Why doesn't anyone ever clean up this dump?"[49] The workers then proceed to select a film as Calvin's dream for the moment. The conversation between the workers reveals the slippery nature of dreams. The evaluations of what is playing in Calvin's mind are telling. One worker labels the movie "awful," while another asks, "Why can't we ever watch anything good?"[50] Just before Calvin wakes up, an exchange between the workers crystallizes the point at hand. According to the first worker, "This makes no sense! What's going on?? Has this been dubbed from some other language?"[51] The worker in the middle of the panel is more direct: "*None* of these make sense! We're splicing them all out of order."[52] The last worker may as well be speaking to anyone who would fix the text's meaning. Attempts to understand the text, like what Calvin is dreaming about, is a "waste of time."[53] There is a clear self-referential point to be made with respect to *Calvin and Hobbes*. On some level the imaginative constructs, like the unconscious, cannot be distilled into an obvious meaning. The corollary point, then, is that attempts to contain the imagination in any respect — be it Watterson's, the text's, or the reader's — gloss over the textual environment that gives rise to various meanings. In this strip's final frame, Calvin substantiates the point when the imaginative characterization of his subconscious gives way to the real context. He comments, "Whoo, I had so many strange dreams!... I wonder what they mean."[54] As Watterson makes clear in the narrative, the dreams can mean anything; the reader is left to wonder what, exactly, is playing on the movies that elicit the strong responses from the subconscious workers. Moreover, there exists an obvious caution against attempts to tease out what Watterson might have had in mind. To clean up the subconscious would require a constant descent (in the form of psychotherapy) to clean up the mess and therefore clarify what Calvin is actually dreaming. The implication echoes the points that Derrida, Cunningham, and Barthes make. Attempts to clean up the text in this capacity restrict the reader's opportunity to imagine what fills the gaps within the text.

This brief discussion highlights an important methodological feature of this book. The texts that Watterson constructs are primarily an imaginative expression of how a six-year-old makes sense of the world. Watterson makes clear that the strip offers Calvin's viewpoint:

> Most of the time, the strip is drawn simply from Calvin's perspective, and Hobbes is as real as anyone. So when Calvin is careening down the hillside, I don't feel compelled to insert reminders that Hobbes is a stuffed toy. I try to get the reader completely swept up into Calvin's world by ignoring adult perspective. Hobbes, therefore, isn't just a cute gimmick. I'm not making the strip revolve around the transformation. The viewpoint of the strip fluctuates, and this allows Hobbes to be a "real" character.[55]

Watterson reiterates the caution not to restrict meanings when reading the text. The basic imaginative construct that allows the strip to function should not be considered a point of critical concern in a textual analysis. The subtext to Watterson's claim, and indeed this lengthy discussion, about the imagination is that it is easy to prove that Hobbes is not real because he is literally a stuffed tiger. To stress this point in order to highlight how the strip is not realistic is to undermine the text and therefore the meanings that emerge through Calvin's imaginative relationship with Hobbes. On this point Derrida sounds a similar caution: "I am wary of the idea of methods of reading. The laws of reading are determined by that particular text that is being read ... we must remain faithful, even if it implies a certain violence, to the injunctions of the text."[56] Derrida's point is well taken; there is much to be gained in reading the text without dwelling on the psychological implications of Hobbes' reality. Furthermore, it is important not to infer any motivation Watterson may or may not have had in navigating the potential for psychoanalysis. As Watterson states, "I hate to subject it to too much analysis."[57] If anything, such readings run against the strip's imaginative grain. In the June 16, 1993, strip, Calvin captures this point succinctly. Susie asks him what a particular cloud looks like, and Calvin answers, "A bunch of suspended water and ice particles ... why?"[58] Susie apparently leaves in disappointment, and the final panel shows Calvin smiling as he says, "Everybody hates a literalist."[59]

Having discussed these salient concerns involving the imagination's role in *Calvin and Hobbes*, a second crucial feature of the strip now requires examination. Specifically, what follows will explore how the imagination manifests the textual space that offers Calvin — and the reader — the opportunity to explore meaning in a real world context. Spaceman Spiff provides one of the most frequent tropes that blends Calvin's imagination and what happens in his life. A particularly helpful example of this overlap occurs in the March 27, 1994, strip. As is often the case with Spaceman Spiff, the first panel locates the specific adventure in a sweeping context. Spiff's spaceship has crashed at the bottom of a gorge. In the foreground of a ridge above the crashed spaceship, Spiff marches, his hands in the air, as a prisoner of the alien that oozes along behind him. Spiff provides a bit more information to round out this first panel: "Stranded on a distant planet, the fearless Spaceman Spiff has been captured by a horrible Yukbarf!"[60] This brief introduction to the scene exhibits several characteristics that fill out the discussion above. First, the narrative takes place in a land that is far from Spiff's home (he does live on Earth). Spiff's capture occurs not just on another planet, but on a distant planet. Importantly, the gap between this world and Earth does not deter one of Spiff signature qualities. He remains fearless even though he finds himself stranded in a place that is decidedly inhospitable.

The Yukbarfs intensify the displacement that frames this strip. In the second panel, Spiff stands before one of the Yukbarfs' leaders. The leader exclaims: "So the Earthling won't cooperate, eh? We'll see about *that*! Take him to the dungeon!" The Yukbarf that captured Spiff punctuates the leader's authority by accepting the order without question: "Yes, Your Most Supreme Odoriferousness!"[61] Despite the threat of his impending torture, Spiff remains unmoved: "You don't scare *me*, you talking blobs of oozing slop! I am impervious to pain!"[62]

With the confrontation firmly established, the gap between reality and the imagination is established on the imagination's terms. The narrative thus moves towards a showdown that is decidedly outside the bounds of reality. At the same time, Spiff's appearance before the Yukbarf leader begins to elide the distance between Spiff's imagined context and the circumstances that give rise to this particular escape from reality. Despite the Yukbarf's threats, there remains a curious link with reality. The Yukbarf leader sits at a desk that looks like any Earthling executive's office. There is a telephone, a nice penholder, and a picture of what is presumably one of its smiling family members. These details seem innocuous, but they initiate a transition that blurs the line between Calvin's imagination and his reality. The fourth panel continues to elide the difference between what is real and what is imagined. Spiff now finds himself in the dungeon, but the ominous, cave-like darkness gives way to a brightly lit living room. Though widely traveled, Spiff is surprised by what he finds. Standing in the presence of a third Yukbarf, he asks, "Hey! What kind of dungeon is *this*?! Aren't you going to torture me?"[63] The Yukbarf responds: "Oh yes! Have a seat and let's see how you withstand a calm discussion of wholesome principles!"[64] The transition that begins with a couple of familiar details now further collapses the gap between the imaginary and the real. In the final panel the reader finds the real context out of which Calvin's imagination escapes. Calvin is sitting on a couch just like the one in the Yukbarf dungeon and yelling at the top of his lungs as his dad gives him a lecture on building character.

The imagination, then, releases and binds Calvin to his actual experiences. Though the link that informs the Spaceman Spiff narrative (and other imaginative characters, such as Stupendous Man) is often not obvious, there remains a thematic parallel that structures the imagination's departure. Consequently, the meaning that Calvin's imagination generates is not completely unhinged. Just as Spaceman Spiff retains his Earthly roots, so too does this imagined identity exhibit a lingering influence from Calvin's world. This specific Spiff adventure exposes this link by retracing subtly, and then clearly, the circumstances that generate the need to find meaning through the imagination's departure.

Though Calvin's imagination tends to indicate a problematic experience in his actual life, there are also examples wherein the imagination provides a way to move beyond such circumstances. For example, in the September 26, 1993, strip, the reader finds Calvin in a familiar groundswell for imaginative departures: school. The difference here, however, is that the Spaceman Spiff adventure that follows the end of school does not function as an escape within an experience, but rather as a way to distance Calvin from an experience that has concluded. When the bell rings, Calvin no longer needs to endure boredom, his teacher, or Moe's bullying (because she lives near Calvin, Susie is always lingering). Still, the end of the school-day slides into another one of Spaceman Spiff's adventures. In this specific example, there is a noticeable distance in that Spiff does not encounter an antagonistic, sadistic monster. Without an alien foe, Spiff is able to fly home to Earth without interruption. The strip concludes with Spiff landing his spaceship in Calvin's front yard — the adventure almost always bleeds back into reality — and Calvin explaining that his imagination gives voice to an appreciated experience from the real world. He explains his day to his mom in a way that clarifies the inverted capacity in which the imagination is functioning: "I enjoyed coming home."[65] Whereas Spiff's adventures usually project Calvin (as Spiff) as far as possible from reality, here the point is to distance one part of reality from another through the imagination. The point, then, is not to discover an alternative way of processing a positive experience, but, rather, to bridge that from which Calvin wants to escape with the anticipated experience of freedom that he will enjoy more fully once he gets home from school (at least until Hobbes pounces).

A further iteration of the permeable boundaries between Calvin's imagination and his actual context appears in another Spaceman Spiff adventure. As he cruises over the surface of Planet Quorg, searching for life, Spiff slowly realizes that the topography is not what it seems.[66] What he originally understands to be "peculiar rock formations"[67] turns out to be giant alien footprints. Hitting the thrusters, Spiff speeds away from an adventure that inverts his expectations: "While Spiff was searching for alien life, it seems alien life was searching for Spiff! No doubt it wanted the earthling for dinner."[68] The unexpected reality Spiff encounters exposes how the text gives rise to the kinds of parallel meanings that stitch together Calvin's reality and his imagination. This particular adventure thus recalls Derrida's discussion of the trace. This is an important dynamic that signs generate within a text: "From the moment the sign appears ... there is no chance of encountering anywhere the purity of 'reality.'"[69] As these two worlds meet in Spiff's realization, the reader comes to occupy a disjointed space. The result, according to Derrida, is an erasure: "What is lost in that complicity is therefore the myth of the simplicity of origin."[70] Without the origin, the text cannot be anchored to a particular reading. Thus, Derrida highlights the failure of these aliens to bring Spiff to dinner (or of his parents to get him to come inside). Consequently, the text remains tangled among the intersecting narrative threads. Calvin speaks as Spaceman Spiff in running away from his parents' footprints in the snow: "Ughh! Spiff blasts into hyperspace!"[71] In this complicated textual space the reader finds in a different capacity the dual influences on Spaceman Spiff narratives (and, indeed, throughout *Calvin and Hobbes*). What panel might come next remains unclear; the reader must interpret what occurs, which depends largely on how the decision to blast into hyperspace unfolds. The sign's dual nature as real and imagined thus exhibits the dynamic Derrida articulates. There is no pure reality to be had in this strip. Moreover, this open conclusion lacks a definitive origin (the strip does not explain what preceded Spiff's decision to explore this particular planet), which lays bare the myth of a simple textual origin. This brief adventure complicates both what precedes and follows the moment wherein the strip accommodates the tension between the real and the imagined worlds that overlap in a footprint, which remains "perhaps a little *too* peculiar."[72]

A final example will cement the point concerning how Calvin's imagination and his actual circumstances intersect, influence one another, and, on occasion, overlap in a way that blurs distinctions between the two contexts. In the strip from January 20, 1991, the reader encounter's Spiff's spaceship in the final moments before a crash landing. The planet — Plootarg — is expansive and, therefore, broadens the imagination's narrative context. In the second panel, Spiff emphasizes both the space in which the episode unfolds and the departure that Calvin's imagination enables. This crash-landing is "just another typical day for the incredible Spaceman Spiff."[73] This time, however, something turns out to be different. When Spiff realizes "the zealous Zarches"[74] have tracked him to the planet's surface, he knows he must act quickly to avoid capture. The problem, however, is that "the planet's soft, granular surface makes him easy to track!"[75] Undaunted, Spiff "runs backward, so his tracks show him going in the *opposite* direction."[76] The plan works, as the aliens lumber past the rock outcropping on which Spiff hides. Up to this point the reader encounters an adventure that is typical for Spaceman Spiff. However, the final panel reveals the actual context that informs the need to compensate for a granular surface that leaves clear footprints. Calvin's parents are looking for him in a snow-covered space. The salient effect in this example is that the real world's influence on the imagination — Calvin's desire to stay outside and his subsequent attempts to avoid his parents — boomerangs and is affected by what occurs in Calvin's imagination. This encounter with aliens is thus not simply an escape from specific life circumstances. As the imaginary context closes, the real world exhibits an imprint from the Spiff narrative, which allows the strip to remain open to further iterations of this adventure.

The two important features discussed in this chapter — Calvin's imagination's ability to transcend his actual circumstances and how this departure informs the textual space at hand — indicate the central role that the imagination has in allowing meaning to emerge. In the world of *Calvin and Hobbes* these dynamics repeatedly generate the narrative context that ultimately invites readers into the space wherein the imagination and reality intersect in a way that accommodates multiple interpretive readings. To conclude this discussion, it will be helpful to look at these dual components not in a context that is primarily imagined (i.e. when Calvin assumes a different identity and occupies a space outside reality), but in a narrative that unfolds within reality. Calvin's battle with a legion of snow goons provides just such an example. Importantly, this narrative arc begins with an imaginative accent that remains firmly located within reality. Calvin is standing over a snowman, and he performs a ceremony that commands the snowman to live.[77] These first two panels do not suggest anything beyond a child's normal imaginative play. In the third panel, however, the imagination as it functions in *Calvin and Hobbes* unhinges the strip from a normal game. The snowman grunts, gets up, and angrily chases after Calvin. Though still in the initial parameters of a child's game, the imagination thus gives rise to an experience that cannot be contained within reality.

As the snow goon strips continue, a variety of complicating matters arises that thickens the plot. Calvin cannot figure how to kill the snow goon in a way that is acceptable within reality. Luring the snow goon into the house — a combination of both the imaginative world and the real world — will not work because Calvin's mom would not be happy about the big puddle that would result.[78] This apparent throwaway line highlights the tension at work in this experience. What Calvin imagines will have tangible effects in his actual life and, importantly, this crossover forbids an action within the imagined narrative. The alternative, then, is to attack the snow goon within the imaginative context that has been established, which, tellingly, extends the narrative. When Calvin and Hobbes attempt to kill the snow goon with a barrage of snowballs, an unexpected thing happens. The snow goon realizes he can make himself bigger by packing on more snow.[79] The idea spills over into the generation of further snow goons.[80] Yet again the storyline condenses the real and the imaginary. Calvin obviously has to make the additional snow goons if others can perceive them.[81] At the same time, Calvin responds to Susie question's about "all those ugly things" with an imagined ignorance: "What do you mean 'all those'?"[82] Taken wholly within the real context that contains the snow goon narrative, Calvin comes across as absurd; he would have to remember making multiple snow goons. The point, however, is the ability of the strip to bracket this obvious point through the imagination. Because the line between reality and imagination blurs, the reader can join the adventure on Calvin's terms.

To doubt the imagination is to deny the underlying dynamics within *Calvin and Hobbes* that allow these kinds of adventures to emerge. The subtext to this point is that the imagination is, in the end, the influence that sustains the strip. As the day winds down and Calvin's mom calls him in, he responds that he has to stay out to kill the snow goons.[83] Calvin's mom does not enter his imaginative context and responds that this supposedly necessary task can wait until tomorrow.[84] Calvin's comment to Hobbes as they walk towards the house captures precisely the imagination's privilege: "Moms and reason are like oil and water."[85] Calvin reverses what constitutes reason. Whereas Calvin's mom speaks reasonably as defined within the real context at hand, Calvin asserts that the imagination's logic transcends such limitations. Not to be deterred, Calvin upholds this inverted understanding of reason when he ignores what is reasonable in order to kill the snow goons. He refuses to wait until the following day, and once his parents have gone to bed, he goes outside to spray all the goons with the hose so they will be "popsicles through July!"[86] Of course, Calvin's parents react to his actions as any reasonable parent would; they haul him inside because kids should not be outside in the middle of the night to spray the yard with a hose.

With the lines between reality and imagination demarcated, the coda to this narrative arc reiterates that the imagination is the primary influence in *Calvin and Hobbes*. When Calvin tries to explain to his parents what he was doing the previous night, he asks repeatedly, "see?"[87] The implication is clear; viewed only through reason's expectations, the imaginative departures that characterize the strip do not make sense. Calvin laments this as he sits in his room: "They never see."[88] The need to see requires that his parents — like the reader — must blend the two parallel influences at work in the narrative. In so doing, the text becomes a membrane between what is real and what is imagined. In recognizing these two distinct features of the strip, the reader can then follow the text as it slides between the strip's divergent contexts. The important thing for Calvin is that the influence of either the imagination or the real world can wax and wane, a volatility that permits the text to accommodate multiple kinds of meanings.

CHAPTER THREE

Stuck on the Sidewalk
Understanding the Human Condition

Having discussed how the imagination generates a specific kind of narrative context in *Calvin and Hobbes,* and having identified this space as a gap between author and reader, there exists the need to define what constitutes a text. The implications of clarifying this point will indicate how meanings in *Calvin and Hobbes* emerge out of the intersection between Calvin's imagination and his real experiences. More specifically, broadening the definition of the text to incorporate the strip's visual elements will recognize how meanings emerge in a multi-layered capacity.

Paul Ricoeur offers a helpful starting point in framing how to conceptualize a text. At a basic level, the text is "any discourse fixed by writing."[1] This definition identifies the crucial feature of *Calvin and Hobbes* that constitutes a text: the act of writing. Though there are other elements to the strip, the baseline for this book is the fact that a written discourse invites readers into Calvin's world. On the basis of this initial definition, one can than incorporate a second, obvious element of *Calvin and Hobbes*: the visual context in which specific discourses arise. The text, then, exhibits the interplay of two discourses that complicate the basic claim that writing fixes meaning. Kearney provides a summary that helps clarify this point: "The poetic imagination liberates the reader into a free space of possibility, suspending the reference to the immediate world of perception (both the author's and the reader's) and thereby disclosing new ways of being in the world."[2] Importantly, this composite definition establishes the uniqueness that characterizes *Calvin and Hobbes.* The various ways in which the verbal and the visual interact allow the thematic and imaginative dualities that have been discussed thus far.

Calvin's wagon is one of the obvious examples of how the strip's visual element complements its verbal exchanges. Watterson summarizes how the wagon functions in the strip: "I think the action lends a silly counter-point to the text, and it's a lot more interesting to draw than talking heads. Sometimes the wagon ride even acts as a visual metaphor for Calvin's topic of discussion."[3] Silly or not, the wagon brings together the two important discourses that invite the reader into Calvin's world. Not surprisingly, this particular feature of *Calvin and Hobbes* opens the text into an intimate space. As Watterson explains, "Calvin rides the wagon through the woods ... [which] is important to the strip, because it's the place where Calvin and Hobbes can get away from everyone and be themselves."[4] The wagon, then, is not simply a fulcrum between the visual and the verbal; it is the threshold into a reflective space.[5]

The wagon has an obvious structuring role in *Calvin and Hobbes*, and, as such, it provides a symptomatic example of how the visual and verbal discourses affect the strip's context. In such instances, the verbal element of a strip occupies the foreground. Often, these exchanges take place in a fixed space that adds little to the content of a particular discussion. For example, during an early strip the reader encounters Calvin and Hobbes sitting under a tree as Calvin shares his thoughts:

> I've been thinking. You know how boring dad is? Maybe it's a big phony act! Maybe after he puts us to bed, dad dons some weird costume and goes out fighting crime! Maybe this whole 'dad' stuff is just a secret identity! Maybe the mayor calls dad on a secret hot line whenever the city's in trouble! Maybe dad's a masked superhero![6]

This imagined alter-ego does not emerge obviously out of the visual markers.[7] More pointedly, the visual context does not advance the narrative energy. If anything, the clear disjunction between the setting and the topic stall what little momentum this particular strip has. Hobbes is not immune to the conversation's pace; he responds in a similarly mild way: "If that's true he should drive a cooler car."[8] Calvin offers a final word that emphasizes how a verbally dominated strip can grind to a halt: "I know. Ours doesn't even have a cassette deck."[9] Any consequential meaning that might have emerged following Calvin's imagined alternative to his dad's generally mundane character evaporates. Whether or not the car has a cassette deck is a decidedly uninteresting point given the conversation that fills the strip's first three panels.

In contrast to the August 8, 1989, strip, the visual is at times the privileged form of discourse. Such instances occur in two distinct capacities. The first occurs when the strip's visual elements provide the context;

any dialogue serves to calibrate what the reader sees. One example of this dynamic occurs in the strip from July 23, 1995. A blazing sun melts Calvin as the top row of panels moves from left to right. By the end of this first row, there is only a puddle of water and Calvin's soaked clothes. The second row of panels conveys a weather cycle at work; the Calvin-puddle evaporates and swells the cloud at the top of the panels, which eventually blows away and leaves the clothes behind. In the third row of panels this cloud begins to rain, a deluge that reforms Calvin. This reconstituted Calvin is naked and he dashes off. The final panel shows his mom picking up his shirt and his underwear and exclaiming with a stern look, "...not again...."[10] The emphasis in this progression is how the hot weather makes Calvin feel, an idea conveyed without any dialogue. When Calvin's mom speaks, she interrupts the visual narrative in a way that extends the narrative that this visual progression establishes. The point is clearly not her frustration that Calvin is running around the neighborhood without any clothes on; rather, this example captures the broader implication of strips wherein the visual provides the primary narrative energy. If one were to remove the illustrations that contain the dialogue, the particular meaning at hand would not emerge.

While this dynamic is most striking in the Sunday strips, which offer the space to enhance the visual narrative, foregrounding the visual part of discourse functions similarly in single-panel strips. For example, in the strip from January 6, 1993, the visual setting coordinates the exchange between Calvin and his mom. She stands off to the left side, looking down at Calvin, without saying anything. A snow chicken — laughing with enjoyment — stands at the center, holding an axe in its wings. As the panel moves to the right, the reader finds a snowman's body resting against a tree stump. The snowman's head lies off to the right, eyes crossed, to punctuate this strange role reversal. Calvin looks sternly back at his mom and says, "Oh yeah? Define 'well-adjusted.'"[11] The words require the visual context to condense the exchange into a broader narrative (and in this case, the story is particularly funny). Because the dialogue appears in a narrative that is already underway by virtue of this strip's visible component, the reader is able to imagine what Calvin's mom said that prompted Calvin's response. Much like the movie in Calvin's subconscious, the effect is to establish a bridge, through the intersection of the visual and the verbal, to the possibility of multiple meanings.

A more pronounced example of the central importance that the strip's visual elements appears when the narrative requires no dialogue. The Sunday strip from December 6, 1992, begins with an alien ship hauling Calvin from his bed, trapping him in a tube filled with green liquid, and replacing him with a robot. Back on Earth, the robotic Calvin proceeds to take cookies, smash a lamp with a shovel, and throw schoolbooks in the trash. Each of these disruptive acts occurs in sight of Calvin's mom, who, rather than speaking, offers essentially the same look of shock at what is happening. Nevin Martell captures what is at stake in considering the visual element of *Calvin and Hobbes* closely: "With Watterson's drawings, you can't be complacent, you need to engage and imagine what is beyond the obvious. In this way, a casual walk across a meadow becomes an afternoon in the woods for the reader."[12] While this wholly visual narrative reveals a bit about Calvin's character, the richness that characterizes the balance between the visual and the verbal is absent in this example. Towards the end of the events at hand, Calvin gestures towards his mom with wide eyes about the events that led to his poor behavior; her look summarizes well the overall tenor for this strip. She does not seem to be listening very closely, because she does not affirm the explanation that Calvin offers. Without any verbal markers, then, this strip manages to articulate clearly how Calvin's imagination and the reality of his mom's suspicions are incongruent. The lack of dialogue, then, speaks again to the critical balance between the visual and the verbal that gives *Calvin and Hobbes* its imaginative spark.

In sliding between these various narrative trajectories, the common textual denominator is clear: *Calvin and Hobbes* is a text because multiple discourses anchor it. The richness this combination can bring emerges after a particular reading of *Hamster Huey and the Gooey Kablooie*. Readers are probably familiar with the basic exchange when Calvin's dad begins the process of reading a bedtime story. He asks Calvin what book he wants to read, Calvin says *Hamster Huey*, and Calvin's dad does everything he can to convince Calvin that they should read another book. As the joke reappears in later strips, the consequences of re-reading the same story over and over again take unexpected turns. By the third panel of the strip from October 6, 1992, the argument over what to read has reached a boiling point. Calvin's dad presents a version of the story between the third and fourth panels. In the latter, the reader sees Calvin and Hobbes sitting in bed, the covers pulled up close to their chins, and reflecting on their story time. Calvin exclaims with something closer to apprehension than excitement, "Wow, the story was different *that* time!"[13] With a similar tenor, Hobbes wonders, "Do you think the townsfolk will ever find Hamster Huey's head?"[14]

There are multiple points to discuss in the wake of Hamster Huey's untimely end. The strip's multiple discourses expand the number of possible meanings that emerge by holding together the various viewpoints at work. In broad terms, this example shows how the verbal and visual discourses combine to produce a text that either on its own would be unable to do. Calvin's remark indicates that something has changed, a point that does not necessarily surprise the reader given the intensity of the argument in the prior panel, as well as other examples wherein Calvin's dad will adlib to provide some variety when reading *Hamster Huey and the Gooey Kablooie*. In this sense, Calvin's verbal contribution bridges the space between the third and fourth panels. The reader can continue to imagine what exactly this story is about because the strip offers no visual or verbal indications as to what is in the actual book. Watterson explains that *Hamster Huey and the Gooey Kablooie* is, like the noodle incident, a purposefully vague idea that invites the reader to let her/his mind wander in regards to the story's content.[15] The verbal discourse, then, encourages the reader to engage imaginatively the tension between Calvin and his dad.

The result is a gap between panels that invites the reader to extend the narrative as s/he wants. Given the basic construct that Watterson develops with this recurring theme, the story is already unknown. The fact that Calvin similarly encounters different versions of *Hamster Huey and the Gooey Kablooie* thus emphasizes the role that the imagination plays in *Calvin and Hobbes*. Moreover, this point appears specifically in this context through the combination of Calvin's verbal response to the story that occurs between panels, as well as the surprised look on his face. According to his dad, he has "memorized [*Hamster Huey and the Gooey Kablooie*].... It's the same story every day!"[16] Even when the reader knows what to expect, the imagination can always generate new readings. Calvin is perhaps too familiar (as his dad tries to argue) with the text, yet the text can still generate legitimate surprise. Calvin's words do not convey the intensity of his reaction to this unexpected story; his expression enhances the effect that his words have.

With respect to a text's meaning, then, this particular strip highlights not only how the visual and the verbal coalesce to expand how the text encourages the imagination, it also indicates how this combination permits the text to juggle multiple perspectives. Three different imaginative responses to the story materialize in the gap between the third and fourth panels. Calvin, as discussed above, responds to the surprise that a text he knows well can still be different. Calvin's dad has obviously imagined a new take on *Hamster Huey and the Gooey Kablooie* because he departs from the text. In this respect, then, Calvin's dad mirrors Watterson's stress on the imaginative freedom this particular trope is designed to engender. Even though the actual text remains elusive, the combination of the verbal and visual components make clear that the text has been re-read in a new way. The importance of both discourses thus leads to Hobbes' perspective, which similarly brings together the strip's two elements. Hobbes' face offers essentially the same expression as Calvin's, a parallel that establishes Hobbes' surprise at the departure from the story's text. This visual likeness opens into a clue as to what Calvin's dad imagined. As a tiger, perhaps it is understandable that Hobbes would feel the effects of an animal character losing his head. The idea is unsettling, and the strip's tone suggests that this even involved some kind of foul play against Hamster Huey. Hobbes' remark thus adds a further layer to the shock that his face registers, a transition that opens the text into a deeper (and darker) reservoir of possible meanings. The reader encounters in this strip the very surprise that Calvin and Hobbes — and perhaps Calvin's dad — feel when the narrative departs from what the actual text of *Hamster Huey and the Gooey Kablooie* contains. This imaginative freedom therefore rests on the nuances that the visual and verbal discourses generate as they mutually reinforce the way in which the text unfolds.

This specific example indicates how the balance between the visual and verbal discourses that *Calvin and Hobbes* achieves offers multiple perspectives, a complexity that ultimately gives rise to a variety of meanings. When the verbal exchanges are at the forefront of a strip, the strip's visual component provides a subtext that enhances the words that are being spoken. Hobbes is perhaps the richest example of how this silent presence weaves into the words that Calvin speaks. Through his expressions, Hobbes is able to react to what Calvin says, regardless of whether he ultimately offers a spoken response. These visual cues provide a second discourse, then, because they absorb the content of what Calvin is saying and therefore express Hobbes' thoughts. Often this dynamic adds a foil that challenges what Calvin is suggesting, while at other times Hobbes' non-verbal communication can amplify the meaning at hand.

This effect builds on the strip's two discourses in a way that expands the text, which in turn provides the reader a deeper space into which s/he can venture in search of meaning. While Hobbes' expressions provide a good example of how the strip's two discourses work together, there are other ways in which the verbal and the visual blend to provide a more nuanced textual space. Calvin's expansive snowmaking portfolio is a good example of how the two discourses reinforce one another. Whereas the visual element within a dialogue ensures that multiple voices are heard, even if only one person is speaking, in Calvin's sculptures the visual often provides the exclamation point that dialogue cannot provide on its own.

The visual element, then, adds a further way to understand a discourse, which in turn expands the definition of a text. By reconfiguring these definitions, one can identify the complexities that generate additional meanings in *Calvin and Hobbes*. Barthes summarizes well how such variations ultimately enrich the text (and thus the reading experience). He writes, "The text needs its shadow: this shadow is a *bit* of ideology, a *bit* of representation, a *bit* of subject: ghosts, pockets, traces, necessary clouds."[17] In a word, the multiple discourses that characterize *Calvin and Hobbes* permit these elements to emerge. Moreover, the interplay between the verbal and the visual generates the space for Calvin's imaginative departures. Ricoeur captures the importance of identifying how these different elements interact within the text: "To explain is to bring out the structure, that is, internal relations of dependence which constitute the statistics of the text; to interpret is to follow the path of thought opened up by the text."[18] In emphasizing the openness that characterizes a text, Ricoeur highlights the need to mind the dynamics that prohibit a definitive reading of any text. Ricoeur continues: "The movement of reference towards the act of showing is intercepted, at the same time as dialogue is interrupted by the text. I say interrupted and not suppressed; it is in this respect that I shall distance myself from what may be called henceforth the ideology of the absolute text."[19] In defining the text, then, incorporating a plurality of discourses as textual anchors preserves the openness that *Calvin and Hobbes* invites the reader to explore. As will become apparent, this invitation is a central feature of the text's freedom to shift between different contexts.[20]

The text's elusive nature reveals a deeper concern that *Calvin and Hobbes* frequently addresses: the tension that characterizes the human condition, and therefore the difficult of making sense of what it means to be human.[21] At this juncture the point to make is simply that the dual discursive nature of *Calvin and Hobbes* balances the various tensions that unhinges the text from hermeneutical moorings. The result is a constant shift in perspectives and consequences that indicate how difficult it is to reconcile human nature with the realities from which Calvin seeks to escape. In *Metaphor, Analogy, and the Place of Places: Where Religion and Philosophy Meet*, Carl G. Vaught examines the importance of narratives as structuring how humans search for meaning; therefore, he enhances a discussion of how multiple discourses and the shifting perspectives they enable in *Calvin and Hobbes*. While a descent into an overly technical analysis is out of tune with the current argument, it is important to highlight how Vaught outlines the specific points that follow. Of particular note is the effect stories have on how humans establish originary hermeneutical anchors. Within the stories that inform our capacity for understanding (and thus for reading the text), Vaught stresses how spatial and temporal considerations refract our experiences and, moreover, anticipate a metaphysical category.[22] He writes, "The context of religion and philosophy involves an interplay among temporal, spatial, and eternal dimensions, each of which moves in two directions, and all of which come to focus on a dynamic and unfolding Place where they converge."[23] While *Calvin and Hobbes* cannot be labeled strictly religious or philosophical, thematically the strip examines themes that fall squarely within these fields of inquiry. As such, Vaught's study offers more depth in considering how the text permits different meanings to emerge.

At this point Vaught's insights into the temporal and spatial warrant more discussion, as they pertain to the issue of the text's composition and its ability to host meaning. Vaught clarifies how the intersection between a tripartite structure of human experience affects the text: "The temporal, the spatial, and the eternal dimensions of experience both intersect and unfold in a Place that makes other places possible, that mirrors their structure at the distinctively reflective level, and that orients thinking with respect to them."[24] The strip from October 7, 1990, offers a symptomatic example of how various (textual) places open into reflective spaces. Once again Spacemen Spiff provides the context; his exploration brings him to a place that "appears to be uninhabited."[25] Ever aware, Spiff notices that the lichen on this planet's rocks form odd geometric patterns, so he gets down on all fours to take a closer look. In so doing, he realizes that the lichen patterns are actually farms, which are close by one-inch-tall skyscrapers.

The narration that follows this realization exhibits the process Vaught describes: "Spiff reflects that human scale is by no means the standard for life forms."[26] In this imaginative narrative (the actual context is that Calvin is looking at some ants on the playground), the reader joins Spiff in recognizing an important point for understanding human nature. Spiff's realization undercuts the human tendency to define their experiences in solely anthropocentric terms. This adventure reminds Spiff that other lives with other normative concerns exist alongside humanity. This particular strip emphasizes the point when "a blimp-sized monster appears over the hillside!"[27] The monster turns out to be Moe, which relativizes the question of scale even further. Among humans there can be no normative understanding because humans, like the creatures Spiff encounters, exhibit a variety of meanings. The specific place at hand — the unnamed distant planet — thus fractures into multiple perspectives, which, once recognized, undercuts any attempt to standardize the text's meaning.

The consequences of multiple places, Vaught explains, are significant when considering how the text's encouraging of the imagination gives rise to meaning. As narratives break into different contexts, one is lead to reflect on the implications of other places as they relate to one's own experiences. Vaught writes, "Mystery requires reflective openness; power demands an acknowledgment of otherness; and structure points to the possibility of philosophical intelligibility."[28] The divergent scale of weighing experiences thus permits an ironic clarity if the text in question is approached with full recognition of the pluralities it allows. The reflective turn provides an opening that allows a structured search for meaning. Vaught continues: "Philosophical categories and the human responses they evoke require a language appropriate to the experiences they generate and to the reflection they provoke."[29] Vaught's argument dovetails with the frequent imaginative narratives that Calvin uses to configure his actual experiences. Contexts such as Spaceman Spiff adventures provide the language that balances the experiential and reflective elements of *Calvin and Hobbes*, which are recognizable in the dual discourses that the text accommodates. When identifying these different places (to employ Vaught's term) within the strip, the "language" at work meets the criteria Vaught maintains is necessary for finding meaning: "[It] must be figurative, performative, and intelligible at the same time; for the mystery of experience requires figurative discourse; the power of existence demands performative discourse; and the intelligibility of life needs comprehensible discourse."[30] The imagination generates this tripartite language by giving rise to contexts that speak to the complex experiential nature of the human condition. As an imaginative text, then, *Calvin and Hobbes* enables through the imagination a discourse that is figurative, performative, and comprehensible.

Moe's appearance adds an important element to these various perspectives. He makes clear two important points as the strip transitions out of the imaginative context. One the one hand, Moe's teasing might tempt Calvin to "abandon philosophical reflection for experiential immediacy, seeking to solve the problem of fragmentation by immersing [himself] in a mode of experience that is free from every form of opposition. In this way, [he] can seek to replace reflection with experience by returning to the experiential origins with which reflection begins."[31] However, Calvin — acting as Spiff would in the strip's actual context — reaches for a weapon (a rock for Calvin; a "stun blaster" for Spiff) to confront Moe (the monster), which makes clear the impossibility of a retreat to such an origin. Vaught continues: "The attempt to move beyond fragmentation by undertaking a quest for complete comprehension is equally defective, primarily because it assumes that we can give every problem, existential or otherwise, a reflective resolution."[32] The need to respond to Moe's abrasive presence stresses the impossibility of filtering one's experiences through a tidy narrative that glosses over the new perspective Moe establishes. Spiff realizes as much, and therefore he cannot take as normative his own humanity. Consequently he must engage the blimp-sized monster as constitutive of his fragmented experiences.

The various influences on the text must coalesce in a way that is intelligible, but at the same time the text cannot be rigid in speaking to the influences Vaught identifies. Rather, in its intelligibility the text must resist the "literalistic mentality" that often characterizes religious and/or philosophical reflection.[33] The result, Vaught explains, is the text's ability to accommodate the kinds of multiple discourses that characterize *Calvin and Hobbes*.[34] An early strip clarifies specifically how this balance has the "ability to provide an orientation for things in space."[35] As Calvin and Hobbes stand at the top of a snow-covered hill with their toboggan, Calvin reflects on the stillness that fills the space.[36] After inviting Hobbes to lie on his back on the toboggan and look at the sky, Calvin describes a condition wherein the temporary absence of distraction that occurs at the top of the hill would be permanent: "Imagine what it would be like without any people or houses around. It would be perfectly still."[37] The crucial departure that characterizes so much of the strip — an alternative context imagined from within a specific textual setting — leads into a panel without a verbal discourse. Calvin and Hobbes thus stare up at the sky, lost in their respective thoughts about the possibility of sustained stillness.

Their shared sense reveals in the text's orientation a way "to speak about [what] can never be comprehended adequately."[38] At the same time, this glimpse of an alternative to the fragmentation that is implicit in the strip cannot be sustained. Though this example imagines stillness, the fact remains that "intelligible discourse forces us to admit that life, thought, and action would be meaningless apart from the presence *and absence* of eternity."[39] As Hobbes comments that the imaginative departure is "very peaceful,"[40] Calvin disrupts the moment. He kicks the toboggan down the hill. Hobbes leaves the trace of a yelp as he disappears from view, while Calvin, with a broad smile, says to the reader, "I hate all that silence."[41] The departure to stillness cannot be maintained; the point at which this condition is imagined must remain absent. The narrative context demands, then, that Calvin eventually break up the reflective moment. The sudden burst of activity (with Hobbes' accompanying scream) highlights the tension that sustains this particular text. The imagined silence takes on new meaning as a (possible) presence when Calvin ensures an absence of silence.

This paradoxical presence and absence is conveyed through the visual discourse's spatial configuration. Both the physical departure from noise and the act that disrupts this departure require this characterization for the strip to unfold.[42] This example, then, highlights the importance of visual discourse in how *Calvin and Hobbes* generates meaning. While the verbal exchange is important insofar as it articulates the imagined alternative, it is the spatial element — conveyed visually — that makes the disruption possible.[43] This combination is crucial to how the strip enables the reader (along with Calvin) to balance the imagined peacefulness and eventual disruption. Vaught explains how examples like this thrive upon multiple discourses: "taken together ... [they] provide an intelligible framework within which philosophical reflection can attempt to attain the satisfaction it needs."[44] Vaught's nuanced language recalls two important features from earlier in this discussion: the need for intelligibility and the impossibility that this textual balance can provide clarity of meaning. The spatial, temporal, and eternal elements that are present in this example enable a reflective context that captures the essential disruption of life and how the imagination can transcend this condition. At the same time,

Calvin's inability to endure the silence reminds the reader that the imagination can only attempt to find meaning in a disjunctive context.[45]

Because the text maintains equilibrium between its verbal and visual discourses, it can sustain an energy that reaches towards the horizon that always recedes. Gianni Vattimo summarizes well how the horizon structures the text's space, and therefore how meaning emerges: "But what in fact matters most about the concept of horizon is the order of things articulated *within* it."[46] Consequently, the accent falls not on the impossibility of what lies ahead, but, rather, on the journey that occurs within the horizon's boundary. By discharging the text into a space without rigid boundaries, Vattimo's analysis indicates how the text can overcome the instability that characterizes humanity's journey within life's horizon.[47]

While the horizon marks the point to which Calvin's imagination can extend the text, this boundary also destabilizes the experiential context out of which he reaches towards the freedom that alternative worlds provide. In the April 16, 1991, strip, one encounters the paralysis that can result when one is aware that the horizon marks a boundary that can never be reached. The context is rather mundane; Calvin and Hobbes have stopped while walking along the sidewalk. Calvin reflects on what this particular experience means with respect to his life:

> Let's say life is this square of sidewalk. We're born at this crack and we die at that crack. Now we find ourselves somewhere inside the square, and in the process of walking out of it. Suddenly we realize our time in here is fleeting. Is our quick experience here pointless? Does anything we say or do in here really matter? Have we done anything important? Have we been happy? Have we made the most of these precious few footsteps?[48]

An important realization materializes in this brief, contemplative moment. Crucially, Calvin begins his thought process by framing life in specifically spatial terms. Because there is a beginning and end to life, a boundary necessarily coordinates how one should understand the human condition.

While the setting establishes a specific point at which life begins, the tenor of Calvin's reflection belies the stability that such a definitive origin connotes. The theme of displacement follows on from the discussion earlier in this chapter concerning the inability of the text to provide meaning that is stable. In addition to the examination of Vaught's work with respect to this point, the theme of textual instability recalls Derrida's stress on the openness of the text as a consequence of a latent and therefore necessary instability. Insofar as the text cannot contain meaning because all signs trace an already absent origin, there can be no clearly demarcated beginning to meaning in the sense that the sidewalk's crack structures a geometric understanding of life. Thus, the stress in this particular strip falls on the space that Calvin occupies: the expanse between the beginning and the end. The outer edge is death, a reality that ultimately destabilizes everything else within the square that portrays human life.[49] Significantly, then, Calvin attempts to understand his human condition only after he frames his reflection with an admission of life's fragility.

In an early, extended narrative thread, Calvin confronts mortality in a different context. When he finds an injured raccoon, Calvin experiences directly the fragility that characterizes life.[50] As he watches over the injured raccoon, Calvin understands acutely the implication of death: it is a devastating loss.[51] Though it intersects Calvin's life for a very small amount of time, the raccoon affects him deeply by and through its death. Calvin reflects: "It's like I found him for no reason. I had to say goodbye as soon as I said hello. Still ... in a sad, awful, terrible way, I'm happy I met him."[52] Meaning in the context of death is paradoxical. The lack of a reason for what is happening is tied to the raccoon's vulnerability,[53] which strikes Calvin as a series of events that is not fair.[54] The difficulty of reconciling the human condition with a sense of goodness/fairness in the universe thus follows on from Calvin's response to the raccoon's death. Death is unfair insofar as Calvin perceives this event as connected with some skewed value structure that characterizes the universal. The raccoon's death does not "make sense"; yet in the unnecessary death, Calvin touches upon the value that others can bring to life. The raccoon's death offers direction in how to understand life, given that death is an inevitable part of it. Calvin cites his mom to explain to Hobbes the lesson he learns: "We don't really understand it, but there are many things we don't understand, and we just have to do the best we can with the knowledge that we have."[55] The basic point this encounter with death reveals, then, is that there are limits to what humans can know. Moreover, death affects specifically where these limits are insofar as death is a deeply subversive part of life.

The sidewalk's limit is the horizon that (to recall Vattimo) fractures meaning. The limit and its hermeneutical consequences thus reinforce the fact that death frames life, and therefore all meaning. Kearney reflects on the implications that emerge out of this fragmented condition: "The limit experience of death is the most sure sign of our finitude. Moreover, it is precisely *because* we are beings who know that we will die that we keep on telling stories, struggling to represent something of the unpresentable, to hazard interpretations of the puzzles and aporias that surround us."[56] The struggle to comprehend life in light of death's inevitability is a narrative that, if taken seriously, can be paralyzing. The April 16, 1991, strip concludes by capturing how disruptive this kind of reflection can be. The final panel shows Calvin and Hobbes staring down at the same spot on the sidewalk without saying a word. Calvin's insight has frozen the two friends in the midst of their journey (across the sidewalk and, more broadly, though life). It is now night, a passage of narrative time that indicates the power of death to extend reflection. The implications of continuing their walk suspend Calvin and Hobbes; to progress towards the other side of this square is to continue an inevitable journey towards the end of life.

In his own imaginative way, Calvin acknowledges that death is a part of life. When he is in the midst of a stretch of creativity in his snowmaking, Calvin cites mortality as the inspiration for making a rather bland snowman. He explains to Hobbes that because snow melts, he is able to "take *advantage* of my medium's impermanence. *This* sculpture is about transience. As this figure melts, it invites the viewer to contemplate the evanescence of life. This piece speaks to the horror of our own mortality."[57] Like humanity, snow's presence materializes into a suspended state.[58] It is water prior to falling, and it returns to liquid form. Calvin harnesses this fluidity in order to articulate an awareness of how such a condition ultimately undermines the self. The snowman will gradually dissolve into a pile of slush and eventually cease to exist as a snowman.[59] Importantly, Calvin asserts that this point follows from snow's latent properties. It is a necessarily unstable substance, which, like humanity, suffers outwardly the effects of its inevitable decay.

On the basis of the snow's temporary nature, Calvin describes an effect that leads the reader to imagine a visual account of the snowman that has yet to occur. The need to consider this aspect of the snowman follows from an awareness of mortality, but, significantly, the other kids who see the snowman are unable to make the leap from what is present in the text — a plain snowman — and the implications that Calvin builds into his snowman. As these kids taunt Calvin for being "stupid" because "it's too warm to build a snowman,"[60] he mutters to Hobbes with disgust, "Genius is never understood in it's own time."[61] The genius that he implies is the ability to imagine what the snowman will become based on its latent characteristics. Conceptualizing how snow will reveal mortality through the process of melting anticipates a visual text (art is a text insofar as it is a kind of discourse) that will extend the point he makes to Hobbes. In this respect, the visual functions in a slightly different capacity; it is in process, yet through its anticipated development it generates significant meaning. Those who are unable to make this imaginative leap do not appreciate the genius at work in this discourse, and in Hobbes' words, are "Philistines."[62] The broader point, then, is that the intersection between the visual and the verbal elements in the text requires an imaginative engagement. Failure to do so will not only restrict the meanings to which the text leads the reader, it also reveals how a lack of imagination is a deeply problematic way to engage a discursive context. This, in turn, speaks to the effects that a lack of imagination can have when one considers the human condition's mortality.

In *The Space of Literature*, Maurice Blanchot provides helpful scaffolding for examining how death's presence affects the text. By drawing on Blanchot's work, the experience captured in the April 16, 1991, strip will enrich the current discussion of how the textual properties of *Calvin and Hobbes* develop the imagination's ability to respond to the implications of Calvin's reflections and the soon-to-melt snowman. As Calvin and Hobbes reflect on mortality, two distinct themes emerge simultaneously: fragility and strength. The first, of course, exposes the human condition as a journey towards an unavoidable end. In this capacity the human condition becomes a series of questions concerning value.[63] An existential crisis[64] lingers with Calvin and Hobbes, as they remain immobile in the final panel. While the strip leaves the reader to dwell with Calvin and Hobbes in this unsettling space, the honesty with which this experience acknowledges the fate that awaits all humans allows the reader to share in the bond that death cannot disrupt — namely, the friendship between Calvin and Hobbes. Blanchot summarizes well the dynamic at work in this scene: "To write is to enter into the affirmation of the solitude in which fascination threatens. It is to surrender to the risk of time's absence, where eternal starting over reigns."[65] This is a decidedly solitary moment for the two friends, as they jointly experience an impending mortality. As Blanchot explains, the point at which the text incorporates the possibility of the eternal[66] is the moment when the text can be released from death's influence. "Whoever is fascinated doesn't see, properly speaking, what he sees. Rather, it touches him in an immediate proximity; it seizes and ceaselessly draws him close, even as it leaves him absolutely at a distance."[67]

Even as their reflection on life's inevitable end roots them to a particular space, Calvin and Hobbes are able in their recognition of death to counter the grip mortality has on the text.

Even though Calvin and Hobbes see death demarcated on the sidewalk, they also see an alternative to death's instability. This point is implicit in the endless consideration the friends share after night has fallen. Their reflections on mortality do not cause either to move; they remain together. This is a specific intimacy that reflects Blanchot's broader point. The text is able in its two discourses to bracket Calvin and Hobbes from the implications of mortality by asserting their shared commitment to finding meaning despite death's effect. There exists a textual reminder (and remainder) that death cannot be overcome completely. To recognize that life is finite is to alter how the imagination functions. According to Blanchot, "This recognition ruins in me the power of knowing, the right to grasp. It makes what is ungraspable inescapable; it never lets me cease reaching what I cannot attain. And that which I cannot take, I must take up again, never to go."[68] The consequence of the imagination's transcendence in response to death is, then, a cord that simultaneously binds the text indefinitely to the unavoidable end that smothers the imagination. This is a crucial tension, given the argument at hand. In the end, the imagination necessarily remains tethered to the real world contexts that it seeks to reorder.

The ability to withstand the text's dislocation despite this fetter is one of the crucial roles that imagination plays. The suspension that Calvin and Hobbes experience on the sidewalk does not preclude them (or the reader) from reconfiguring how to understand the space between the sidewalk's beginning and end. In this still-to-be-determined space, then, death can be transformed into the horizon that always beckons the imaginative journey. Blanchot explains: "In the heart of the distress and weakness from which it is inseparable, [the text] again becomes a possibility of plenitude, a road without any goal at the end, but capable *perhaps* of corresponding to that goal without any road leading to it."[69] The text, then, is a journey, sustained through the imagination's ability to depart from life's realities while never forgetting the essential influence that demands an imaginative release in the first place.

One sees this effect in Spaceman Spiff's continued fearlessness to travel to the farthest (and furthest) places from Calvin's life, thus revealing a willingness to embrace the journey as a process. The goal is rarely to return to Earth; most Spiff adventures conclude with his retreat from some antagonist.[70] In Spiff, the reader finds the plenitude that grows out of this moment on the sidewalk. Consequently, the invitation to explore takes on added meaning insofar as Calvin leads the reader across a text without direction. The road does not lead home; it meanders through an imaginative world that is always aware of but never tied solely to life's fragilty.[71]

As Calvin and Hobbes remain on the sidewalk, the text's deconstructive implications emerge. The line that constitutes death's horizon obscures the initial line that is, according to Derrida, already absent.[72] Blanchot explains how the suspended movement ultimately opens the text towards further adventures:

> This absence makes it impossible ever to declare the work finished or unfinished. The work is without any proof, just as it is without any use. It can't be verified. Truth can appropriate it, renown draws attention to it, but the existence it thus acquires doesn't concern it. This demonstrability renders it neither certain nor real.[73]

The absent textual origin takes on narrative significance and therefore announces the importance of the imagination's freedom to respond to life's fragility. The imagination's lack of demonstrability ultimately affirms the text's intelligibility. More specifically, by unhinging the text from the notion of a stabilizing anchor one can recognize what is at stake in Calvin's adventures. The text's lack of a fixed center holds it open to an endless number of adventures, a freedom that ultimately affirms the imagination's importance in finding meaning within life's fragility. Whether one is following Spiff's daring escapes or joining Calvin and Hobbes on the sidewalk to reflect, the unmistakable result of the two discourses at work in *Calvin and Hobbes* becomes clear. In the end, the imagination has the ability to transcend the challenges that life poses. No context is immune to Spiff's fearlessness (though Susie-like aliens tend to put up a good fight), a reminder of the enduring stillness at the end of the April 16, 1991, strip. Like Spiff, the friendship between Calvin and Hobbes remains undaunted in the face of the horizon's limit. Whenever this text's implied closure occurs — Calvin and Hobbes have to leave the sidewalk at some point — the bond between the friends resists the rupture that death's ultimate closure will bring. Undaunted, the imagination holds the two friends together.

Blanchot offers a helpful metaphor to characterize the balance between the instability and freedom that set *Calvin and Hobbes* apart as an imaginative text: exile. Blanchot frames this concept by stressing the implications of the writer's decision to release the text towards the reader.

His explanation is particular insightful with respect to Watterson and the texts he creates, so a lengthy quotation on this point is helpful:

> [The author] is exiled from the city, from regular occupations and limited obligations, from everything connected to results, substantive reality, power. The outward aspect of the risk to which the work exposes him is precisely its inoffensive appearance. The poem is inoffensive, which is to say that whoever submits is deprived of himself as power, consents to be cast out from his own capability and from all forms of possibility.[74]

The author is free to invite the reader into the text's world because as an author s/he undertakes a journey. The purpose of this journey is to imagine, which, as discussed earlier, is a generative property that characterizes how *Calvin and Hobbes* unfolds. A corollary absence of obligation to concerns that are tangential or altogether unconnected to this search for meaning is, infamously, a hallmark of Watterson (his decision not to license *Calvin and Hobbes* for merchandise speaks to the importance of preserving the text's power).[75] Moreover, the strip's narrative baseline is innocuous in its appeal lies in its invitation to readers. Just as Watterson yields the text to the reader's imagination (through Calvin's imagination),[76] the reader also yields in accepting the invitation; to find meaning, s/he must enter the text on its terms.

Watterson's decision not to license *Calvin and Hobbes* was in this respect a serious moment and, consequently, a legitimizing aspect of the world Watterson created. There are multiple analyses of his decision that can be consulted for more on this point, but Watterson's own words summarize well the stakes of his decision: "Each product I considered seemed to violate the spirit of the strip, contradict its message, and take me away from the work I loved. If my syndicate had let it go at that, the decision would have taken maybe 30 seconds of my life."[77] Watterson's approach to the issue of licensing echoes a point made by Gaston Bachelard in *The Poetics of Space*:

> There is also the courage of the writer who braves the kind of censorship that forbids "insignificant" confidences. But what a joy reading is, when we recognize the importance of these insignificant things, when we can add our own personal daydreams to the "insignificant" recollections of the author![78]

The joy of the strip — its surprises and its willingness to accommodate analogous readings — develops in part because of Watterson's refusal to condense the world that Calvin explores into a marketable package. The strip's identity transcends such boundaries because, paradoxically, Watterson expands the strip by maintaining its insignificance with respect to marketing. He could have made a fortune selling stuffed tigers, but to do so would sacrifice the integrity of the adventures that emerge when a stuffed tiger is around.

Caught amidst exile's tension, the text becomes the space that experiences simultaneously a real and an imagined departure. Blanchot explains that within exile, one "belongs to the foreign, to the outside which knows no intimacy or limit."[79] Herein lies the corollary to the text's ability to bring the horizon intimately close and impossibly distant. At once the text is both of these experiential contexts, which, as Calvin makes clear on the sidewalk and frequently throughout the rest of the strip, gives rise to the textual space wherein the reader can join Calvin in attempting to find meaning amidst paradoxical influences. The result, according to Blanchot, is a recalibration of how one crosses the text: "Exile ... makes [one a] wanderer, the one always astray, he to whom the stability of presence is not granted and who is deprived of a true abode."[80] Displaced from this true abode (and thus from a textual origin),[81] one realizes that any conclusion gives way to the process of looking for such a thing, which, of course, can never be found. Calvin and Spiff are explorers and therefore wanderers who lack "the ability to abide and stay. For where the wanderer is, the conditions of a definitive here are lacking.[82] In this absence of here and now what happens does not clearly come to pass as an event based upon which something solid could be achieved."[83] This is the text's identity: displacement compounded and overcome through the imagination. The interpretive freedom that comes with the lack of a definitive here indicates why the imagination surfaces as the way to incorporate the two discourses that structure *Calvin and Hobbes*.

An important consequence of how the visual and the verbal interact is the ability to bend the structuring effects of space and time. Clark explains how the breakdown of specifically temporal limitations releases the text: "The essential nature of language, rather than being harnessed to mimetic or cognitive ends, was set free to effect itself in its own textual space. Once representation is eschewed, the order of the text need no longer submit to the sequentially of mundane time."[84] Thus unhinged, the text can transcend the categories that would otherwise restrict the imagination: "There would be a dislocation of time, as there is a dislocation of place, yet belonging neither to time nor place. In this dislocation we come round to writing."[85] Here Vaught's loosening of temporal and spatial significance is apparent. The text's intelligibility does not require the clearly defined effects that space and time exert on the human experience. As a space disrupted once it is loosened from the moorings, the text becomes in its exile a journey of possible meanings in response to the definitive end of space and time in humanity's mortality.

In conceptualizing the text as an exilic space, Blanchot accommodates the multiple perspectives into which *Calvin and Hobbes* often splinters. This is not to say, of course, that the narratives that populate the strip lack meaning; in fact, sanctioning paradoxical features ultimately enriches how one can read the strip. Calvin's world is truly a space wherein the lack of a here provides the stepping off point for the content that welcomes readers in sustained, significant numbers. The disjunctive features that might otherwise come across as meaningless point to the imagination's power to generate meaning.[86] On this point Bachelard provides an insightful approach to the text. In navigating the uneven topography that characterizes the text's exilic space, the reader is forced to engage in a capacity that cannot ignore that lack of clear hermeneutical signposting. Bachelard explains that the text's various shades are "not an additional, superficial coloring. We should therefore have to say how we inhabit our vital space, in accord with all the dialectics of life, how we take root, day after day, in a 'corner of the world.'"[87] In Bachelard's conception, the text's paradoxical element is what substantiates the ability to find meaning. In not making sense, this quality outlines the context in which humans can make sense of their experiences. This possibility (never to be confirmed) is, for Bachelard, an unavoidable and privileged part of the text. Insofar as the text — like the human condition — cannot escape the disruption the life's various shades cause, a familiarity with the unknown is crucial. Humanity's condition is defined by uncertainty. A willingness to acknowledge these parameters is important if one is to endure the text's paradoxical implications.

The question, then, is whether the reader is willing to reach elbow-deep into the text's unknowable space, or whether the reader will attempt to skirt what cannot be avoided. Calvin, of course, encourages the former course of action. In the March 4, 1991, strip, Calvin stands before his mom in his adventurer's helmet. His mom asks how his day is going, and Calvin responds that nothing of consequence has happened so far. His mom grabs onto the qualifying phrase: "'So far?'"[88] Calvin explains what he means in a way that also clarifies why he is wearing the helmet: "Well, you never know. Something *could* happen today. And if it *does*, by golly, I'm going to be ready for it!"[89] This willingness accepts that there is no way to know what life will bring, and, more importantly, refuses to back down from the challenges that are implicit in this uncertainty. Calvin's mom echoes the thoughts of many: "I need a suit like that."[90]

Calvin's imagination, then, reaches out towards the text's horizon despite the unsettling effect this boundary has on the text (and on life). By undertaking this journey, he reveals another paradoxical feature of the world that he occupies through his imagination: In his departure from reality he ultimately bends meaning back to the context that he seeks to escape. Or, in Bachelard's words, "Here we touch upon a converse whose images we shall have to explore: all really inhabited space bears the essence of the notion of home."[91] On the one hand, this essence is an assertion of the text's crucial absence; there is no home (Blanchot's here) and therefore no hermeneutical stability. On the other hand, this trace of what has been lost in departing always lingers in the text, which in turn allows the person who occupies the text on these terms to orient her/his reading back towards the home that has been lost.

Amidst the allure of the home from which the text has departed, there exists a significant risk that threatens to undermine the fearless adventurer. As Bachelard reminds his readers, "When we dream of the house we were born in, in the utmost depths of revery, we participate in this original warmth, in this well-tempered manner of the material paradise."[92] The appeal is obvious, but in journeying towards the recovery of this warmth, one risks the encounter that reiterates the text's exilic parameters. For example, the January 5, 1990, strip begins with Calvin and Hobbes returning home after a day out in particularly cold conditions. Calvin's eyes are barely open, and an icicle dangles from Hobbes' nose. As he opens the door to the warmth of his house, Calvin remarks, "This is the part of winter I like best ... when you come inside, freezing cold and soaked ... and you put on fresh dry clothes, and run up to the warm kitchen, where mom's got a steaming mug of hot chocolate waiting for you!"[93] The home's essential invitation structures the text, just as the thought of hot chocolate no doubt sustains Calvin while he trudges home through the biting wind. This expectation is the participation wherein the text nearly grasps that which is absent throughout exile — namely, the welcome, stable space that a home provides.

The problem, of course, is that this originary warmth remains out of reach because exile is, by definition, a space that does not contain a home. Calvin senses this bitter reality when he walks into the kitchen, only to find it empty. He calls, "Mom?... Mom?? *Hey Mom!*"[94] The crescendo in his tone anticipates the *other* possibility to returning home and finding a warm mug of hot chocolate — namely that no one will be there to offer this welcome. Hobbes finds a note with this cruel reminder: "Calvin, I'm next door. Don't have anything to eat, or you'll spoil your appetite. Mom."[95] Calvin, with his hands in his pockets and an expression of disappointment that is remarkably similar to the look on his face as he opens the door in the strip's first panel, laments, "It's going to be a long, cold, dark winter."[96] Calvin lays bare the harsh reality that the text occasionally speaks. As Bachelard states, though "we flee in search of a real refuge,"[97] a second essential trace fills the text's space: the reminder that one can only dream of experiencing the essence that the text implies. The home that welcomes one in out of the cold thus becomes "centralized solitude."[98] As a result, the home's anticipated warmth is a reminder of exile's indefinite character. That which invites the reader forward is, in the end, a sign of "prolonged waiting."[99]

Fortunately for Calvin, not every winter is as dark as this single experience suggests. At other times, a trip back through the snow finds the warmth that he anticipates. In the January 17, 1988, strip, the reader encounters Calvin as he trudges uphill against a strong wind. His eyes are nearly shut in the same capacity as the January 5, 1990, strip. The first panel emphasizes the intolerable cold that winter can bring: "I've got to go in. Another five minutes out here, and I'll be frozen solid."[100] Hyperbole aside, the urgency Calvin feels helps to capture the allure that the home's warmth can have. Given that Hobbes is not with Calvin, and, moreover, that Calvin does not even consider Hobbes in his desire to be inside, this experience offers a different view. Bachelard explains: "A reminder of winter strengthens the happiness of inhabiting. In the reign of the imagination alone, a reminder of winter increases the house's value as a place to live in."[101] Several important points arise from Bachelard's comments on winter. First, the bitterness that Calvin experiences brings into focus the home's warmth as a counterbalance to his exposure to winter. He is so cold that home provides a refuge, regardless of past instances (or future ones) wherein the home is not a place he wants to dwell.

Importantly, Bachelard stresses that the text characterizes the home as safe space from within a context that is the antithesis to what is desired. It is through this contrast, moreover, that the true value of the home as a refuge materializes fully within the exilic winter though which Calvin plods. He realizes this value fully when he enters into the warm, bright space of his house. His mom greets him with the very thing that elsewhere portends a dark winter: a mug of hot chocolate. She then directs him to the fire — the source of warmth within the warming context — and brings him a comic book. Calvin's sincere reflection captures what the imagination's desire, now fulfilled, means: "Nobody knows how to pamper like a mom."[102] Calvin encounters exile's opposite; for a moment he understands and appreciates the stability of his home.[103] Heidegger offers an understanding of dwelling that is helpful to the point at hand. Specifically, the text permits humans to dwell — albeit temporarily — because it can establish a momentary refuge amidst humanity's thrown condition. Like Bachelard, then, Heidegger captures the desire that the text's exilic character gives rise to: an impossible home (or origin) that steadies the text.

Calvin's comfort is, unfortunately, short-lived. Hobbes reacts to the pampering that Calvin receives in an uncharacteristically selfish way. As Calvin appreciates what his mom has done, Hobbes interjects, "So are you going to eat all those peanut butter crackers yourself, or what?"[104] Whereas Hobbes' friendship usually provides a secure feeling amidst life's chaos, here he is the presence that interrupts the serene moment that Calvin enjoys. Moreover, Hobbes' comment draws attention back to his original absence in the narrative. This is one of the few adventures involving a sled of which Hobbes is not a part. As a result, he does not share the cold of winter's exile with Calvin but, rather, undermines the momentary break from winter that greets Calvin when he returns home. Consequently, Bachelard's analysis holds true insofar as Hobbes re-establishes the contrast between the home as a safe space and the impossibility of experiencing this valuable feeling for any length of time. Even during a moment's respite, the text cannot outpace its exilic character. There is always a reminder of the dislocation in human experience, even during the moments that suggest the wanderer has finally arrived at a safehouse.

A look at winter in the strip of December 26, 1988, will provide an illuminative coda to the various themes discussed in this chapter. A single panel covers two-thirds of the strip. This uncommon visual construct allows Calvin and Hobbes to look out at the moon-streaked yard from the comfort of their house. The shadows obscure their faces slightly at the far left of the panel, which establishes a contrast with the moon that hangs brightly at the top right corner. Calvin's reflection summarizes what is at stake in the different contexts that this strip brings together. He tells Hobbes, "There's nothing prettier than new fallen snow on a clear, freezing moonlit night."[105] The next and final panel pulls the reader back into the house with the two friends as Calvin makes clear how he understands the scene's beauty: "...through a window, that is."[106] Exile's vast context can be beautiful when viewed from within the safe confines of the home. The corollary point is that this can only be appreciated from within; as Calvin makes clear, things are decidedly different when viewed from the outside. This outside is close; it encloses the house and thus foreshadows the inevitable departure from the house back outside.

Winter is a delicate context, one that frequently brings together the two discourses that constitute *Calvin and Hobbes*. Calvin's appreciation for the night's beauty responds to and pre-empts the scene that unfolds in the December 26, 1988, strip. The visual and the verbal coalesce into a winter night that captures the instability of the human condition, and therefore structures how the text speaks to this reality. As Calvin shows in a variety of circumstances, winter is the space wherein different and often discordant influences converge. Following Calvin's adventures, one can recognize how the imagination opens the text to examine deeply rooted experiences that define the human condition. While the text does not ultimately spare Calvin from the realities that prompt his reflection, it does offer still moments with Hobbes to slow, even if momentarily, the pull that so often collapses life back into a reminder that reality cannot be escaped. All that is left, then, is the ability to transcend winter's chill imaginatively and momentarily, a calmness that balances the multiple interpretive paths leading through the text.

CHAPTER FOUR

Irony

The Real World's Uncomfortable Lesson

When it comes to Susie Derkins, Calvin's imagination can develop some good schemes. The problem is that his plans tend not to work out. A particularly good example of this contrast occurs in the June 21, 1987, strip. Calvin can hardly contain his excitement as he runs across the top panel. He revels in the "sheer *genius*"[1] of his plan; he has been saving snow in the freezer for months to throw at Susie in the middle of the summer. After Calvin sneaks up behind Susie, the story pauses just as he is poised to throw the snowball at Susie. He stands behind her in mid-windup as she plays on the sidewalk, unaware of what is going on behind her. As Calvin releases the snowball, he exclaims, "*Hey Susie!!*"[2] Perhaps it is just bad luck, but even from a few feet away Calvin manages to miss her. The snowball slams into the sidewalk and Calvin unleashes his frustration as he tries to understand how he missed: "There must've been a cross breeze! I can't believe it!"[3] Meanwhile, Susie scoops up the snow and reforms it into her own snowball. Calvin stops complaining long enough to realize the tables have turned. With a wicked grin plastered on her face, Susie throws the snowball squarely into Calvin's face (notably, Susie manages to overcome the cross breeze that caused Calvin to miss from the same distance). As Calvin lies on the sidewalk covered in snow, Susie walks away with a look of satisfaction on her face. The final panel from this strip offers Calvin's reflection on the chain of events that led him to this point: "The irony of this is just sickening."[4]

There is little doubt that what happens here is ironic. In fact, Calvin's analysis reveals a common — and crucial — textual feature of *Calvin and Hobbes*. An excursus into how irony affects a text will thus provide the stepping off point for this chapter and, in the end, indicate how irony permits the text to pivot towards readings that extend beyond the specific context in which it appears. In his classic treatment of irony, *A Rhetoric of Irony*, Wayne C. Booth outlines the steps for understanding how irony unfolds within the text. The reader must "reject the [text's] literal meaning,"[5] try out "alternative interpretations,"[6] decide "about the author's knowledge or beliefs,"[7] and, finally, "choose a new meaning or cluster of meanings with which we can rest secure."[8] This progression establishes a format that reflects a common understanding of how irony works. Its purpose is to suggest a new meaning in the text through particular disjunction.[9] Though in identifying this purpose Booth rightly cautions against literalizing meaning in an ironic context, he fails to stress in full irony's ability to accommodate multiple meanings. As a result, he regresses into claims about authorship, which, while often true (most authors who use irony do so intentionally), is a distraction from what is at stake when irony makes its appearance in the text.

This off-center focus is apparent in the suggestion that irony can lead the reader towards secure meanings. Booth distances himself somewhat from these implications in highlighting that irony produces "the inevitable presence of victims, real or imagined."[10] This point is well taken insofar as irony thrives on subverting some expectation (both characters and readers tend to suffer this linguistic blow). However, like his outline of how irony functions, Booth's comments on irony's victim eventually circle around to a conception that finds in irony a stabilizing effect. Booth writes, "Even irony that does imply victims, as in all ironic satire, is often much more clearly directed to more affirmative matters."[11] Behind this claim lies an optimistic hermeneutic that does not cohere with the destabilizing wake that irony leaves in a text. Irony leads away from stable meanings; it pulls the reader into the rubble of the text that anticipates clarity. As Calvin's experience shows, the presence of irony does not afford this kind of clarity. He assumes his plan will work, which foreshadows the inevitable failure that he experiences. His confidence is ironic because it is doomed to fail. The irony is that the victim[12] is the one who intended to hit Susie with the snowball. Victimhood is thus reversed, and in this inversion the unsustainability of Booth's positive reading of irony becomes apparent. He even admits the problem, despite the trajectory of his argument: "I shall work on the ... assumption unproved: that with certain kinds of irony the mind's irrepressible desire to be clear is the very source of whatever pleasure or profit is to be found."[13] The whole point of the strip in question is to deconstruct this critical expectation and therefore to emphasize that irony does not function in the capacity that Booth suggests. While the premise is acceptable — the mind, like the text, anticipates stability — the results that this critical approach suggests are not tenable. The text does not grant profit in that it cannot accommodate the clarity that Booth claims irony can provide.[14]

At this point it would be a good idea to recall Calvin's analysis of what occurs. It is sickening because irony's role is to deny constantly the expectations that things will go according to plan (which is particularly troubling when the Dictator-for-Life of G.R.O.S.S. is involved). On this point, D.J. Enright is helpful in recasting irony's role as something that resembles what Calvin realizes: "The art of irony, ostensibly less abrasive, may be the more disturbing because it is 'an enquiring mode that exploits discrepancies, challenges assumptions and reflects equivocations' but doesn't presume to hold out answers."[15] While Enright echoes Booth's suggestion that the author's motivation is a key factor in irony, there is an obvious divergence with respect to the textual effect that irony causes. Whereas Enright stresses irony's disjointed (and disjointing) nature, Booth argues that irony ultimately brings clarity to the text. Booth writes, "Any written or spoken word of stable irony, I have assumed, is a structure of meanings, an order which rules out some readings as entirely fallacious, shows other readings to be partially so, and confirms others as more or less adequate."[16] Though Booth then cautions that all but the simplest ironies are bound to give readers some trouble,[17] the structuring energy he grants to irony is unmistakable. The notion of adequacy belies any softening of his assumptions; to suggest that irony brings clarity to the text is to miss the more subtle disruptions that irony generates.

In broad terms, Enright makes clear that irony does not crystallize meaning. On the contrary, it breaks apart the assumptions that presume meaning. Part of Calvin's sickening experience is this unexpected inversion. The reader never finds out what exactly caused the snowball to miss Susie. Perhaps it was a crosswind, or simply Calvin's over-zealous wind-up that altered the trajectory ever so slightly. What the reader does encounter is the moment when the plan's certain success (in Calvin's mind) disappears and the tables turn on Calvin's expectations. His reflection in the final panel reveals the effect that irony produces. In Enright's words, this result produces the effect that Calvin experiences: "The detection of an ironic twist is supposed to make us feel better. In this instance it can only make us feel slightly worse."[18] If Booth's analysis were correct, the reader would encounter a text that arrives at what irony is *supposed* to do. However, as

Calvin realizes painfully, irony produces the opposite of such expectations, which is why the text leaves the reader — and Calvin — with a sickening feeling. When expectations are not met, one is left with a clear awareness that something did not happen as it was supposed to, which in turn invites a lingering doubt into the text. An important thematic shift thus occurs in irony's wake: attempts to understand what went wrong turn into reflections on why things went wrong.

The ability to undermine assumptions allows irony to destabilize the text, an effect that, when recognized, asserts the indefinite instability from which the text cannot escape. Another clear example of irony from *Calvin and Hobbes* condenses what is at stake when exploring how it affects the text. The strip in question begins when Susie walks up to Calvin with her stuffed bunny, Mr. Bun, as he and Hobbes are sitting on the sidewalk (because this panel includes a third person, Hobbes appears as a stuffed tiger). Susie enthusiastically suggests that the four friends can play together: "You and I can be the parents, and Hobbes and Mr. Bun can be our children."[19] Calvin's response is dripping with irony: "Oh right. Hobbes and I are gonna put our big plans on hold so we can play house with a stuffed rabbit? Forget it!"[20] Given her perception of Hobbes (which the reader shares in the first three panels), Susie's response is more than fair: "I don't see why you'll play with your dumb ol' tiger and not with Mr. Bun and me. You're just mean, that's all!"[21] After Susie leaves, Hobbes amplifies the irony at work in this strip. As Calvin shares his thoughts on girls, Hobbes reflects on the exchange: "Mr. Bun seems comatose. Did you notice?"[22] Given that the main tension in the strip is between Susie and Calvin, Hobbes' comment appears to be little more than an afterthought. However, this observation announces clearly the ironic texture that characterizes this encounter. Hobbes appears as an inanimate tiger throughout the exchange, yet his supposed activity is the reason that Calvin will not play with Susie. The effect on Susie is to unsettle how she understands the experience. Enright's analysis of irony's effect thus rings clearly; for her there is no perceptible reason that she and Mr. Bun cannot play in the same capacity in which Calvin and Hobbes are supposedly playing.

If the strip were to end in the third panel, the irony would be obvious enough in its subversive effect. However, there is more to the story. Hobbes calls specific attention to the fact that Mr. Bun appears to Calvin as Hobbes appears to Susie. Moreover, in this specific instance Hobbes also perceives Mr. Bun as an inanimate stuffed animal. Despite the contrast to which irony calls attention, Hobbes' word choice implies that he *might* be able to see Mr. Bun in a different capacity. The tenor of his comment does not confirm that Mr. Bun is comatose in the same way that Hobbes is comatose to everyone but Calvin. There are instances when Hobbes is with Susie and not Calvin[23] wherein Hobbes may have interacted with Mr. Bun in the same imaginative way that Calvin interacts with Hobbes. If this were the case — and there is no way to say for sure one way or another based on the textual evidence at hand — the irony would only thicken. Hobbes would thus reveal the limits of Calvin's imagination insofar as Calvin would not be able to perceive Susie's "real" relationship with Mr. Bun despite the fact that he frequently laments others' inability to see his own imaginative relationship with Hobbes. Thus, her invitation that Calvin rejects based on what she cannot see is valid if the reader shifts the perspective at work in the strip.

Because Susie and Mr. Bun mirror Calvin and Hobbes, irony's effect is pronounced. David Jasper offers a helpful explanation of how irony is at work in this kind of circumstance: "Irony is never satisfied in itself, and arises out of the peculiar requirements of each situation."[24] Hobbes' comment would not be as pointed without the specific context because the text feeds off of the contrast (and similarity) between Hobbes and Mr. Bun. There is a particularly biting effect at work in this ironic exchange. Hobbes undermines Susie's relationship with Mr. Bun in a way that destabilizes his friendship with Calvin. There is, then, an obvious target at which irony aims. Its presence is not simply to suggest a new way of reading this exchange; the point is to call into question the imaginative construct at work in this particular strip (and, indeed, throughout *Calvin and Hobbes*). In the October 1, 1987, strip, a state of play involving kids, imagination, and stuffed animals leads to an exchange that frustrates everyone involved. If the reader were not aware of what is at stake when Calvin rejects Susie's offer, Hobbes makes the point clear. In so doing, he actually undermines Calvin, which, as Jasper writes, extends the disjunction that irony causes: "Endlessly self-reflexive, irony engages in a perpetual redescription of established beliefs and assumptions in order to break free from their power."[25] Irony thus casts into doubt the very imaginative dynamic that provides the foundation for Calvin's friendship with Hobbes. If Mr. Bun is simply a stuffed rabbit, then Calvin effectively undermines his best friend. This is the subtle feeling that Enright identifies; the irony that infuses this exchange suggests — even if only in this particular strip —

the limits of Calvin's imagination. Both friends thus destabilize their friendship, however slightly, following a decision that supposedly rests on the strength of their friendship. If they are unwilling to play with other kids and stuffed animals imaginatively, then perhaps their own adventures should be called stupid. In turn, this label would fracture the very imaginative construct, and thus the strip's meaning, by virtue of irony's destabilizing effect.

Despite its clear, if subtle, effect on the text, irony can be difficult to identify. Jasper highlights this elusive nature as an important consideration when discussing irony: "Irony, inherently unstable and destabilising, happily works against its own narrative discourse and against its own textuality. The best irony is barely perceptible."[26] During one of Calvin's camping trips with his parents, this quality affects the text long before the irony is obvious. After a string of frustrating experiences, Calvin finally loses his temper when he cannot escape the annoyance of bug bites. Hobbes offers some practical advice: "Don't scratch the bites or you'll just make the itching worse."[27] This comment establishes irony's presence, but Calvin does not realize how disruptive the suggestion will be. He merely retorts, "What am I supposed to do then? It's driving me crazy!"[28] Yet again, Hobbes makes a practical suggestion: "Think about something else."[29] At this point irony saturates the narrative, but Hobbes' seeming pragmatism obscures just how bad things are going to get for Calvin. In the final panel, irony comes into focus; when Calvin asks what he should think about that can take his mind off of the itching that overwhelms him, Hobbes says matter-of-factly, "Maybe stepping out of all that poison ivy."[30] This exchange captures the subtle, creeping manner in which irony operates. Hobbes' role is ironic; in attempting to make things better, he ultimately makes things worse. Whereas Calvin starts this strip thinking that he has reached a limit based on how badly the bug bites itch, by the end he is acutely aware that bug bites are a mild concern. Poison ivy is a longer-lasting, more deeply rooted source of discomfort. Hobbes knows this, but he leaves Calvin unaware of how things are getting worse. His actions make manifest irony's willingness to work against the text's narrative momentum and, moreover, how irony's presence unsettles the space at hand rather than resolving the issue that Calvin faces. Everything about Hobbes in this strip coheres with his usual nature, but one cannot help but wonder why he helps Calvin in a distinctly unhelpful way. As Calvin's friend, Hobbes' suggestions should alleviate the frustration Calvin feels, but, through irony, the opposite occurs.

The complex exchange between Calvin and Hobbes in the July 27, 1989, strip indicates a further property of irony. Though it unsettles the text, irony paradoxically sustains an element of that which it undercuts. Enright explains this counter-intuitive dynamic: "If irony is to work there must be truth, centrality, and representativeness in the vicinity; it cannot be enforced through the words or actions of a crackpot or a tiny eccentric minority."[31] The subtlety with which irony undermines the text is, in effect, an inside job. It thrives on the kinds of expectations that permit it to enter the text without being noticed. In Calvin's case, his trust in Hobbes does not expect to result in the one thing that could aggravate an already intolerable situation. The July 27, 1989, strip develops because of the truth — Calvin's friendship with Hobbes and the expectations for sympathy that come with their bond — that ultimately leads to the opposite of what Calvin expects. One can see the same familiarity at work in both of the previous examples cited. The sickening irony that Calvin experiences when attempting to hit Susie with a snowball thrives in part because the plan is clever and because Calvin's feelings towards Susie really want to bring the plan to a successful conclusion. Because these expectations are understandable when viewed through Calvin's character, the unraveling control over the situation is all the more unsettling. Similarly, Hobbes' comment about Mr. Bun is sharp because he embodies the observation that he voices. If here were not another stuffed animal, then his comment would not undermine the very act of speaking about Mr. Bun.

In this example Calvin suffers irony's disruption, but he is frequently the vehicle of irony's unsettling influence as well. A particularly striking example of this dynamic occurs early in the strip when Calvin wakes up his dad on Father's Day. Calvin announces, "In appreciation of your service as dad, today I am living according to the principles of your fatherly wisdom."[32] Calvin's dad is not amused; it is five in the morning.[33] Calvin explains the early hour in accordance with his dad's wisdom: "Yes, 'Early to bed, early to rise,' you always say...."[34] Calvin then offers another example of how he is living in accordance with his dad's principles: "I was going to buy you a nice present, but a 'penny saved is a penny earned,' as you say ... so I'm now earning 6 percent on the money I didn't spend. Yes, dad, thanks to you I'm a happier, better person."[35] As with the poison ivy, irony is unmasked in the strip's final panel. Calvin's dad grumbles, "I knew we'd made a mistake the minute I saw that little bologna loaf in the hospital bassinet."[36] On the day that Calvin's dad should celebrate that Calvin actually takes his father's principles to heart, the reverse occurs; there is little appreciation for the gift despite the fact that Calvin's dad would otherwise be happy to see these guidelines embraced. Quite simply, Father's Day is not an occasion to be celebrated because, ironically, Calvin's dad has passed on fatherly wisdom. The principles that help him to enjoy life are the source of an obviously unenjoyable experience. Calvin's ironic gift thus subverts the notion that trusting in certain virtues can enrich life because those same values can also prove disruptive in a rather frustrating way.[37]

The grumbling Calvin's dad offers in response to his gift leaves irony's mark on the text, but the comment Calvin's mom makes to his dad adds an additional layer of irony. Her offhand remark — "Nice work, Socrates"[38] — constitutes a double irony. From Calvin's dad's perspective, the wisdom passed on should not result in an early morning highlight reel of moral principles. Indeed, virtue should lead to an enjoyable life, yet Calvin's temporary appreciation of virtue results in the opposite of what his dad hoped to accomplish. The second irony, which is more subtle still, undermines this inverted expectation. There *is* wisdom to Calvin's disruption because Socrates was a disruptive figure in this respect. He meant for his questions to dislodge those whom he encountered from their assumptions.[39] Calvin *is* happy, but not for the reason one might expect if his happiness derives from Socratic wisdom. Knowing Calvin's relationship with his dad, this happiness stems from the fact that he has turned his dad's emphasis on character against him.

To anticipate a more extended discussion in the second part of this book, it is worth noting the strong similarities between Calvin's ironic use of wisdom and the Noble Lie that Plato ascribes to Socrates in *The Republic*.[40] The noble lie is how Socrates justifies the idea that there are different classes of people in the state. Each class is determined by the kind of metal that constitutes its being. Even though this is not true — and those who claim to have gold in their selves know as much — the lie is justifiable because when people believe it, an orderly society will follow. At its core, the idea requires that the unwise remain unaware of the lie that extends their ignorance. Calvin, then, exposes the flaw in this conception of how the ruling class should manipulate the masses. If wisdom is truly part of human nature, then all humans should search for truth. Calvin does just this and, consequently, undermines his dad's authority (with irony, of course).

The angle from which irony affects the text constitutes an important consideration. In each of the examples from *Calvin and Hobbes* discussed in this chapter, a particular disruption arises from the narrative arc that eventually reveals irony at work. While the text can be slow to reveal irony's full effect, irony often leverages its presence out of sight. Gregory Currie emphasizes this subtle nature in discussing how the narrative context is not antecedent to irony's disruption: "We have seen that narrators who orient their narrations according to the point of view of a character may do so with a degree of irony. Irony is crucial to a proper understanding of narration."[41] Currie then expands on this point: "Ironic narration ... is not the same thing as the use of irony in narration."[42] Though his distinction is precise, Currie identifies an important consideration. Irony is not simply derivative; usually it is firmly embedded within the narrative, and therefore it cannot be isolated in analyzing its effects. Consequently, one cannot accept as normative the explanation that irony is a simple textual foil. According to Currie, "The traditional view according to which irony is saying one thing and meaning the opposite is badly wrong."[43] In rejecting this simplistic understanding of irony, Currie enriches the discussion at hand. To distill irony's presence in *Calvin and Hobbes* into a kind of metaphor is to misunderstand irony's deconstructive nature. The ability to recognize irony's effect does not lead to clarity of meaning. On the contrary, irony casts the text into a state of hermeneutical mayhem, which frustrates continually the expectations that often derives from the normative understanding of irony that Booth posits and Currie (like Enright) rejects.

In making this point, a word is needed to head off a criticism that emerges from a specific, ironic strip. When completing an assignment for school, Calvin deconstructs those who would use Deconstruction when approaching a text critically.[44] There is, then, an obvious irony in this chapter; yet by grounding this analysis in the text as a communicative space, the result falls closer to the literary study that Parker offers, and therefore resists floating into the more abstract understanding of irony that Albert Cook brings to bear on Marcel Duchamp.[45] As discussed in Chapter One, there is always the risk that one can overreach in analyzing the text, a risk that is especially pronounced when irony is mishandled. That being said, the current discussion finds its response to this potential criticism in Hobbes' own academic achievements. When Calvin attempts to simplify the question of how tigers hunt their food, Hobbes responds defensively and explains that a lot more than hunger goes into the pursuit of food. In fact, he explains sternly to Calvin that his dissertation on ethics "was *very* well received."[46] This comment mitigates to some extent the risk that bringing critical theory (or any academic methodology) to bear on a text can shut off the text's energy. As Hobbes makes clear, sometimes a bit more depth can provide significantly more insight; used appropriately (Hobbes is not one who is prone to hyperbole), academic studies can expand the text's parameters. As Calvin states (ironically) upon learning that Hobbes is an accomplished scholar, "I never realized killing was so grounded in the liberal arts."[47]

Currie, then, recalibrates irony in a way that extends the discussion at hand. Because irony is part of the text's structure, it has a role in developing the specific narrative that reveals irony. Thus, Currie states, one must recognize "that irony is essentially communicative, that it is essentially linguistic, that it is essentially critical."[48] Given irony's ability to undermine the text of which it is part, the essential communicative function that irony serves complicates further the dislocation that irony causes. Certain texts are communicative spaces that require irony's presence, even if this presence ultimately produces a space that proves unsettling. Irony constitutes a kind of textual rebel that sustains as it undermines. Though tucked away in a note, Currie pinpoints this effect as crucial to understanding irony: "ironic utterances embed."[49] In light of the previous chapter's discussion about the text's exilic character, one can see the dangerous implications of examining irony. On the one hand, recognizing irony's communicative role in the text is necessary to engage the text's world, yet in so doing the reader — like the character(s) in question — cannot escape the displacement that irony ultimately brings about.

As it undermines the text, irony is able to uncover meanings that can otherwise be ignored. The ability to expose how the text suggests an untenable meaning is a particularly incisive way for irony to be unsettling. The first panel of the February 9, 1995, strip shows Calvin standing in front of a snowman he has made.[50] The snowman lies on its stomach in deference to Calvin, who shakes his fist as he explains what is happening to the snowman (and the reader): "As I have created you, so I can destroy you! Therefore, in recognition of my supreme power, you must worship me! Yes, bow before mighty Calvin and tremble for I am the eternal, all knowing...."[51] The ability to create — which is a necessarily imaginative act — provides Calvin with a sense of power. He is literally able to mold the snow in a way that will bow down to the influence he has over his environment. In addition to this basic relationship between Calvin and his world, one encounters a specific conception of this creative power in the words he uses to explain to the snowman why this is a significant interaction. First and foremost, Calvin claims responsibility for existence, which echoes any number of creation stories. This, in turn, leads to the specific characteristics he cites as relevant, given his role as a creator of snowmen. His eternal, omnipresent qualities demand the response that the snowman offers. Importantly, however, he does not use a few key terms that he implies in describing his power. There is no mention of divinity; Calvin says he is merely mighty, as opposed to an almighty creator. This omission is important, as it grounds this particular strip in the real-world context out of which Calvin is able to fashion this exchange.

While this is an interesting, imaginative act, the scene quickly unravels. Before Calvin can finish extolling his power over the snowman, Susie appears and hits Calvin with a snowball. The shot is a good one, so much so that Calvin flips over with enough force to send his shoes flying. The immediate point, then, is a rather obvious irony. The same process that allows Calvin to fashion a worshipping snowman allows Susie to make a snowball to announce clearly that Calvin's power over snow is similarly available to others. He may be able to make snowmen, but this ability does not protect him from other creative acts involving snow.[52] There is, then, a clear ironic effect at work in this strip.

While Susie's appearance exposes through irony the fragile nature of Calvin's claims to the snowman, there is a deeper irony that is less perceptible but far more significant with respect to this text's possible meanings. She reveals that Calvin's control is limited in scope; he is subject to other forces that he cannot manipulate as he does the snowman. Currie offers a helpful explanation for understanding how Susie's ironic act conveys an important point in response to lording over the snowman: "Irony [is] a communicative device; the author or narrator — or for that matter one character speaking to another character — generally engages in an ironic act for communicative purposes, aiming to express their attitude (often a negative one) concerning someone or something."[53] The communicative effect is in this instance clear; Susie offers a strong rebuttal to the power Calvin claims. Her intention is important insofar as her ironic act affects Calvin in a way that establishes a broader point concerning his claims to be mighty. By revealing Calvin's weakness as he claims to be strong, Susie binds Calvin to the very thing over which he claims to have absolute power. Even if the power is actual, it is essentially useless insofar as it cannot accomplish anything beyond making a snowman in a prone position (which is going to melt anyway). A thousand snowmen bowing down would do nothing to protect Calvin from Susie's snowball (had they been standing, he would have avoided lying in the snow without his shoes; this is another good example of how the visual and the verbal play off one another to enhance meaning).

Susie's snowball no doubt wounds Calvin's pride, but the crucial point is that she uses the same medium to express her power that is the basis for his similar claim. Both ultimately mold a natural element in order to express a conception of individual power, but the irony at work in Susie's act hints at her own limitations. Herein one finds the tendency of irony to inject the text with a negative claim. The specifically negative idea at hand in this strip is that humans are essentially powerless. The tenor is pessimistic because it is precise in its dislocation of Calvin's claim that the opposite is true. He cannot even finish explaining why this snowman should worship him. The point at which the snowball hits him is the point at which his speech should mention that in addition to his all-knowing self, he is also all-powerful (assuming he continues following a classic tripartite characterization of the divine: omniscient, omnipresent, and omnipotent). It is just as well that he does not characterize his power as divine, because the very thing he supposedly controls is the very thing that marks his weakness. This, in turn, yokes Calvin to the natural world and therefore establishes his fragility through his claim to power. The summary moral is simple in its unsettling reminder: The natural world should not be understood as something that humans can control because humans are a part of that world.[54]

The desire to transcend the world's limits often leads to an inflated sense of confidence. Another example from Calvin's snowmaking oeuvre will round out how irony functions in such contexts. Throughout *Calvin and Hobbes*, the first Sunday strip from the New Year offers a reflective scene on some kind of meaning. Because of the time of year, these texts usually involve Calvin and Hobbes discussing something either while exploring the snow or, as is the case in the January 3, 1993, strip, using snowmen as vehicles for examining what the New Year portends. The initial snowman that the reader encounters in this strip is leaning slightly forward, his hand on his brow to indicate that he looks ahead to what awaits at the New Year's horizon. There is an air of confidence about this snowman, which prompts Hobbes to remark that this is a "very inspiring"[55] work of art. Calvin appreciates the comment, a fact evident in his expression that occurs in an inset panel. In the broader panel in which Calvin accepts the compliment, there are several snowmen who are doing various things while the confident snowman looks ahead. A couple are arguing, a few lounge about under a tree, and, most importantly, two snowmen laugh cynically at the snowman who greets the New Year with enthusiasm. The contrast is marked, and Hobbes announces the irony by stressing that these snowmen are "the *real* world."[56] The effect is piercing in its critique of the idea that the New Year brings about a new template wherein people can strive ahead and, in so doing, jettison the troubles that build up during the course of the year.

The expressions on the two snowmen who mock the confident member of this crowd dovetail nicely with Calvin's response to Hobbes. He elaborates on what the irony of confidence reveals in this particular scene: "This is why we're always glad when the old year is over."[57] There is value in the transition that the New Year marks, but in his ironic comment Calvin reveals the veneer of striving into the New Year. Any new year is, more often than not, going to be similar to the previous one. The things that the confident snowman wants to leave behind will almost certainly reemerge before he sets forth towards another horizon in a year's time. The scene emphasizes the cyclical nature of life insofar as it stresses that life cannot outpace its inherent shortcomings. As it progresses, time breaks things down; so to determine somewhat arbitrarily that a particular point in time overcomes this trajectory is indeed laughable. The further irony is how the confident snowman remains unaware of the reality from which he looks towards a new year. He is a recurring joke; the best part of the New Year for the other snowmen is the chance to laugh once more at the fool who thinks things will somehow be different in the coming year.

This strip makes clear that for the person who would ignore the instability that characterizes the human condition, irony becomes an inescapable hermeneutical trap, that because it is part of the text, cannot be countered fully. Thus, the appeal of the classic definition of irony is apparent. An irony that provides a foil can be overcome; Booth suggests as much in arguing that irony helps to bring about clarity. In truth, however, irony casts the text into disarray, which frustrates the kind of readings Booth derives from ironic contexts. As *Calvin and Hobbes* makes clear, irony's disruption engenders multiple readings, exposes unstable expectations, and often leaves many questions unanswered. Hobbes' ironic comment about Mr. Bun invites concern about his motivations, while Calvin's ironic birthday present to his dad opens the text into a legitimate question of how valuable principles really are. Herein lies part of irony's value. Because of its complex and troublesome nature, Currie suggests that "irony requires the capacity to engage imaginatively with another's point of view even though one may think it defective; lack of this capacity is a frequent feature of those characters whose faults, great and small, arise from thinking everyone must see the world as they do."[58] While irony's disruption cannot be erased, it does privilege the imaginative response that is the basis for finding meaning amid life's dislocation. Irony protects the text's freedom to accommodate multiple perspectives by undermining simplistic readings of a text.

Calvin's dad, then, turns out to be a bit more like Socrates than Calvin's mom's comment suggests. As mentioned elsewhere,[59] there is a risk in reading too much into Watterson's allusions. While the analysis that follows will not delve too deeply into whether Watterson purposefully uses the name in the June 15, 1986, strip to invoke Socratic thought, it is worth noting that in Book IV of *The Republic*, Plato stresses that happiness should benefit everyone, not just an individual.[60] The emphasis in Book IV is not only that happiness should benefit all, but also that this happiness is a product of virtue. As Socrates tells Glaucon, "And now at last, it seems, it remains for us to consider whether it is profitable to do justice and practice honorable pursuits and be just, whether one is known to be such or not, or whether injustice profits, and to be unjust, if only a man escape punishment and is not bettered by chastisement."[61] Even Glaucon admits that the point is obvious: "I think that from this point on our inquiry becomes an absurdity."[62] There is a simple calculus at work in this exchange: Virtue leads to happiness, which benefits everyone. When this passage is read alongside the examples above, the irony is obvious. Calvin's virtue brings about unhappiness for all but himself, which is precisely the conception of happiness that Socrates deconstructs in Book IV of *The Republic*. The coincidence (if it is a coincidence) between Calvin's mom's aside and the fact that Socrates is often considered the first true ironist thus demands attention insofar as the irony that Enright, Jasper, and Currie discuss departs noticeably from how Socrates uses irony.

Søren Kierkegaard spends a significant amount of time addressing the issue of Socratic irony in his work *The Concept of Irony*.[63] Brad Frazier summarizes well how Kierkegaard approaches Socrates: "*The Concept of Irony* is a diffuse, subtle, and complex work. The first half of the work, constituting the bulk of it, focuses on Socrates and Socratic irony. Socrates is a main topic of Kierkegaard's discussion because Kierkegaard takes Socrates to be the first ironist, that is the first person who exemplifies irony as an existential stance."[64] Frazier's explanation leads him to characterize Socrates' approach as "pure irony,"[65] which indicates a "comprehensive stance as 'infinite absolute negativity.'"[66] In Kierkegaard's mind, Socrates swings irony's pendulum to the extreme that is opposite to Booth's sterilized understanding. Irony's disruption is totalizing, which rejects the suggestion that irony can lead to clarity. At the same time, however, Kierkegaard's critique of Socrates in *The Concept of Irony* serves to pull back the negative associations that Frazier captures in his summary. The result is to bracket irony's impetus to textual play and therefore to recover the multiple readings that irony enables. In this sense, Kierkegaard provides a further resource in examining how irony functions within the text. A reading of irony that balances its various influences on the text will be helpful in clarifying further what is at stake when Calvin's mom calls his dad Socrates.

While *The Concept of Irony* offers a helpful critique of Socratic irony, another of Kierkegaard's books, *Concluding Unscientific Postscript*, offers a more nuanced and thus more insightful discussion of irony for this project. Before examining specifically how Kierkegaard situates irony within the human condition, it is important to summarize briefly his notion that there are three "spheres of existence: the aesthetic, the ethical, the religious."[67] Among the three stages, there are two "boundary zones ... irony, constituting the boundary between the aesthetic and the ethical; humor, as the boundary that separates the ethical from the religious."[68] As a fulcrum between the aesthetic and the ethical, irony constitutes a kind of threshold between the individual who dwells in the immediacy of experience (the aesthete)[69] and the individual who seeks meaning in a commitment to some duty (the ethicist). Irony brings into tension the dislocation that characterizes the aesthete's understanding of life and a desire to find stability through ethical actions. According to Kierkegaard, "Irony arises from the constant placing of the particularities of the finite together with the infinite ethical requirement, thus permitting the contradiction to come into being."[70] Irony thus reveals in its disruption "that the speaker has exercised the infinite movement [towards the ethical], but proves nothing more."[71] In this capacity irony focuses on the tension in the exilic instability that defines the human condition, as well as the anticipated recovery of the text's absent origin. As it undermines a specific narrative, irony thus opens towards the ethicist's value structure a release that finds in the ethicist's commitment to duty a meaning that counterbalances life's difficult circumstances which the aesthete cannot outrun.

Read alongside Kierkegaard's analysis, the role that irony plays in *Calvin and Hobbes* thus comes into focus. Irony calls into question how the individual's desires relate to the values that irony brings into question, be they Calvin's, his dad's or Hobbes.' Its effect is not to privilege one over the other, but rather to explore the gap between a commitment to some value and the unstable contexts in which those values emerge. More specifically, Calvin's dad can value certain principles, but Calvin shows in that living in accordance with these virtues does not necessarily provide a panacea for a meaningful life. Kierkegaard explains that irony is relational in bringing these different threads together, and thus it is a communicative presence in its disruption. At the same time, irony cannot unhinge the aesthete from the immediacy that usually characterizes human life. Irony, then, is "a synthesis of ethical passion which infinitely accentuates *inwardly* the person of the individual in relation to the ethical requirement — and of culture, which infinitely abstracts externally from the personal ego, as one finitude among all the other finitudes and particularities."[72] In the example involving Calvin's plan to hit Susie with a snowball during the summer, these effects are clear. Irony offers through its inversion new perspectives on value, but it does not make manifest outward change. Tellingly, this plot's failure does not dissuade Calvin from pursuing further schemes against Susie. The founding of G.R.O.S.S. makes this point clear enough, both with respect to Calvin's motivations and the unsuccessful nature of his best schemes.[73] Even as it invites refection that can lead to new sources of meaning, irony also makes clear that it does not transcend in and of itself the displacement that initiates a search for meaning in the first place.

As a bridge between the aesthete and the ethicist, irony characterizes an understanding of the human condition that orients the individual's search for meaning. In Calvin's case, irony infuses the imagination with the ability to balance the real — his aesthetic tendencies — and the imaginative wherein he often assumes an ethicist's commitment to duty (the frequency of the Spaceman Spiff adventures as a way to depart from life's reality reveals this dynamic; it is not surprising, then, that when the reader encounters Calvin in real life he frequently resorts to irony when characterizing his experiences).[74] Kierkegaard explains how deeply rooted irony can be in this respect: "Whoever has essential has it all day long, not bound to any specific form, because it is the infinite within him. Irony is a specific culture of the spirit, and therefore follows next after immediacy."[75] This description captures the complex nature of irony, particularly as it relates to the texts this chapter has considered. Irony is fluid in its form, but its effect remains the disruption of the narrative context in which it materializes. Thus, Kierkegaard explains, irony has "an existential determination."[76] As an infinite within, irony's outward appearance thus exhibits the elusive nature discussed above. As a state of being, more than a specific action, irony can speak to a variety of circumstances in a variety of ways. Read through this critical framework, one can see how irony infuses the June 15, 1986, strip with a particular rebalancing of values. By calling Calvin's dad Socrates, Calvin's mom calls into question the static assumptions about value that Calvin reconfigures with his Father's Day gift. The implications of this reversal seep into the narrative as a double irony because the displacement of that which would otherwise direct Calvin through life undermines the broader construct that Kierkegaard mentions. Irony calls into question how a specific set of values and Value function within the space between the aesthete (which Calvin often is) and the ethical (which Calvin's dad often is).

Irony's role as a threshold between the aesthete and the ethicist permits the transition to the comical, which similarly acts as a constitutive presence as opposed to an acute literary trope. The comical similarly provides a measure of structure in articulating the difference between the ethicist and the religious person. According to Kierkegaard, "The ethicist is ... ironical enough to perceive that what interests him absolutely does not interest the others absolutely; this discrepancy he apprehends, and sets the comical between himself and them, in order to be able to hold fast to the ethical in himself with still greater inwardness."[77] Given that Calvin's dad usually functions as an ethicist, this explanation clarifies how irony encircles the strips in which Calvin and his dad interact. Whereas the June 15, 1986, strip stresses Calvin as the source of irony, in other cases Calvin's dad brings irony into the text. A good example of this dynamic occurs in the December 20, 1987, strip. After buying a Christmas tree with his mom, Calvin races in to get his dad to bring the tree into the house. Calvin's dad, however, does not share Calvin's enthusiasm and responds ironically, "This year I thought we'd just keep the tree in the garage."[78] Not only does this strategy save Calvin's dad some labor, it also saves the trouble of decorating. As Calvin becomes more and more anxious, Calvin's dad continues his ironic approach to the conversation: "If you get a present ... you can take it out to the garage to open, and pretend the tree has lots of lights, and...."[79] At this point Calvin runs away to his mom, which is a sure sign that he perceives irony's effects rather acutely. Calvin's dad is aware that Calvin is not interested in his values, and, as a result, he resorts to the comical to contain the difference. By subverting Calvin's aesthetic desires regarding the Christmas tree, Calvin's dad clings to his own understanding of life. This strategy ultimately opens the text to the comical, which is subversive in revealing the limits of the ethicist's principles.[80]

The contrast between Calvin's values and the values his dad would like Calvin to have direct attention to an important feature of irony and the comic in Kierkegaard's analysis. Both the ironic and the comic function because there exists some norm against which the text is measured. Robert C. Roberts explains the role that a norm plays: "A sense of the normal is basic to any sense of humor. You won't find anything funny if you don't find anything to be normal, and this sense for the normal is what constitutes a person's perspective."[81] If one recalls briefly the scene wherein the snowman strives forward and is mocked, s/he will likely recognize Roberts' point (especially if the reader in question finds the snowman scene funny). Crucial is the contrast between one's normative understanding of the world — with respect to values, meanings, expectations, or any other such framework — and what occurs when an experience does not cohere with this expectation.[82] By peeling away the text to expose some deeper consideration, irony exhibits its disruptive character.

The comical, then, functions similarly to irony. In fact, Kierkegaard suggests that the comical is more pervasive; it "is present in every stage of life ... for wherever there is life, there is contradiction, and wherever there is contradiction, the comical is present."[83] Despite its ubiquity, one must specify that the comical is "*the painless contradiction.*"[84] As a contradictory force, the comical thus affects the text in a disruptive manner, yet it also achieves in its contradiction a kind of imaginative direction when searching for meaning. The painlessness of the comic's contradiction is thus a milder form of irony's bite. As Will Williams explains, the comic is, in this capacity, "not necessarily an unqualified force for chaos or randomness. While, through the contradiction, some form must be subverted in the comic, this form must be subverted from some *position*, which may turn out to be a new norm supplanting the old."[85] In this conception, the comic, like irony, unhinges the text in order to permit alternative readings. Williams continues: "The comic appears to function like a kind of fulcrum, which dislodges but only by putting down weight in a new place."[86] By mirroring irony's effect, the comical thus moves towards a paradoxical stability within the text (without realizing as much). Both the ironic and the comical structure a response to life circumstances, and therefore both speak to the search for meaning in response to life's destabilizing experiences.

When she walks into the living room and finds a broken lamp and Calvin shouldering a baseball bat, Calvin's mom experiences the disjunction that both the ironic and the comic texts contain. As one not always prone to surprise at Calvin's antics, her face says everything, which enhances her cry of disbelief: "You've been hitting *rocks* in the *house*? What on earth would make you *do* something like that?"[87] The question is ripe for an ironic response, which Calvin readily provides: "Poor genetic material?"[88] The context that elicits the question is an ironic twist on baseball; it very much unsettles Calvin's mom's expectations. His response — which is seemingly earnest, given his expression and demeanor — aggravates this disjunction. Calvin's mom not only experiences the pointed disruption that Calvin's game brings, she also absorbs an explanation that she is implicitly responsible for what occurred. The point that emerges in her shock is clear, but the answer is subtle in its ability to cut more deeply than she probably expected when asking her question. Calvin shoves her into irony's morass, which is ultimately worse than hitting rocks in the house. As Calvin sits in his bed reflecting on what just happened, his comment is telling: "Bad guess."[89] One could easily gloss over irony's presence, but the narrative implies that the punishment he receives is for his comment. By reflecting the question of motivation back onto his mom, Calvin subverts her authority as his mom, and therefore her understanding of what constitutes appropriate behavior in the house. At no point during this strip does Calvin show any surprise or remorse about hitting rocks in the house. This, in turn, suggests that within the context of whatever game he imagines, hitting rocks in the house is perfectly acceptable. Consequently, the tense exchange with his mom establishes the negotiation[90] between Kierkegaard's spheres (and should make the reader laugh; this is a decidedly funny strip).

Irony, of course, cuts both ways and often does so rather deeply. An excellent example occurs when Calvin's mom is sitting at the table, Calvin walks by, waves, and exclaims, "Hi. It's me. Your big accomplishment in life!"[91] The next panel shows Calvin's mom slumped on the couch as his dad ties his tie. She mutters, "I'm depressed."[92] Calvin undermines a crucial value that supports parenthood. If he is not his mom's big accomplishment in life, then she is exposed to questions about her ability as a parent. On the other hand, if Calvin's statement is true, then she must reconcile Calvin's character with the extent to which his existence affects how she understands life. Either way, Calvin's comment dislocates her mood and sends her reeling to the couch in order to find meaning amid irony's textual disruption.

The oscillation of responsibility and judgment in this strip captures how irony's subversive effects can enrich a text. Enright explains how irony's dislocation establishes an alluring presence within the text: "Irony lives in the ample territory between those two extreme states; it acknowledges what must be, contends against what should not and need not be, and intimates what conceivably could be."[93] Irony brings expectations into proximity that creates friction within the text. While subversive and often uncomfortable to experience, these moments ultimately provide the opportunity to recalibrate how one's values respond to the expectations concerning these values. At times the results can be surprising and help one to realize that what has been trusted without assumption is, perhaps, not the only viable way to make sense out of life's circumstances. Calvin's mom certainly does not expect Calvin to explain his decision to hit rocks in the house by referring to his genetic material. However cutting the remark, there exists a certain truth; Calvin's genetics are a part of his life and therefore the decisions that he makes. Herein lies the discomfort that irony embeds into the text: "On occasion as close as the pen can come to the sword, alternately anodyne and tonic, until nothing on earth can sustain us any longer it is a source of endurance and courage and even, in its oblique and tentative way, of hope. Another ambiguous gift, it may be, but a gift all the same."[94] If irony is a gift, then it is unexpected and burdensome. This is, however, the paradox that irony accommodates, and therefore indicates how irony assists the imagination's efforts to make sense even in the most senseless contexts. What this gift reveals may startle, upset, or engage the reader, but in the end it is a gift that helps the text speak meaningfully to the unpredictable nature of the human condition.

CHAPTER FIVE

When Roses Smell Like Flowers
The Individual's Relative Value

Calvin understands money in a way that makes sense when he shows an aesthete's sense of value. He watches what he has closely and is always looking for a way to make more with a minimum amount of effort. This is a relatively constant feature of Calvin's character, a fact evident in one of the last strips when Calvin finds a quarter on the ground. His expression leaves the reader to believe he has stumbled upon some great treasure as he exclaims, "Look! A quarter!! Wow! I'm rich beyond my dreams! I can have anything I want! All my prayers have been answered!"[1] This barely controllable verbal stream reveals much about how Calvin frames this unexpected experience. Several salient features emerge, all of which help to frame a discussion about Calvin's individualism and its consequent values. The first, obvious point is that the imaginative scales Calvin uses to determine value are not entirely balanced. Having discussed the lengths to which Calvin's imagination can travel, a quarter is, in the scheme of things, a paltry find. There is certainly the option to read this strip as a child's encounter with money. Calvin's response makes sense because to a six-year-old a quarter can seem like a lot.[2] However, such a reading is simplistic, given that Calvin exhibits elsewhere a more nuanced response to his search for money. He frequently has entrepreneurial aspirations that seek to maximize his income at as small a cost as possible.[3] This tendency might indicate a businessman in the making, except he frequently attempts to sell things that have little or no value for consumers. Moreover, when he attempts to squeeze money out of others, he does not set the bar for success as low as the August 28, 1995, strip suggests. He feels genuine excitement about the unexpected material benefit his find will generate. Calvin's excitement results largely from the extent to which material things can be normative for a person in determining what, exactly, constitutes value in life.

The surprise that nearly overwhelms Calvin sets the stage for a more telling insight into his sense of value. After reflecting on the lengths to which this quarter will go, Calvin pauses to consider what he has just said. This third panel suspends the narrative momentarily between two possibilities. On the one hand, Calvin might gain some perspective on what he just said and realize that both the actual value and the perceived value of this quarter are skewed. The other possibility — which ultimately is the direction Calvin takes this strip — is to get down on the ground and hope that "maybe there's more."[4] The individualized standard that determines value for Calvin is pervasive in this sense; the irony of his comments induces a reflection that strengthens his desire for fulfilling his dreams at a pretty cheap rate. Moreover, his desire to find more money in the field undermines the initial value he ascribes to the quarter. Rather than be satisfied with realized dreams, everything he wants, and answered prayers to boot, he would rather look for more. Relative values can be quite alluring.

A corollary to this example occurs in the strip from March 11, 1986, when Calvin *loses* a quarter. His despair is similarly out of balance with the amount at stake. When Hobbes tells him that he will just have to wait until the snow melts to find the coin, Calvin reacts rather strongly: "*Till the snow melts? It's 25 cents!!*"[5] The final panel in this strip is hyperbolic, but it emphasizes just how important this quarter is: Calvin is out in the field where he lost the quarter with a hairdryer. One can admire his determination, but, as with the strip discussed above, the value he places on this quarter far outweighs its monetary value. The idea of having money is more important in the end than the money itself, which is why Calvin is willing to search for the proverbial needle in a haystack. Stated differently, he is willing to go to great lengths to recover the quarter because of the value it represents as money lost, not because of its literal value. He never registers that there are seemingly several alternatives to laboring in this capacity. He could probably earn four times as much[6] if he spent that time elsewhere, but the immediacy of the value he ascribes to the quarter clouds his ability to maintain perspective about what he has lost (and, of course, this ignores the question of why he would carry something so valuable on his person in a space that will require significant angst to recover the item should something happen to it).

Any objective sense of value with respect to money gives way to the subjective value the individual places on such things. On the one hand, there is no reason to begrudge Calvin's decision insofar as he can determine how important money truly is in his life. Strictly speaking, this is the case, and if Calvin deems the best use of his time is to search for a quarter in a field of snow, then there is little one can say with respect to what he considers valuable. Such concessions, however, shift the discussion in a way that obscures the problematic attachment Calvin has to quarters. There is a lack of depth in such a choice of what one considers to be valuable, and, moreover, the argument that upholds Calvin's actions as the best path towards finding the meaning he desires is problematic. In the end, the question of value that emerges in each of these examples is for Calvin a question of immediacy. Unless Calvin's investment strategy involves a significant amount of liquidity,[7] then the value of money has more to do with an idea of what money can buy as opposed to true buying power. This, in turn, reveals the transient nature of the things that will generate greater value for Calvin; the quarter is a means to an end. This approach to the money is common enough, to be sure, but this does not mean that finding value in the ability to acquire material things through one's wealth will generate lasting returns when it comes to the search for meaning in life.

In transitioning out of an examination of specific textual features, Calvin's unexpected find and consequent reaction offer a helpful example to consider how an individual's sense of meaning is distortive. To smooth the transition, a return to Kierkegaard and the concept of the aesthete as it relates to value will be helpful. In *Concluding Unscientific Postscript*, Kierkegaard summarizes how the aesthete's values are at odds with a common Western sense of value: "Avarice, vanity, envy, and so forth, are thus essentially forms of madness; for it is precisely the most general expression for madness that the individual has an absolute relationship to what is relative."[8] These qualities capture Calvin's response to the quarter. He exhibits an obvious avarice both in the desires he thinks this quarter will buy and, of course, the desire for more. If greed is an unsatisfiable appetite, then Calvin is most certainly greedy in this respect. The subsequent characteristics that Kierkegaard mentions follow on from the underlying avarice that the strip reveals. The point of this example is precisely what Kierkegaard links with the qualities that characterize the aesthete. For such people, value is relative to the point of absurdity. Calvin's appetite for satisfaction is in this instance strongly material and, as he makes clear, something that cannot be fulfilled.

To recall the previous chapter, irony provides the threshold between the aesthete who exhibits avarice (and other comparative standards) of value and the ethicist who would labels such virtues vices. The disjunction eventually opens the text towards the comical because, Kierkegaard explains, "the comical is always rooted in the contradictory."[9] The contradiction, of course, comes from those who understand value in more objective terms (the ethicist or the religious person) and thus can understand how Calvin's reactions are hollow. If dreams can be bought so cheaply, and if they never satisfy, then the aesthete who thinks such things are possible, or even normative, is bound to be disappointed in life. This is the point at hand; the contradiction between Calvin's values and a detached look at those values elicits a wry smile. Treating a concept such as value in a way that can easily be called vice is, from certain perspectives, an absurd undertaking.

Though one can easily critique Calvin for his actions when he finds or loses a quarter, a few additional comments are necessary. First, Kierkegaard explains that the contradictory elements that are embedded in irony also convey a nuanced version of the comical; in such cases the textual disjunction is simply a point of view brought to bear on the aesthete from someone who does not share these values. The aesthete also has an appreciation for the comical. Kierkegaard explains: "It is madness, and from the aesthetic standpoint comical, that a being whose nature is dedicated to the eternal, uses all his strength to lay hold of the perishable, clinging to what is precarious."[10] Though one can locate value beyond the immediate satisfaction material things can bring, an unavoidable reality is that humans remain bound by the inevitable decay that characterizes such things. To deny value within this sphere is to undertake a similarly contradictory stance, as this standard belies the context out of which one seeks to define value.

The initial experience that opens this specific text into these questions involves a quarter, which, as money, signals the broad question of value at the heart of this contradiction. By drawing on Kierkegaard, the goal is to emphasize that when discussing values, one almost inevitably engages in a discussion that is relative, particularly when one takes into account the fact that those who value one thing or another are individuals. The approach with which Kierkegaard examines the individual and questions of value is often contained within an existentialist label. While this term will be helpful in digging more deeply into Calvin's identity, a few words of caution are necessary at the outset when drawing from this philosophical reservoir. Diogenes Allen and Eric O. Springstead provide a helpful summary of how the term existentialism applies to Kierkegaard. They write, "The label 'existentialism' refers to *themes* that occur in a number of writers who in other respects differ from Kierkegaard and from each other as well."[11] The particular themes that link Kierkegaard with other existential thinkers are, according to Allen and Springstead, "the irreducibility and primacy of the individual, and a stress on choice."[12] The thematic stress here is particularly important in bracketing Kierkegaard's Christianity from an analysis of *Calvin and Hobbes*. As mentioned in Chapter One,[13] there is no distinctly Christian element within the strip. Any parallels between this faith tradition and the strip are thematic similarities.

Thus, in drawing heavily on Kierkegaard, there is no intent to suggest that Watterson has somehow smuggled a particular kind of Christianity into his work. In the particular example above, one can readily identify how Kierkegaard's ideas are manifest without any reference to Christianity. Calvin's response to finding money is decidedly individualistic, a characterization that does not require any religious additives. To be clear on this point, it is worth emphasizing that the implications Calvin draws from the experience reflect only his interests and the things he imagines this money will buy to serve his individual desires. Moreover, the choice he makes after reflecting on these possibilities advances these concerns. For a single panel, Calvin has the opportunity to choose what he will do next. His choice to look for more money condenses two salient concerns for an individual: value and what to do with that value.

While the specific example at hand is not an event with significant experiential ballast, the salient concerns it speaks to anticipate broader existential concerns. As Allen and Springstead explain, "Kierkegaard and the existentialists also focus on extreme situations in which the normal and familiar ways of understanding and dealing with life break down."[14] Life is not about finding quarters; life is about what to do with the experiences that stress the individual's values and need to choose. The consequence of this responsibility is significant. It "reveals to use our own individuality and ... [makes] us take responsibility for our own actions and the kind of people who are without the support of philosophy, science, or religion. The individual thus is to face the universe, with no rational scheme with which to master or control it."[15] In choosing (or valuing), the individual thus confronts her/his own understanding of the universe and, moreover, s/he recognizes (if s/he is paying attention) that any such conception remains incomplete. Bound by and within exile, the individual confronts the limits of her/his understanding as choices reveal perhaps more than the individual can bear. There is, in the end, no recourse that can unbind this burden; everyone must confront the reality that life is constrictive in its mystery. Because there is no metanarrative to which one can attach meaning, one must discover the truth about oneself—which can be a trying and ugly thing because most people do not know what they will find—in deciphering the meanings that serve as signposts in this disjunctive context. Every choice thus becomes a reflection of both the individual's instability and the loneliness that comes from realizing that nothing can assuage this isolation.

Allen and Springstead add an important postscript to this dislocating analysis. Kierkegaard is responding in part to a Hegelian emphasis on the ability to use rationality to decode the world around us. Kierkegaard retains the unknown in conceptualizing humanity's condition, which, Allen and Springstead point out, creates space for other ways of understanding: "[Kierkegaard's] stress on the limitations of reason does not arise from wrestling with the philosophical problem of the connections between things in nature or the limitations of reason in science. It is rather Hegel's excessive claim to be able to comprehend the ethical and religious life by reason that aroused him."[16] As Calvin shows routinely, the imagination is, perhaps, one of the few reliable ways that the individual can overcome the existential instability that undermines all meanings. Read alongside Kierkegaard, the imagination thus provides a release from a life that attempts to fix these meanings in material things. With recourse to his imagination, Calvin is able to discover new kinds of value, which is crucial for transitioning out of the aesthete's sphere and into the ethical sphere. The result is to reconfigure the things in life that he does not like in a way that provides enjoyment. For example, through the imagination Calvin can overcome his personal desire *not* to brush his teeth,[17] and, when imagining himself as Stupendous Man, suggest as parting guidance that kids always brush their teeth.[18]

In this conception the ultimate motivation for moving towards the ethical and thus beyond the kinds of values that speak only to an individual's immediate desire is boredom's paralysis. The aesthete will recognize—if s/he is wiling to admit as much—that the world's fleeting sources of value will not overcome the fragility of the human condition. This realization emerges, Allen and Springstead argue, when the individual encounters in her/his values "intolerable boredom or even despair."[19] Blaise Pascal expands on the connection between the kinds of things an aesthete values and the end to which they lead: "Anyone who does not see the vanity of the world is vain himself. So who does not see it, apart from young people whose lives are all noise, diversions, and thoughts of the future? But take away their diversion and you will see them bored to extinction."[20] Pascal stresses the inability to realize boredom's effects, which, as will be discussed below, is a crucial impediment to finding meaning in life. Moreover, his label for the kinds of things an aesthete values — the diversions of life — indicates how such interests ultimately direct one's attention away from that which can provide more satisfaction. There exists, then, a paradox that characterizes the aesthete: focusing on one thing alters the individual's perception of reality to the point that other ways of understanding the world cannot be accommodated.

Calvin struggles with each of these things to a great degree in his real life. He makes clear that the aesthete's risk, then, is inaction, which inevitably collapses along with the things s/he values. Kierkegaard offers a helpful summary of this point: "The perishable is nothing when it is past, and it is of its essence to pass away, quickly as the moment of sensuous enjoyment, the farthest possible remove from the eternal, a moment in time filled with emptiness."[21] It is not surprising, then, that when boredom grips Calvin, he resorts to his imagination, not only to find meaning[22] but to do so in a way that is decidedly virtuous when compared with his self-interested musings after finding a quarter.

Meaning appears in many guises for Calvin, but when the imagination is pronounced, this meaning tends to emerge through the experiences of his alter egos. The two most common identities he assumes are Spaceman Spiff and Stupendous Man, both of whom exhibit virtues that transform Calvin's experiences into adventures wherein he is heroic. In each case there is a clear interest in virtues that traditionally underscore Western thought: courage, strength, and justice. It is worth noting that even when Calvin's imagination does not cast him into one of these roles — his frequent escapades involving dinosaurs are a good example — he usually occupies a role in the narrative that is characterized by qualities that reflect the virtues just mentioned. If one takes a sampling of contexts wherein Calvin morphs into a dinosaur, one will notice that he is almost always a carnivore, which reflects the dinosaur equivalents of courage, strength, and justice (if justice is the rule of that which is, in the end, "so much cooler"[23]).

Moreover, these virtue-laden narratives contrast sharply with Calvin's decided inability to be imaginative when he is watching television. In such circumstances, the pointlessness of the television's immediate gratification is apparent to everyone but Calvin.[24] This disjunction highlights, therefore, the imagination's freedom to construct meaning; When Calvin is a passive recipient rather than a creator, meaning fades (though the irony is still present; in such circumstances, the meaning about our culture's addiction to television is obvious).

There exists, then, a significant counterpoint to the imagination's freedom throughout *Calvin and Hobbes*: a false sense of direction that results from an aesthete's values. In the May 2, 1991, strip (in one of the last strips before Watterson went on sabbatical), Calvin and Hobbes are talking about where meaning can be found. Calvin explains to Hobbes that his attempt to pause in life and consider how simple things can open into unexpected possibilities has failed: "You know how everyone says you should stop and smell the roses? Well, this morning I did. *Big deal!* They smelled like a bunch of dumb flowers. It was the most mundane experience I've ever had!"[25] Calvin obviously misses the point; stopping to smell the roses is not about what roses smell like. Rather, the point is to take time to appreciate the things in life that are often present but underappreciated. In a world defined by his immediate interests, such nuances do not register with Calvin. Despite his own warnings elsewhere,[26] he takes the advice to smell the roses literally. Because this does not cohere with the kinds of things wherein he does find meaning, he reduces what can be good advice to something mundane (this is, of course, ironic insofar as Calvin exhibits elsewhere some truly mundane interests).[27]

If the strip concluded with Calvin rejecting the notion that the smell of roses can provide value to his day, this example would provide a helpful look at how Calvin's self-interest can prune his imagination. As one might expect, however, when Calvin gets on a roll, there is more to the story. The momentum of his frustration with the flowers continues when he tells Hobbes, "Who's got time for this nonsense! I'm a busy guy! I've got things to do! The *last* thing *I* need is to stand around with my nose in some silly plant!"[28] The punch line that follows in the fourth panel explains why Calvin is so busy; He has a television program he wants to watch.[29] The irony at work in this strip brings the issue at hand into sharp focus. While the specifics about the show are not mentioned, Calvin's commitment to a television program in the midst of complaining about mundane experiences announces forcefully how his imagination can fail to embrace the different meanings that his experiences offer.[30] It seems unlikely that the television program in question would provide a qualitatively better experience than the silly flowers he smells (which is in itself an irony; roses actually smell rather nice), yet he is wholly unaware of this disjunction. He is clear where value lies in this context, and he specifically emphasizes that he has better things to do than stick his nose into roses. By claiming responsibility for discarding the flowers so clearly, Calvin ultimately exposes the absurdity into which a lack of imagination can lead.

It is no accident that elsewhere Calvin's desire to watch television is similarly limiting with respect to how he determines meaning. There are frequent examples of Calvin's desire to watch television and, moreover, the lack of imaginative content in the programs he likes. Two consequences of the television's ability to stunt his imagination are worth noting to round out the point that the strip from May 2, 1991, reveals. The first, more common state that Calvin exhibits when watching television is absolute boredom. For someone with such an expansive imagination, he shows a remarkable willingness to let his brain do nothing of consequence.[31] This tendency might explain the second recurring consequence — namely, Calvin's willingness to allow advertisements to convince him that he needs a particular product. This impressionable submission to advertising indicates a similar — though perhaps more troubling — failure to find meaning through his imagination. By accepting that he needs a product to find meaning in life, Calvin admits that when watching the television he is unable to choose for himself what really matters in his life. Thus, boredom exhibits the same failure that Calvin cites as the reason that the flowers are not worth his time. Just as he cannot imagine why the smell of the roses offers anything of value with respect to the world as he understands it, his willingness to embrace the materialism he watches on television speaks to a kind of reverse failure of the imagination. When smelling the roses, he refuses to expand his thoughts beyond the fact that he would rather be watching a program; while when watching these programs he is unable to exercise the choice he privileges so dearly in different circumstances.

The contradictory ways in which Calvin pursues meaning deconstructs the notion that value is something that can be discussed outside the context of an individual's experience. Three specific vignettes in Plato's work speak to the question of whether value is relative or if it can be construed objectively.[32] This question constitutes a key theme in Plato's *The Republic*. When examining whether justice exists, Glaucon casts into doubt whether goodness (i.e. justice) is anything beyond self-interest. To make the point, he recounts the story of Gyges — a shepherd (and a poor man) in the service of the king of Lydia — who finds a ring that, when worn, makes him invisible.[33] Realizing the freedom this ring offers to provide whatever he wants, Gyges proceeds to seduce the king's wife, kill the king, and take over the kingdom. Free from any consequences that might befall him because of his invisibility, Gyges suggests that upholding objective value is merely the result of facing consequences. Glaucon thus makes the following statement concerning value:

> If now there should be two such rings, and the just man should put on one and the unjust the other, no one could be found, it would seem, of such adamantine temper as to persevere in justice and endure to refrain his hands from the possessions of others and not touch them, though he might with impunity take what he wished even from the marketplace, and enter into houses and lie with whom he pleased, and slay and loose from bonds whomsoever he would, and in all other things conduct himself among mankind as the equal of a god.[34]

The argument is clever, and it poses a serious question: Is the good by virtue of some innate property, or is the good merely that which some agree is good? If the latter is the answer, then questions of value are relativized. One can usually assume that the unjust man would run amok if given the power to act freely; the real test is whether a just person would continue to behave justly if s/he had a ring that allowed the user to exist within a society yet not be bound by that society's values. Thus, Glaucon concludes, "No one is just of his own will but only from constraint, in the belief that justice is not his personal good, inasmuch as every man, when he supposes himself to have the power to do wrong, does wrong."[35]

In *Discipline and Punish: The Birth of the Prison*, Michel Foucault offers an insightful look into the role the body plays in structuring society's ability to enforce a particular understanding of good. More specifically, Foucault notes how modern conceptions of justice drift away from overt corporeal punishments to imprisonment.[36] Implicit in society's ability to imprison is the modern stress on punishment as the loss of liberty.[37] This punishment is still visible[38] and thus functions in the same capacity as public disciplines that were common throughout most of history. This may seem a departure from Plato's example, but the thematic development is important with respect to an existentialist stress on the individual's choice. The implicit standard at work in Foucault echoes the example that Glaucon provides — namely, the visibility of actions, even if what is outwardly visible is a failure to behave in accordance with a given standard. Social values thus remain in tension with a stress on the individual's choice, which highlights what is at stake in the myth of Gyges' ring. The important issue is to release the question of value from a social context in order to understand how an individual in her/his freedom of choice understands her/his experiences.

If value turns out to be relative, then a stress on the individual's choice as determining what is meaningful in life takes on added significance. Given Kierkegaard's claim that the cultural institutions that set value — science, religion, and the like — cannot ultimately provide normative structures, the strength of Glaucon's claim increases. Without the threat of consequences that a cultural norm provides (or enforces), the individual will pursue her/his self-interests. Frequently, Calvin's own actions make this clear, but a specific example echoes the myth of Gyges. When he imagines an elixir that, when drunk, makes him invisible,[39] Calvin offers support for Glaucon's claim. Thus released from detection, Calvin realizes that he is free to indulge his desires: "I can perpetrate any crime undetected! I have complete freedom! I can get away with anything!"[40] The threat of punishment that would otherwise curb his behavior is gone, and Calvin responds at first by realizing that he is no longer bound by a social definition of value. His first act reveals a great deal about his desires: He raids the cookie jar. For all of the opportunities his (imagined) invisibility affords, he remains tied to the immediate satisfaction that one expects from Calvin's aesthetic tendencies.[41] Though constructed, this example links together Gyges' ring, the question of the individual, and how society informs how we understand value. The insight that follows reveals, in the end, a look into the individual that can be challenging in its authenticity.

A corollary example from Plato will extend and enhance this discussion. The issue is not merely that individuals will pursue their own interests when they are free from social convention; there is also the concern that what individuals define as valuable in such contexts will ultimately fail to provide meaning that is fulfilling. As Calvin shows in the examples discussed thus far, there is a strong proclivity to define value in terms that are material and immediate. In *Gorgias*, Plato offers the example of a leaky jar to characterize the difficulty a person faces when trying to keep up with the need to satisfy these kinds of value structures. Importantly, Plato sets up the contrast so that the thing valued — "the sources of each of these supplies were scanty and difficult and only available through much hard toil"[42] — is objective in its conception. Thus, he is able to explain the contrast between the person who seeks immediate gratification and the person who recognizes the value of the thing in question. The virtuous person, "when he has taken his fill, neither draws off any more nor troubles himself a jot, but remains at ease on that score."[43] When this person encounters a thing that is valuable, s/he stores it safely and thus is able to appreciate the thing's intrinsic worth. S/he finds satisfaction without the need to overindulge. The other person, however, struggles when s/he desires to enjoy continually the thing in question. Plato writes, "The other finds, like his fellow, that the sources are possible indeed, though difficult, but his vessels are leaky and decayed, and he is compelled to fill them constantly, all night and day, or else suffer extreme distress."[44] Trying to satisfy a desire that is unending will suffer the inescapable toil of trying to fill up a jar that always leaks. The one who desires constant or immediate fulfillment is unable to appreciate the real value of the thing in question, which, in turn, dislocates this person from being able to find an "objective" enjoyment in life.[45] Plato's recognition thus parallels Kierkegaard's warning: The aesthete risks a life defined by paralysis because this person finds value in something that cannot be sustained.

One sees this dynamic in the August 28, 1995, strip. The thing in question has a value that is equal for anyone; the quarter's buying power does not shift from person to person. What does change, however, is each person's understanding of how that value will affect her/his life. For Calvin, there are dreams to be fulfilled; but again, this value is fleeting. There needs to be more because, recalling Plato, the leaky jar must be filled continually. Those who are not content with things that provide meaning in life do not find a measure of satisfaction beyond the briefest of moments. The constant search for more money will inevitably drain Calvin because even if he were to find another quarter, presumably his response would be the same. The new find, like the old, would fail to provide any lasting satisfaction.

A final example from Plato will round out the picture of the shortcomings that Calvin often exhibits when pursuing immediate gratification. In Book VII of *The Republic*, Plato explains his famous Allegory of the

Cave.[46] Humanity is trapped in its ignorance, able to see only the shadows of puppets cast on the cave's wall by a fire. Because those who dwell in the cave are chained in such a way that they have seen only these shadows, their understanding of reality is distorted.[47] Once a prisoner finally breaks free from these chains, the fire's light — which has cast the shadows and is thus the "true" source of knowledge in the cave — is blinding. Plato's description captures the effect this reorientation has on the person who has been trapped in ignorance: "When one was freed from his fetters and compelled to stand up suddenly and turn his head around and walk and to lift up his eyes to the light, and in doing all this felt pain and, because of the dazzle and glitter of the light, was unable to discern the objects whose shadows he formerly saw."[48] Such is the effect of knowledge on the ignorant; it upsets completely the ignorance that used to be normative. Once the prisoner recovers his sight, however, he travels out of the cave and into the world of the Forms, where he discovers the true nature of things.[49] The broad point that the Allegory makes is clear enough: The journey from ignorance to knowledge can be painful, but if completed, one can understand the human condition infinitely better than if one remains ignorant.

What many readers fail to register is what the prisoner, now enlightened, decides to do next. Socrates poses an important question: "If he recalled to mind his first habitation and what passed for wisdom there, and his fellow-bondsmen, do you not think that he would count himself happy in the change and pity them?"[50] Glaucon answers that the prisoner would return to his fellow prisoners in order to share with them the knowledge he acquired during his journey. Upon this prisoner's return, however, Socrates asks what his fate will be: "Would it not be said of him that he had returned from his journey aloft with his eyes ruined and that it was not worth while even to attempt the ascent? And if it were possible to lay hands on and to kill the man who tried to release them and lead them up, would they not kill him?"[51] Glaucon affirms the point at hand; those who are still ignorant will not welcome knowledge to the point of killing the person who suggests an alternative to life in the cave. Suggesting an alternative to ignorance can be a dangerous thing.

An implicit choice for the released prisoner throughout the allegory of the cave thus concludes the narrative in an unexpected capacity. He must decide continually during his ascent to continue seeking knowledge, as it would be easier to return to the condition that he knew prior to his freedom. Given the reception his fellow prisoners would provide upon his return, the escaped prisoner's fate emphasizes the relative value of knowledge versus ignorance. The former can provide clarity about life, but for the majority of people the latter is preferable as a way of understanding the world. Freedom and knowledge are powerful things in the Allegory, but they are not necessarily desirable. One can see in this example, then, another example of the aesthete's limited scope of meaning. There is a kind of comfort when living in ignorance, which not only binds the aesthete to her/his impossible search for meaning, but also prevents her/him from welcoming a new way of experiencing the world. In the Allegory of the Cave, knowledge is first defined by the prisoners' very narrow experiences. Thus, the knowledge they have appears to be normative; yet because they lack awareness of the machinations behind them (and, more importantly, above them), they remain trapped within a skewed awareness of their experiential context.

For a precocious six-year-old, Calvin occasionally shows a strong preference for ignorance. More specifically, when presented with the opportunity to acquire knowledge, he will demure loudly. For example, in the strip from January 5, 1993, he explains to Hobbes just how little interest he has in learning: "I don't want to go to school. I don't want to know anything new."[52] At first glance this comment does not reveal anything beyond his usual morning grumpiness (or even the attitude towards school that many a six-year-old probably has). However, in the second panel Calvin expands on why he does not want to learn: "I already know more than I want to! I liked things better when I didn't understand them!"[53] Several important points emerge from this clarification. The first is visual. Whereas Calvin's initial comment does not exhibit any obvious intensity, in the second frame his arms are crossed and a scowl has appeared on his face. This outward defiance amplifies the reasons he offers for desiring ignorance. It is not simply that he supposedly has enough knowledge; he wants *less* knowledge, and he does not want anyone to force him to learn. There is a logic at work here that would presumably be welcome in Plato's cave. Knowledge lacks ignorance's appeal because of the demands that knowledge makes on the individual. As the escaped prisoner shows, remaining in an ignorant state of existence is an easier way to live, especially given the consequences that await the person who returns with knowledge. Calvin thus echoes Plato in his desire not to be challenged insofar as he states an obvious preference for ignorance. He is aware, then, of what knowledge demands and makes a conscious decision to value ignorance more highly than knowledge because the former is, in his eyes, a less burdensome state in which to live.[54]

Elsewhere, Calvin qualifies his desire to remain ignorant in a slightly different capacity. His knowledge of history may not be the best, but he "can recite the secret superhero origin of each member of Captain Napalm's Thermonuclear League of Liberty."[55] The willingness to invest in a kind of knowledge that he admits is "thoroughly useless"[56] dovetails with the point at hand. As Aristotle explains, happiness requires knowledge *and* action: "Happiness is an activity of soul in accordance with perfect virtue."[57] For Aristotle, merely knowing what is good will not suffice; one must also act in a way that manifests this goodness. By disassociating knowledge from any activity that can be construed as virtuous or even meaningful, here Calvin exhibits a further slant towards the aesthete's way of determining value. Calvin's mom captures the point more succinctly in the strip from August 4, 1989: "How can kids know so much and still be so dumb?"[58] Calvin explains that he actually is not dumb and has plenty of common sense; he just "choose[s] to ignore it."[59]

By the third panel in the January 5, 1993, strip, Calvin's rant has assumed an agitated posture. He shakes his fist in the air and growls, "The fact is, I'm being educated against my will! My rights are being trampled!"[60] At this point Calvin injects his desire for ignorance with a pronounced irony, which in turn parallels further the restrictions that ignorance places on the individual as portrayed in the Allegory of the Cave. Ignorance is rarely a province where facts support one's claims, yet this is the certainly with which Calvin asserts his desire to reject a path to knowledge. Thus, his ironic comment undermines either his supposed ignorance or the desire to remain in this state, whether he knows anything or not. Similarly, the preference for ignorance that one finds in Plato's cave belies a different fact — namely, that the prisoner who eventually breaks his chains does so through his own volition.[61]

This desire anticipates the fourth panel of the January 5, 1993, strip, which brings this example back around to the initial discussion of Kierkegaard. Hobbes finally chimes in and asks: "Is it a right to remain ignorant?" To this Calvin responds, "I don't know, but I refuse to find out."[62] It is important to note that in this final panel the reader only sees Calvin's back. This different perspective suggests the same reorientation that occurs in the Allegory of the Cave, only in this case the pivot is reversed. Whereas the prisoner in the Allegory turns *towards* the light that represents knowledge and thus a reorientation away from ignorance, Calvin turns away from his vigorous assertions concerning his right to be ignorant. Much like the passion that occurs in panels two and three, in the final panel his posture emphasizes the claims he is making. As with the prisoner's agency, Calvin's physical orientation reflects his choice to prefer ignorance. In revealing his strong inclination towards ignorance, then, Calvin brings into the question of knowledge versus ignorance the matter of choice. Just as knowledge is ultimately a matter of seeking and enduring the disruption that a release from ignorance brings, remaining ignorant requires a commitment to resist the possibility of acquiring knowledge. The prisoners who have not escaped exhibit this choice in their willingness to kill the one who returns to the cave and speaks of a different way to understand the world. Choice and value thus converge while Calvin waits at the bus stop in a meaningful way, even if he insists on knowing as little as possible. He does not give up the awareness that he can choose between knowledge and ignorance. There exists, then, a lingering trace of value that ultimately resists the closure that is seemingly at hand when he answers Hobbes' question — insofar as to answer requires at the very least that one has heard and understood the question.

The strip from February 4, 1993, is a particularly sharp example of Calvin's awareness of the balance between knowledge and ignorance. When he brings a snowflake into class, he waxes lyrical about its individuality and how this uniqueness dissolves in the context of school. Calvin understands how institutional contexts often constrain an individual, while his classmates seemingly remain unaware of their ignorance. In this case, Calvin is the one with knowledge who returns to share the truth of the world. Moreover, he exercises his choice in leaving the context that extends his classmates' ignorance. This exchange reveals that Calvin is decidedly not ignorant. In the circumstances wherein he professes a desire to be such, there is more at work. Specifically, he never relinquishes the freedom to choose to be ignorant or to be knowledgeable; there are just some instances in which, for whatever reason, he opts to regress into ignorance.

Despite the seeming consistency with which Calvin adheres to an aesthete's value structure, there are times when this wholly self-interested way of understanding life collapses. Importantly, Hobbes is often the one who turns Calvin's value system inside out and, in so doing, reveals how these values cannot provide lasting satisfaction. A particularly striking example of this revelation occurs during a walk in the woods. Calvin tells Hobbes, "I don't believe in ethics any more. As far as I'm concerned, the ends justify the means. Get what you can while the getting's good — that's what *I* say! Might makes right! The winners write the history books!"[63] One finds in this monologue a good summary of not only the aesthete's preference for immediate gratification, but also the justification for pursuing such things at the cost of anything, even others. By relativizing ethical standards, Calvin ultimately ignores his own experiences and, moreover, exposes the unstable nature of his claims (Calvin's constant struggles with Moe, who epitomizes the might-makes-right value system, undermines this claim; irony, then, does well in temporarily masking ignorance — or, rather, the choice to present oneself as ignorant). Once he has finished his diatribe, Hobbes does not even bother to voice a response; he simply pushes Calvin into a puddle of mud. Incensed, Calvin yells, "*Why'd you do that?!?*"[64] Hobbes undermines the argument Calvin makes by explaining, "You were in my way. Now you're not. The ends justify the means."[65] Here Calvin experiences the full implications of his willful ignorance and consequent claim to justify any action. By defining this standard only in terms of his own interests, Calvin proves (perhaps unwillingly) that he structures his values in a way that will inevitably crumble so long as other aesthetes are out there. He emphasizes the point when, after hearing Hobbes' perfectly rational explanation, he retorts, "I didn't mean for *everyone*, you dolt! Just *me*!"[66] Ignorance takes a subversive turn in this counterclaim, as Calvin clings to a logical inconsistency. The freedom that underwrites his desire to do whatever he likes at whatever cost to others rests on the assumption that others will not behave likewise.

Hobbes proves otherwise, yet this act does not result in Calvin's acceptance of the impossibility of living life in a way that completely disregards other individuals' freedom to choose. Calvin shows no awareness of the disjunction between the final claim he makes concerning his allegiance to might makes right and the fact that he affirms this right while covered head-to-toe in mud (much like the reversal in which Susie hits him with a snowball while lording over his snowman). For those who would expand on the link between Hobbes' character and his philosophical namesake, this is a helpful strip. The point Hobbes makes to Calvin echoes the point Hobbes the philosopher makes in *Leviathan*. Hobbes stresses that humans are essentially equal, despite physical differences: "Nature hath made men so equal, in the faculties of the body, and mind; as that though there be found one man sometimes manifestly stronger in body, or of quicker mind than another; yet when all is reckoned together, the difference between man, and man, is not so considerable, as that one man can thereupon claim to himself any benefit, to which another may not pretend, as well as he."[67] Because of this essential equality, one cannot claim the right to act in a particular way and then claim that others cannot act likewise. The relative equality of humans ensures that no one person should make the argument that Calvin does here. More broadly, because humans are all to some degree self-interested, everyone must confront the same limitations that Calvin encounters here in searching for self-fulfillment. If everyone insists on her/his right to do as s/he pleases, then chaos will reign. This is the launching point for (the philosopher) Hobbes' discussion about the importance of a social contract, an idea implicit in the conflict of interests that Hobbes the tiger captures by pushing Calvin to the ground.

Experiences like those found in the April 9, 1989, strip identify a crucial shortcoming in the aesthete's value structure: intolerance for others' freedom to choose their own values. Calvin is clear that he is unwilling to extend the right to act freely of any consequences others might experience in pursuing his own desires. Another pointed example — from July 10, 1987 — strengthens the link between the aesthete's values and the inability to accommodate others' freedom of choice. In the first frame, Calvin poses an important question: "What do you think is the secret to happiness? Is it money, power, or fame?"[68] These two questions establish the context as defined by an aesthetic sense of value in response to a question of meaning. Happiness matters to Calvin (as it does to most people), but the ways of achieving happiness are limited to standards that fall squarely within the aesthete's range of things that matter. Already limited in how he imagines the route to happiness, Calvin continues: "*I'd* choose money. If you have enough money, you can *buy* power and fame. That way, you'd have it all and be *really* happy."[69] There is, apparently, a holy grail of meaning if one defines the measures of value in these terms: "Happiness is being famous for your financial ability to indulge in every kind of excess."[70] Kierkegaard could hardly provide a better summary of how the aesthete defines value, and Plato would no doubt explain that this is precisely the point he makes with the leaky jar. Things that can be acquired through hard work become for Calvin a hollow freedom. Pursuing excess highlights the stakes for the aesthete; there always has to be more if there is to be any value. If this is the baseline for the aesthete, then Calvin's goal of enjoying every excess highlights the depths to which this kind of value structure can lead a person. It is no wonder, then, that Plato recognizes in the person who continually attempts to fill the leaky jar the possibility of descending into madness.

The ideas Calvin presents are extreme, a point Hobbes makes in rolling his eyes in response to Calvin's notion of happiness. If this were the final act in this strip, then the point would be clear: The aesthete's search for meaning is doomed by virtue of the narrow range of values that inform the aesthete's understanding of life. Calvin, however, is not finished in discussing how money will provide happiness. Because of the power this money can buy, he envisions a further enjoyment: "The part I think I'd like the best is crushing people who get in my way."[71] Calvin is not willing to extend a might-makes-right approach to satisfying his desires, but he is willing to crush people who attempt to do so. Read alongside the April 9, 1989, strip, the irony at work is piercing in its ability to undermine Calvin. Even as he asserts his strength, his weakness is made manifest by the very other he supposedly will not mind crushing. There is, then, a further irony at work in the July 10, 1987, strip. Calvin seems unaware of telling his best friend that he would happily crush him if he got in his way. Presumably this blanket statement would apply to Hobbes if the circumstances demanded as much, yet one can hardly imagine that Calvin would act in accordance with his claims if it meant giving up his relationship with Hobbes.

Calvin's attitude reveals the difficulty of embracing fully the aesthete's value structure. His experiences echo the instability that Kierkegaard attaches to the aesthete's endless pursuit of something that is, in the end, unsustainable. Another example will offer a further layer to the question of how the individual in her/his freedom cannot always find fulfillment. Safe within a snow fort, Calvin dares anyone to make him do something against his will: "Nobody can make me go inside! I've got 200 snowballs that say I'm staying *out*! No one's gonna make *me* come in the house!"[72] Such defiance is neither out of place, given Calvin's tendencies, nor unexpected, given his willingness to protect his desires against any influence beyond his own. The second panel in this particular strip shows Calvin glaring over the top of his fort. The third panel softens this aggression slightly as boredom begins to take over. In the final panel, Calvin is back inside (through of his own free will) to yell, "*Doesn't anyone miss me?!?*"[73]

Yet another rich irony speaks to the value structure that denies the other's influence at all costs. Calvin longs for the chance to assert his individual values freely, yet, paradoxically, to do so requires someone else to storm his snow fort. Absent this encounter, the energy that drives his anticipation fizzles, and he encounters the limits of self-interest. Even though he does not seem to be aware of the irony behind his question when he asks for someone to engage his impenetrable fort, the contrast is clear for the reader. The need for someone to play a particular role in order to fulfill his expectations undermines the very thing he longs to prove.

Throughout the various examples from *Calvin and Hobbes* discussed in this chapter a pattern emerges. For Calvin, the question of value is usually filtered through self-interest and thus constitutes a relative measure. At the same time, he will go to great lengths to act as though his specific understanding of a given situation should be seen as normative. In this paradoxical attitude — and irony is frequently the revelatory presence in the text — Calvin encounters the limits of this standard, particularly when his claims to self-interested value boomerang and unsettle his stated values. He thus makes manifest the tension between the immediate desires that pull the aesthete through life and the fact that any number of circumstances can frustrate these expectations. The delays and denials that punctuate Calvin's experiences thus provide a thematic link with the broader context that defines the human condition.

As discussed in Chapter Three, the human experience is a kind of exile to be traversed. How the individual understands the various moments in this journey often informs both the capacity in which an individual approaches a given context and the consequences for any action (or lack thereof) during any such moment. In conceptualizing life as a journey, then, Calvin O. Schrag's *The Self After Postmodernity* offers another layer of human identity to consider when examining how individuals define value. Schrag frames his book in a telling manner: "Knowledge of self is as much rendering an account, the telling of a story, as it is the discernment of perceptual profiles — and indeed it is the telling of a story in which the self is announced as at once actor and receiver of action."[74] One can see how Schrag provides a helpful structure in considering the various shades of Calvin's character. His explanations ultimately reveal his journey through a variety of concerns. The specific meanings that arise from his proclamations, his imagination, and his struggles speak to the dislocation that he shares with all people. He is trying to make sense of the world as best he can. At times he assumes a particular approach to find meaning that produces unexpected results, which range from boredom to crisis. What becomes clear in each of these circumstances, as well as those in-between, is the limits that his profound individualism and his desire to choose his own way in life can achieve.

The ultimate failure of a search for meaning occurs for a variety of reasons. Often the text's latent dynamics refuse the clarity that one seeks in finding meaning. At the same time, this resistance to closure enables further possibilities to explore; and while this opportunity can be considered a great freedom, at time life's continual openness can be burdensome. On occasion, the simple desire for a safe space in which to rest is the strongest desire, despite (and in response to) the fact that a foundational instability continually frustrates this desired conclusion to life's journey. The result, Schrag explains, is a loosening of the parameters that seem to structure how the individual arrives at life's meaning(s): "Questions about self-identity, the unity of consciousness, and centralized and goal-directed activity have been displaced in the aftermath of the dissolution of the subject."[75] To continue on life's journey, then, Schrag explains how a shift in perspective is necessary: "If one cannot rid oneself of the vocabulary of self, subject, and mind, the most that can be asserted is that the self is multiplicity, difference, and ceaseless becoming."[76] Thus redefined, the self loses its footing yet encounters a rich freedom of possible journeys. The self is thus able to endure because it is no longer bound by a particular experience or consequent value.

In stressing narrative as the context in which the self takes shape, Schrag invites the influence of the two discourses that characterize *Calvin and Hobbes*.[77] Though a concept that resists stability, discourse "provides its own resources for self-unification and self-identity, and it does so specifically in the form and dynamics of narratives."[78] Any resources remain, of course, fractured, an instability that similarly defines all narratives. At the same time, it is through discourse that identity can emerge and speak to the individual's experiences. This is precisely the balance that Spaceman Spiff achieves for Calvin. The narrative he imagines is able to construct an identity that compensates for the dislocation Calvin's actual self experiences.

The ability to conceptualize a self through discourse can be sustained through life's vicissitudes. Schrag emphasizes that the self generated through narrative "provides the ongoing context in which the figures of discourse are embedded and achieve their determinations of sense and reference."[79] As the locus for this generation, the text's openness thus serves an important role in how the self can be understood. The text's dislocating properties ensure that the narrative is always ongoing, a resistance to closure that appears in the final strip of *Calvin and Hobbes.*[80] This openness is crucial for Schrag in understanding how a self can emerge; rejecting normative understandings of the self as a fixed identity is a necessary step to undertaking the journey of discovering the self. He writes, "We must stand guard to secure the space of discourse as temporalized event of speaking *between* the objectification of speech acts and language on the one hand and the abstractions and reifications in the structuralist designs of narratology on the other hand."[81] By stressing the between that provides the context for various discourses, Schrag resists the move away from this communicative gap and therefore preserves the imagination's ability to discover new meanings.

The risk in finding one's identity through life's journey is to adopt a particular meaning and resist any subsequent experiences that challenge the standard one has constructed. Schrag cautions against any attempt to project a contextualized self into a baseline for all meaning: "In this move to narrativity, however, one must be duly vigilant about another danger on the path toward self-understanding, namely, the solidification of narrative into a narratology that disconnects itself from the concrete temporality of the who of discourse."[82] The starting point for delineating the self through narrative is to affirm, always, that narratives are ongoing; no narrative can be complete insofar as every story can be retold (or re-read). This openness — which, recalling Derrida, is a crucial feature of the text[83] — ensures that a particular meaning can take on a different shape. As Calvin's imagination makes clear, there are no fixed outcomes, and therefore no definitive way to tell a particular story. As the imagination gives way to the real world — and then as Calvin releases himself back into an imaginative context — the way that he conceptualizes himself shifts, an openness that affirms the point that Schrag raises. The who at stake in discourse remains bound by temporality, or, more broadly, by the limits of the human condition.[84] Death, of course, is foremost among these limits, but the broader point is that temporality moves the search for meaning forward whether one likes it or not. These underlying conditions must be incorporated into the narrative, even if only implicitly, for the narrative context to accommodate a possible sense of self. Time is an elusive thing, and staking an identity to it is ultimately an impossible task. It is "misleading," then, "to speak of the narrating self as being 'in' time or existing 'throughout' time."[85] To act as a narrative self requires a constant rebirth; every time the text is read, it begins anew. Thus, the self that emerges through the text's motion cannot be abstracted from the process that makes this self manifest. The emerging self is always a beginning that unfolds in the act of discourse, which is framed in temporal concerns.

The narratives that one finds in *Calvin and Hobbes* retain temporal boundaries even against the fiercest of deconstructive efforts. There are certain beginnings and ends — the physical borders that constrain the drawings, for example — that cannot be ignored in full. They can recede into the background as the reader engages the narrative that unfolds through these spaces, but to erase time completely from the text is a denial of features that are part of the strip's identity. As such, Schrag argues that temporality (as opposed to time) assists the genesis of a self: "The story of the self is a developing story, a story subject to creative advance, wherein the past is ... a text, an inscription of events and experiences, that stands open to new interpretations and new perspectives of meaning."[86] The need to hold the text open to new readings requires that this series of pasts ensures that any reading is a new reading that presents again the opportunity to find meaning. This journey is, of course, related to these pasts (and life is an accumulation of past moments), but it transcends these parameters as it seeks out meaning.

While a lengthy discussion of temporality is best pursued elsewhere, a comment from Schrag on this point is necessary to extend the argument at hand.[87] Quite simply, time is a constituent part of what it means to be human. At the same time, there exists a tension between time and the narrative context that can constrain attempts to articulate an understanding of the self. As Schrag explains, "Because of traditional habits of thought that picture time as a flowing stream, a rapid succession of instants in which things come to and pass away, it is difficult to find the appropriate grammar to articulate the sense of temporality at issue in narrative identity."[88] When Calvin is sitting in class, bored (again) to no end, his imagination releases him into a narrative self. As a self that emerges with each new adventure — which in turn is based on a new context from Calvin's actual life — Spaceman Spiff touches upon a world in which time ceases to function in conjunction with these metaphors. Spiff's "dangerous mission" involves a departure from time's ability to constrict meaning.[89] The narration reveals much about the imaginative context's ability to bend time: "[Spiff] fires his hyper-jets and ... blasts into the fifth dimension! Into a world beyond human comprehension! Into a world where time has no meaning!"[90] In escaping his boredom imaginatively, Calvin discovers again how a release from time's constraints can provide the grammar for narrative identity. Calvin may be stuck at his desk, but his imagination explores the new conceptions of meaning that Schrag aligns with a loosening of time. The visual component of the strip reiterates this point. As Spiff journeys towards and then passes into the fifth dimension, the visual discourse becomes blurry and then breaks into a universe of pastel rings. This new world is made possible by the emergence of a narrative self who escapes time through his imagination.

One of the most clearly referential strips[91] in *Calvin and Hobbes* brings together the various points Schrag raises in elaborating on the self's emergence through narrative. In the May 1, 1992, strip, Calvin walks past the table where his mom is sitting and exclaims, "Paul Gauguin asked 'Whence do we come? What are we? Where are we going?'"[92] Life is about answering these questions; in quoting Gauguin, Calvin ultimately reveals how life is suspended in the space between asking and answering. In the second panel of this strip, Calvin transitions to the latter: "Well, I don't know about anyone else, but *I* came from my room, I'm a kid with big plans, and I'm going outside! See ya later!"[93] His confidence belies what occurs in the fourth strip, when Calvin comes back to ask his mom, "Who the heck is Paul Gauguin anyway?"[94] The identity that Calvin implies in answering Gauguin's questions so earnestly dissolves, which in turn undermines his answers. He does know that he is an individual with big plans; he stresses both to his mom as he walks by the table. The subsequent discourse with her makes this point clear. Any answers to these questions will be tentative and subject to the ongoing journey's always unrealized arrival.

Faced with the limits of narration, the individual still has recourse to understand the self. That opportunity lies in discourse's structure. To engage in a search for meaning through discourse is to engage someone beyond the individual. Schrag emphasizes that for the self to emerge, the narrative must "be told by someone to someone. If the narrative does not tell a story to someone, then it is not narrative; if discourse is not a rendition by someone, then it is not a discourse."[95] In Calvin's passing comments, one can see Schrag's standards at work. His confidence speaks to his mom because he is defining himself to her. Elsewhere, this same dynamic is at work. There are very few situations in *Calvin and Hobbes* that do not involve multiple characters. In the cases where there is only one character present, another person, though absent, is implied through the language, the drawing, or the context that the two generate. The practical implications of requiring someone (or, at the very least, something) else to construct a narrative are clear in examples discussed throughout this chapter. Whether Calvin tries to justify a standard of value that ignores other people, or simply complains to Hobbes, one can recognize in the subtext the requirement that Schrag outlines. Even when he rejects others as having freedom or an influence on his own choices, Calvin implicitly invites these others into the narrative context that gives a particular manifestation of the self. Just as Spaceman Spiff still requires an antagonist to undertake his fearless journeys, so too does Calvin need someone else — even Susie Derkins — to make sense of his world.

The narrative that posits meaning thus folds in on itself, which in turn fractures the identities that humans construct in their respective searches for meaning. The consequence is, as Calvin shows in returning to his mom, that attempts to stabilize the self will eventually break down. This inevitability casts the self as determined through discourse into a troubling paradox. Blanchot captures the plight that is unavoidable and inescapable for the person who seeks meaning through narrative: "The tragic difficulty of the undertaking is that in this world of exclusion and radical separation, everything is false and inauthentic as soon as one examines it."[96] This caution applies both to the aesthete who locates meaning in immediate gratification and, more broadly, in the searches that precede any actual experience of these things. Meaning is elusive and, when finally glimpsed through narrative's discourses, tentative. Though all meanings suffer the breakdown that Blanchot describes, the aesthete's need to regenerate meaning frequently exposes these values to life's underlying instability. To counterbalance this tragic end, one must begin anew in search of a different kind of meaning, which, as Kierkegaard suggests, can be found in the ethicist's commitment to something with a bit more staying power.

CHAPTER SIX

True Value
The Friendship of Calvin and Hobbes

The movement from the aesthete's value structure to the ethicist's commitment to duty demands that a person reorient her/his approach to life.[1] A particular aspect of life that such a shift affects deeply is how a person relates to others. As discussed in the previous chapter, the aesthete frames her/his relationships with other people in terms that advance the pursuit of immediate gratification. The implication, of course, is that others are expendable if circumstances demand as much. In choosing to live in a different way, however, this way of engaging others is no longer viable.[2] Given the significance of this transition, a discussion of how Calvin understands other people will provide the basis for exploring the relationship that anchors the entire strip: Calvin and Hobbes' friendship.

Later in *Calvin and Hobbes*, Calvin approaches almost every major secondary character with a contract that addresses what he perceives as a person's respective shortcomings with respect to his life. Moe has to take responsibility for bullying Calvin[3]; his dad has to promise compensation should his parenting fail to provide Calvin with the life he wants[4]; Ms. Wormwood must own the consequences of any failure that can be traced to Calvin's education[5]; and Susie must agree not to anticipate a romantic relationship with Calvin.[6] In each instance Calvin seeks to codify responsibility at some future point for the way he thinks each person may disrupt his life. Interestingly, each of these figures is at some point conceptualized as a monster in one of Calvin's imaginative departures. According to Kearney, this is a significant detail: "Monsters ... signal borderline experiences of uncontainable excess, reminding the ego that it is never wholly sovereign."[7] The need to extend a contract to particular people thus echoes the need to confront these figures when Calvin imagines them as monsters. In each case Calvin encounters a threat to his individuality; he is acutely aware that these people constrain in some capacity what he values and how he tries to live his life. Kearney captures this point with precision: "While morality often speaks abstractly of the relation between virtue and the pursuit of happiness, it is the task of narrative imagination to propose various fictional figures that comprise so many *thought experiments* which may help us see connections between the ethical aspects of human conduct and fortune/misfortune."[8] Calvin's imaginative characterizations of his anxieties emerge out of a general awareness of his fragility, and their effect is immediately perceptible. In each case Calvin absorbs their effects as a disruptive presence that undermines his narrative self. As a result, he conceptualizes these unsettling figures in terms that allow him to overcome the instability in life that each person-turned-monster aggravates.

The irony in this particular strip is worth highlighting. Given that Calvin's dad is a lawyer, it would seem that approaching him with a contract is a risky move, something Calvin realizes when he is sent to his room. It is also worth noting that Calvin's mom and Rosalyn are the only two significant minor characters whom Calvin does not approach in this capacity. There may or may not be a reason for these respective absences, but the argument at hand does not suffer because of these exclusions. Calvin's relationship with Rosalyn will be discussed shortly (it is distinct), and Calvin's mom may not get a contract because the point is made in Calvin's approach to his dad. In both cases, then, the capacity in which irony functions reveals the particularities about these characters that frame a broader consideration of how they influence Calvin's life.

The link between the secondary characters in *Calvin and Hobbes* and the antagonistic role these people play in his imaginative departures from reality thus speaks to the unstable nature of his life. More specifically, the familiarity of these individuals manifests the intimate ways in which others can unsettle how a particular person understands her/his life. As Kearney explains, "Most strangers, gods and monsters — along with various ghosts, phantoms and doubles who bear a family resemblance — are, deep down, tokens of fracture within the human psyche. They speak to us of how we are split between conscious and unconscious, familiar and unfamiliar, same and other."[9] These monsters reveal the anxieties that Calvin recognizes in life, and moreover hint at a disruption beyond the contractual concerns he seeks to address. In the other, Kearney indicates that the individual can recognize her/his own unstable individuality.[10] As a result, one must find a way to reconcile these dual implications in a way that alleviates the insecurity that these figures expose. In Calvin's case, it is not surprising that these people transform into exotic monsters. Kearney explains, "The key is to let the other be other so that the task is *narrative understanding*: a working-through of loss and fear by means of cathartic imagination and mindful acknowledgement."[11] Just as Schrag locates the emergence of the self in a narrative context, Kearney recognizes that the freedom to imagine alternatives to life's instability is the first step towards balancing an individual's search for meaning with the impossibility of achieving the stability implied therein. The imagination becomes the vehicle that releases the individual to suggest sanctions in response to the instability exposed in how others affect her/his life. For Calvin's life, this takes the form of offering contracts to those who generate this anxiety.[12]

The underlying insecurities that motivate Calvin to offer these contracts open the text into a related theme from existentialist thought. More specifically, the stress on an individual's choice of value will inevitably encounter the absurdity of existence. Following on this point, the existentialist stress on choice can easily lead to the notion that life is absurd.[13] In *No Exit*, Jean-Paul Sartre drags any notion of friendship into the realm of the absurd. The character Inez captures this basis of hell: "I prefer to choose my hell."[14] The stress on choice is but one aspect of hell; the other, Inez famously claims, is that in the end "hell is other people."[15] In others, then, one finds the deeply unsettling realities of humanity, which ultimately provide a mirror of one's own absurd condition. Thus, one may as well choose one's hell. As will be discussed in Chapter Seven, Sartre is extreme in his notion of how choice fractures attempts to understand the human condition. At the same time, he brings together the reality of choice to make a helpful point. If every individual can choose and no one can exercise this ability in a way that transcends the emptiness to which all choices lead, then every person will remind every other of their shared hellish reality.

One of the final extended narrative threads in *Calvin and Hobbes* offers an example of how the imagination's freedom can overcome this anxiety. Rosalyn arrives to babysit Calvin one more time, which portends a long night for both. As Kearney explains, when encountering such an other, "The challenge now is to acknowledge a difference between self and other without separating them so schematically that *no* relation is possible at all."[16] Whereas other characters in Calvin's world convey specific risks that require a contractual response, Rosalyn's threat to Calvin's self is more elusive in its ability to disrupt his life. There is a clear difficulty in attempting to articulate why, exactly, Rosalyn affects Calvin so deeply to the point that Calvin does not imagine her as a monster. Her influence on his life is such that she cannot be transformed into a monster that Calvin can in turn conquer as Spaceman Spiff. This suggests that her presence invades Calvin's world in a particularly intimate capacity.[17] However, in this narrative the two combatants are able to relate to one another on common ground when Rosalyn's offer to play any game Calvin wants launches the strip into a final game of Calvinball.[18] The decision constitutes a significant concession for both. On the one hand, Rosalyn relents in her authoritarian presence, while Calvin invites her into one of his favorite pastimes. The difficulty of this gesture is apparent in Kearney's analysis. The two must relate in a way that overcomes their shared enmity while resisting a stance towards the other that prohibits any value from materializing.

The bond that develops between Calvin and Rosalyn as they play Calvinball thus dissolves the conflict that previously linked (and, paradoxically, still links) them together. The result is crucial insofar as it reveals the imagination's ability to transform the threat of the other into a tolerable or even welcomed presence. On this point Derrida's ideas on hospitality are illuminating. Accepting the other is a "decision [that] is made at the heart of what looks like an absurdity, impossibility itself.... Pure hospitality consists in welcoming the *arrivant*, the one who arrives, before laying down any conditions."[19] The choice to welcome the other is the crucial step that occurs in this instance. By inviting Rosalyn into his imaginative world, Calvin performs what could be absurd in light of their past relationship. However, because the rules of Calvinball are what they are, Calvin is able to engage Rosalyn without the conditions that predate this particular encounter. As a result, Calvin undertakes what Michael Nass labels "a negotiation between two seemingly contradictory imperatives, the imperative to unconditionally welcome the other ... and the imperative to effectively welcome someone in particular and not some indefinite anyone."[20] While playing Calvinball, Rosalyn ceases to be the general other who disrupts Calvin's world, and, more specifically (and more importantly), she is not perceived as his babysitter. This second point is crucial. As Watterson explains, Rosalyn is "the only person Calvin fears."[21] In a space defined not by rules but by a freedom to let the game unfold without preconditions, Calvinball offers the space for the two to engage one another in a way that balances the actual relationship — one of power — with the common ground they share in this narrative.

When discussing hospitality, it is important to remember that the individual must choose to engage the other in the capacity Derrida describes. Elsewhere, Derrida emphasizes this point: "This is the double law of hospitality, to calculate the risks, yes, but without closing the door on the incalculable, that is on the future and the foreigner. It defines the unstable site of strategy and decision."[22] Derrida strikes an important middle ground in the context of this discussion. To be hospitable is not to blindly welcome the other in; the decision to extend this opening is one that carries certain risks. As Calvin well knows, Rosalyn is not risk-free, so to speak. Their shared, antagonistic history warrants a deliberate choice to play Calvinball, yet herein lies the power of choosing to gesture towards the other. The narrative thread opens with another example of this friction,[23] yet both Calvin and Rosalyn reach an agreement that constitutes a choice to be hospitable.[24] In weighing the risk and deciding to engage the other despite antecedent conflict, new meanings become possible. Just as the freedom to choose can preclude any acknowledgement of the other — and certainly welcoming the other in looking for meaning — it is also the groundswell of the gesture that opens the text into new meanings (by all indications, Calvinball is a multi-player sport). It takes a particular context — a space characterized by imaginative freedom — to accommodate both the individuals who refuse to embrace the other and a mutually enriching meeting.

The movement towards the other in a space that remains infinitely open to meaning requires not only the common ground on which Rosalyn and Calvin play, but also a refusal to retreat from a relationship that has moved beyond a calculation of risks. This points bends back to the initial narrative discussed in this chapter. After Calvin has offered a contract to those infringing upon his particular sense of self, he attempts to have Hobbes sign a contract that binds their friendship well into the future. Calvin's intentions are seemingly good, as this suggestion attempts to cement the positives that Hobbes brings to Calvin's life. The tenor, however, is entirely wrong, a point Hobbes makes when he responds vigorously, "People are friends because they *want* to be, not because they *have* to be."[25] Nonplussed, Calvin responds, "That's what this fixes."[26] Hobbes does not relent and instead highlights the need to overcome risks if the friendship is to continue flourishing by handing the unsigned contact back to Calvin: "If your friends are contractual, you don't have any."[27] Quite simply, friendship requires a continued willingness to engage another at the expense of one's individual values; any attempt to infringe upon this mutuality runs against the grain of what friendship is supposed to provide to both parties. This exchange aside, the friendship between Calvin and Hobbes illustrates how the glimmer of Calvin's ability to coexist with such a combative figure can transcend even the starkest examples of his self-oriented perspective on life.

During on of the few bedtime stories that does not include *Hamster Huey and the Gooey Kablooie*, Calvin and Hobbes listen to Calvin's dad tell a story about a boy and his tiger. Calvin may resist the story's morals about behaving and eating sugary cereal, but the climactic moment captivates both Calvin and Hobbes. The story ends abruptly, and Calvin makes his frustration known: "*Good night*?! That's not the end! You didn't even get us to lunchtime!"[28] Calvin's dad tucks him in, kisses his forehead, and explains that Calvin and Hobbes will write another part of the story on the following day. The final frame of the strip shows Calvin hugging Hobbes as he excitedly anticipates their next adventure. As he hugs Hobbes, Calvin exclaims, "This *is* a good story about us if it doesn't end! That's the kind of story I like best! Good night, ol' buddy!"[29] Hobbes rubs Calvin's head affectionately and agrees: "Me too! See you tomorrow!"[30]

This brief exchange captures the foundation of *Calvin and Hobbes*: the adventures of two friends. Though multiple characters intersect with the adventures that Calvin and Hobbes embark upon, their relationship is the axle around which the strip spins. They encounter a range of emotions in their adventures: anger, frustration, sadness, an awareness of mortality, philosophical pondering, and, most noticeably, a deep and abiding love for one another. The bond that anchors *Calvin and Hobbes* invites closer exploration about what exactly drives their friendship. More than any other character in the strip, Hobbes inspires in Calvin a reason to let go of his self-interested attitude, or, as has been discussed in previous chapter, sometimes Hobbes merely endures Calvin's proclivity towards immediate desires, foolish errands, and the occasional insult. Whereas his encounters with others — especially his parents and Rosalyn — undercut Calvin's various attempts to define value only in his terms, Hobbes precludes these shortcomings in Calvin and, in so doing, supersedes Calvin's most difficult moments.

While the accent in this chapter falls upon Hobbes' role in helping Calvin move beyond his aesthetic desires, it is important to note that Hobbes is by no means a blameless partner in the question of how each individual's way of living life affects the other. Hobbes routinely causes

Calvin suffering, both physical (in the numerous examples wherein Calvin returns home and Hobbes pounces on him from inside) and psychological (there are similarly more than a few occasions when Hobbes sneaks up on Calvin to disrupt what he is doing with the mere threat of an attack). These psychological traumas in particular call into question any thesis that treats Hobbes as rising above the shortcomings in Calvin's identity. It is worth noting, finally, that Hobbes is not entirely immune from a standard of value defined in the terms of his own experiential context. Hobbes makes several comments to Calvin about animals' superiority to humans. Such instances reveal how anyone can regress into an aesthete's way of understanding the world.

The friendship between Calvin and Hobbes is the single most important feature in the strip's world, a narrative anchor that holds open the possibility that Calvin can look beyond his own interests. Hobbes' presence ensures that there exists another perspective for most of Calvin's experiences, which in turn expands the meanings into which the strip ventures. Moreover, because Calvin's imagination is the genesis of this structuring relationship, their ability to challenge one another's conceptions of the self constitutes a crucial entry point into the text. Though I focus on the fact that Hobbes is a stuffed animal in Chapter One, it is helpful to reiterate the point, given the extended discussion on the friendship between Calvin and Hobbes that follows. Literally speaking, the friendship is one-sided insofar as Calvin prescribes everything that happens when he spends time with Hobbes. For the critic who would insist on this point, one can grant the need to suspend disbelief in order for the argument in this chapter (and throughout this book) to function. At the same time, this admission ultimately strengthens the broader point at hand, namely that through the imagination meaning can be found in *any* context. Calvin's ability to incorporate his stuffed tiger into the most intimate, vulnerable moments in his life speaks to the imagination's power to generate meaning, even in the most difficult circumstances. Given the stress in the previous chapter on Calvin's often narrow way of viewing the world, his willingness either to reflect upon his attitude (at times) at Hobbes' suggestion or, more tellingly, to admit on occasion that Hobbes' viewpoint on an issue makes more sense indicate that his aesthetic tendencies are not permanent. In turn, this echoes Kierkegaard's belief that one can choose to admit the limits of this aesthete's value system and seek instead a life characterized by commitment.

By turning to ancient philosophical sources to explore the idea of friendship, one can understand more clearly what both Calvin and Hobbes find valuable in their relationship with the other. In turn, this exploration clarifies what is at stake in the broader narrative structure of *Calvin and Hobbes*. A valuable and unsuspecting lesson about an ancient ideal flows beneath the surface of the adventures that these two friends share. The way that their bond anchors *Calvin and Hobbes* echoes strongly how Aristotle conceptualizes friendship in his *Ethics*. In broad terms, Aristotle understands friendship as a necessary condition for living an enjoyable life. Friendship, he explains, is "a kind of virtue, or implies virtue, and it is also most necessary for living. Nobody would choose to live without friends even if he had all the other good things."[31] Quite simply, friendship provides the basis for finding meaning in life. The things that appear to offer value in the aesthete's life pale in comparison to the satisfaction that friendship affords. A friend encourages a person to live a good life, a motivation that transcends the impossible search for meaning that those who seek to fill their leaky jars undertake. The bond that underwrites friendship is available to anyone who is willing to invest in her/his relationship with the other. Everyone can take "refuge"[32] in her/his relationships, a measure of safety that one cannot find solely on one's own.[33]

This dynamic emerges clearly when Moe steal's Calvin's truck on the playground.[34] After trying to reason with Moe to return what he took, and then receiving only the threat to get beaten up in response, Calvin spends several strips trying to muster the courage to confront Moe in order to get his truck back. When his courage fails him, Calvin then tries to imagine how Moe might be receptive to an appeal based on a moral standard. On the basis of this idea, Calvin then returns to Moe and demands his truck back, a request to which Moe responds with another threat. Disheartened, Calvin trudges away and decides that his truck is not worth the trouble. As discussed in Chapter Five, Calvin experiences the effects of the individual freedom he posits when demanding that the world fit his perspective. As with Hobbes' push into the mud, Calvin encounters the corollary to his professed values and, given the outcome, is frustratingly aware of the limits that define the aesthete's value structure. Even if he never recognizes this at the time, Calvin's vulnerability in the infringement of others' choices emerges clearly in this exchange with Moe. The fact that in this instance he seeks Hobbes' help reveals his tacit acceptance that in the end he cannot endure life only on the strength of his frequent claims to individualism.

The narrative thread involving the stolen truck concludes with Calvin and Hobbes walking in the woods as they discuss what transpired. Calvin laments, "You know, sometimes the world seems like a pretty mean place."[35] Hobbes responds as a friend should: "That's why animals are so soft and huggy."[36] The final scene is two frames wide, a visual departure from the norm that emphasizes the point that follows. Calvin sighs, "...Yeah," as Hobbes envelopes him with a hug.[37] Hobbes thus responds in good Aristotelian fashion. He offers the refuge that Calvin needs in the wake of such a destabilizing experience. Moe exposes Calvin's weakness, which in turn frustrates his sense of fairness. Calvin feels alone and helpless, but Hobbes' friendship brings a measure of calm. Beneath the tree, in the arms of his best friend, Calvin can diffuse the extent to which his conflict with Moe aggravates the sense of displacement that characterizes his life. The value he derives from this is a significant departure from the lesson Moe's bullying teaches. Even when he seems to be at the mercy of the one who would act in his own selfish, immediate interests, the safety that friendship brings is unmistakable. As is so often the case, Hobbes provides the comforting space that Calvin does not find elsewhere.[38]

The importance that Aristotle ascribes to friendship invites a more detailed analysis, which in turn helps to appreciate more fully the bond that Calvin and Hobbes share. This more finely grained picture of how friendship affects the life of those who call one another friends reiterates the importance of finding value beyond oneself. As a point of entry into this analysis, it is worth stressing that Calvin and Hobbes frequently disagree with one another; their activities together result consistently in biting, name-calling, bumps, and bruises. As mentioned above, Calvin rarely comes home from school without Hobbes' enthusiastic and painful greetings, and Hobbes' recreation often includes sneaking up and pouncing on Calvin, which more than frays Calvin's nerves.[39] Still, despite Calvin and Hobbes' rough and tumble friendship, one cannot deny the bond between the two. Their mutual affection points towards an underlying and necessary quality to friendship. As Aristotle explains, in friendship; "it is generally accepted that not everything is loved, but only that which is lovable; and that this is either good, or pleasant, or useful."[40] Based on this definition, one can conclude safely that Calvin and Hobbes find something genuinely valuable in one another's company because they both exhibit qualities that grate on the other. Despite these differences (and often because of them), however, Calvin and Hobbes offer to one another something lovable, which, given their often abrasive exchanges, only accents the depth of their friendship. Otherwise, there would be no reason to endure the qualities that do not enhance their relationship.

In Aristotle's understanding, the basis for that friendship results from one of three possibilities: utility, pleasure, or genuine goodness. By utility, Aristotle is referring to a friendship wherein each person derives some kind of benefit from one another without any kind of true affection.[41] That is, friendship based on utility treats the other not as a genuine object of affection but rather as a means to an end.[42] At times, Calvin and Hobbes' friendship seems to fall into this category. For example, while waiting at the bus stop with Calvin, Hobbes is eating a sandwich and drinking from a thermos top. Calvin expresses his thanks to Hobbes for waiting with him, to which Hobbes responds, "My pleasure."[43] On the surface, Calvin seems to derive some benefit from Hobbes' company, while Hobbes apparently waits without any obvious self-interest. In the final frame, however, Calvin notices that his lunchbox is a little light. It turns out that Hobbes also took away some benefit by waiting with Calvin; he got to eat. Thus, an apparently genuine example of Hobbes' affection for Calvin turns out to be a mutually beneficial exchange, though Hobbes' gain is exactly what Aristotle means when he speaks about a friendship of utility.

An inverse example that suggests Calvin and Hobbes' friendship might be based on utility occurs when Calvin sets off to mail his Christmas letter to Santa.[44] Hobbes accompanies Calvin on the walk to the mailbox, and during the trip Calvin cannot stop complaining to Hobbes about the letter's weight; Calvin stresses the frustration he feels, given that the package will cost $2.40 to send.[45] Hobbes listens patiently and then asks Calvin if he has included anything for Hobbes on the list. Calvin reverts to his selfish nature and responds, "What, and pay more postage? This package is breaking my arms already! Go write your *own* list!"[46] Calvin's response reveals his self-interested motives in this particular moment. This utility becomes obvious when Calvin requests Hobbes' help to put the bulky envelope in the mailbox because Calvin is not tall enough to do so himself. His initial response to Hobbes and his later request for help suggest strongly that Calvin appreciates the friendship only insofar as it can provide some benefit. Importantly, Hobbes recognizes Calvin's motivations and thus responds in a way that projects his interests. If Calvin is unwilling to request a present for Hobbes, then Hobbes will not help Calvin. As Calvin struggles, Hobbes sticks his tongue out and tells Calvin, "Tidings and comfort of joy to you too."[47] This tit-for-tat results from each individual's refusal to transcend the thing that he finds important in this context. Moreover, Calvin's initial, selfish statement ultimately elicits Hobbes' response. In a friendship of utility, then, there exists an obvious risk.

When utilities clash, neither person will end up with the thing that s/he desires. When utility is a normative value, this kind of disappointment inevitably follows, which is precisely the point Plato makes in the image of the leaky jar, and that Kierkegaard stresses in characterizing the aesthete. No matter how hard one tries, if one defines value only in terms of the self, and then makes decisions only based on this standard, then one will race to achieve something that is difficult at best and maddening at worst. With respect to friendship, there exists an implicit critique of this approach to determining value, as well as a caution against serving only one's own interests. The desire to protect one's own interests in a friendship characterized by utility thus undermines the help one seeks in relating to the other.

There is, then, an interesting take on a classic philosophical question: the Prisoner's Dilemma. Though the specifics of this exercise vary, the basic construct is that two prisoners who have been working together are caught and placed in separate rooms. The authorities then give each prisoner a choice: either to confess the crime or to remain silent. If both prisoners confess, then both of their prison sentences will be lesser than if either they both do not confess or if only one confesses. There is enough evidence to convict these prisoners, so should both decide to stay silent, then both will face longer prison sentences than if they were both to admit their crime. The twist is that if only one prisoner confesses while the other stays silent, then the one who stays silent will go free while the one who confesses will serve a life sentence for the crime. Both prisoners are given the same information, and they have no way to communicate with one another.

If one develops a matrix to weigh the consequences for each of the four possibilities in this example, the "safest" choice is to stay silent. Because each prisoner has no control over what the other does, the decision to stay silent avoids the worst outcome (i.e. a life in prison). However, because both prisoners will presumably realize this, both will stay silent, which ultimately produces a result that is worse for both than if each were to confess to the crime. If each prisoner cooperates, then each will serve some time in jail, but not as much as if both stay silent. In *Evolution of*

Cooperation, Robert Axelrod offers a thorough and insightful analysis into the dynamics in this philosophical question. His argument is that over the long run, cooperation is a better strategy, as it permits both sides to maximize the benefits derived from their relationship and therefore avoid a way of interacting that is mutually harmful. His conclusion dovetails with the issue at hand with respect to friendship: a willingness to set aside one's own interests will be mutually beneficial in the long run.[48]

Despite the possibility that Calvin views Hobbes' friendship as one of utility, Hobbes' response makes clear that no such bond exists. Aristotle is clear that friendships of utility require a mutually beneficial exchange within the context of friendship.[49] Hobbes leaves no doubt that such a quality does not exist when he refuses to help Calvin lift the envelope into the mailbox. If utility were the only consideration in this context, then Hobbes would presumably leave Calvin by himself. The fact that Hobbes remains with Calvin, despite his self-interested errand, emphasizes that utility is not the basis for their friendship, even if Hobbes' refusal to help is reactive. For Aristotle, friendships of utility end when the mutually beneficial exchange dissolves.[50] The supposed pleasure of a friend's company thus requires a tangible benefit that cannot be reduced solely to a measure of utility. While Hobbes certainly enjoys the irony of Calvin's struggle, to claim that he remains at the mailbox *only* to watch Calvin try to do by himself what he could easily do with Hobbes help is misguided. Hobbes' continued presence thus dismisses the possibility that he and Calvin spend time together solely for some kind of utility. In fact, as good friends do, Hobbes refuses to allow his friendship with Calvin to become a question of utility. By not indulging Calvin's selfish request, Hobbes reaffirms that their friendship is based on more than utility.

A bond based on pleasure presents the second possible basis for friendship in Aristotle's conception. That is, when two people find mutual enjoyment of the moment, they may find themselves in a relationship in this category. This kind of friendship can be deceiving because often times it "has a resemblance to perfect friendship, because good men give each other pleasure."[51] Calvin and Hobbes often exhibit this kind of mutual exchange, especially when they embark upon their outdoor adventures. For example, following a snowstorm, the two set out of build the "greatest snow fort ever," complete with turrets every fifty feet.[52] Despite these grand ambitions, poorly packing snow and Hobbes' chills eventually move the project indoors. Calvin and Hobbes sit on the floor next to the fire as they draw out a plan for the fort once they get better snow with which to work. They sip hot chocolate as they discuss the merits of their design, with their paper, crayons, and the entire afternoon at their disposal. One expects this particular strip to conclude by reinforcing the notion of mutual enjoyment based on their shared interest.

Despite an apparently mutual benefit in a friendship of pleasure, Aristotle sees this second kind of friendship to be clearly defined by self-interest.[53] In the final frame, Calvin asks where the icicle spikes should go. Hobbes answers, "All along the outer wall, after the moat."[54] His mind, however, has drifted elsewhere. As he responds, Hobbes is staring into his mug of hot chocolate, which clearly occupies most of his attention. Hobbes adds, "Say, I think you got more marshmallows in your hot chocolate than I did."[55] Thus, Hobbes acknowledges an important detail in the joint building project, but he also affirms his own self-interests by comparing who has more marshmallows. The distinction is slight, but it is enough to suggest that, according to Aristotle's framework, perhaps Calvin and Hobbes' friendship does not rest on a foundation of mutual pleasure. Even when the two friends are sharing an experience, a hint of self-interest often remains. Just as Hobbes derives some satisfaction from not helping Calvin, here the need to compare who has more marshmallows is a reminder that even within the context of friendship self-interest cannot be scrubbed away entirely. Thus, a friendship that seemingly transcends utility actually suffers the same limits, as self-interest will eventually clash with the mutuality that a friendship affords.

Given the extent to which Calvin and Hobbes often protect their own interests, it is tempting to understand their friendship as one of mutual pleasure only. Other telling examples of their ultimately self-interested motives emerge when the two will blame one another for adventures that run afoul of Calvin's parents. Mutual enjoyment lasts only as long as no one gets in trouble. In one of the first strips, Calvin shows his willingness to ascribe blame to Hobbes if doing so might save himself. When they cause a racket in bed and Calvin's dad comes upstairs in a fit, Calvin quickly blames Hobbes, who happens to be holding a bicycle horn.[56] Of course, Hobbes is more than willing to return the favor. When they argue during the Christmas season, Hobbes is only too willing to tell Santa that Calvin has been misbehaving.[57] These two examples capture a dynamic that occurs throughout *Calvin and Hobbes*. They are friends, but often times their reactions suggest that friendship lasts only as long as the fun does. As soon as activities go awry and consequences become a reality, both Calvin and Hobbes will pass guilt onto one another. Such examples hardly argue for a truly sincere friendship, as a willingness to escape punishment at the expense of one's friend suggests that the strength of the bond between Calvin and Hobbes might not be as resolute as it appears on the surface.

A consistent example of the strain that their friendship endures can be found in several strips that involve Susie. Calvin routinely gets angry with Hobbes whenever Susie enters into their friendship as a playmate. In most cases when Calvin and Hobbes allow Susie into their world, Hobbes sides with Susie. One telling example comes when the G.R.O.S.S. plan to capture and ransom Susie's doll, Binky Betsy, falls apart.[58] Susie tricks Calvin into leaving Hobbes unguarded, and she quickly steals Hobbes. After Calvin and Susie eventually trade their respective friends back, Calvin cannot fathom why Hobbes did not resist Susie's kidnapping (because the entire situation remains grounded in Calvin's imagination; obviously Hobbes cannot resist Susie when Calvin is not around). Hobbes is unapologetic and even reveals that he almost told Susie the secret code that he and Calvin used in the first place to hatch the plan — but only when she rubbed his tummy. Furious, Calvin questions Hobbes' commitment to their friendship.

Despite the occasional descent into their own values, Calvin and Hobbes ultimately transcend the notion that their friendship relies solely on pleasurable activities and outcomes. Though they will blame one another frequently, or even sell one another out, Calvin and Hobbes exhibit the qualities of a truly good friendship. According to Aristotle, a sincere interest in the other's well being defines such relationships[59] because both people "desire the good of their friends for the friends' sake ... [they] are most truly friends."[60] The contextual standard at work here clarifies an important point. When discussing what constitutes a true friendship, Aristotle resists any notion that such a friendship can be contained in a preset formula. One cannot outline ahead of time what a friendship must do because the commitment to the other person precludes any specific experience. As discussed above, when Calvin attempts to codify his relationship with Hobbes, the response captures this exact point. Thus, despite their shortcomings in the context of their friendship, Calvin and Hobbes exhibit a bond that manifests consistently this genuine interest in one another's welfare.

A revealing example of this point occurs during Christmas when Calvin has forgotten to get Hobbes a present. It is important that this strip occurs in the early stages of *Calvin and Hobbes*, as it sets a precedent for their friendship. Though ten years later they will still be arguing, they always return to the loving foundation that they exhibit in this first Christmas exchange. Contrary to his otherwise self-interested concerns during the Christmas season, Calvin feels sincerely devastated that he has nothing for Hobbes. Sheepishly, his hands folded in front of him, Calvin admits that he forgot to get Hobbes a gift: "Uh, Hobbes?... I forgot to get you a present. I didn't even make you a card."[61] Hobbes admits that he, too, forgot to do anything for Christmas. Based on other interactions between the two when one does something that neglects the other, the reader might expect a more explosive result to the exchange. Hobbes, however, erases any tension or fault by grabbing Calvin and giving him a big hug. The final frame extends this embrace and thus emphasizes that Hobbes' affection for Calvin outweighs any material interest. Calvin responds tenderly and honestly, "Not so hard, you big sissy. You squeeze my tears out."[62] Hobbes has a content look on his face as he responds simply, "Merry Christmas."[63] From the outset, Calvin and Hobbes can always return to this state of mutual affection from the selfish, material, and immediate desires that cause friction in their friendship. The ability to embrace despite past (or future) conflicts echoes the transcendent effects that Aristotle ascribes to true friendship: "[This] enduring quality ... is good both *absolutely* and *for his friend*, since the good is both good absolutely and useful to each other."[64] When everything else is stripped away, Calvin and Hobbes exhibit this deep, lasting, and selfless love for one another. They do not need to get one another presents to express their affections, a departure from self-interest that allows the friends to act in service of the other. Their mutual presence transcends the need to be friends for mere utility or pleasure. In a truly good friendship, such qualities come naturally.

A further example will indicate in more depth how Calvin and Hobbes' friendship reflects deeply influential values in Western thought. In his dialogue *Lysis*, Plato provides a simple explanation of the quality that defines true friendship: "Friends are said to have everything in common, so that here at least there will be no difference between you, if what you say of your friendship is true."[65] Calvin and Hobbes certainly have no shortage of shared interests. A capsule of one summer day reveals a multitude of moments wherein Calvin and Hobbes' interests genuinely overlap.[66] They both jump eagerly out of bed to start the day. Over break-fast, they share the comics, and, once finished, they run outside. They play against one another in a game involving dart guns. They take photos together and they swim together. After a game of Calvinball, they lie in the grass and stare at the sky, absorbed in conversation about what they see in the clouds. After an intense wrestling match — which shows not every moment is harmonious — they conspire to soak Susie with a water balloon. They marvel at the moon as daylight fades, and then they punc-tuate their shared experience by capturing fireflies. The full slate of activ-ities conveys how much they enjoy one another's companionship. More tellingly, as they sit in bed, they lament that they did not have more time to spend on their daily agenda. Calvin remarks, "Summer days are sup-posed to be longer, but they sure seem short to *me*."[67] Hobbes is thinking the same thing. "I'll say," he replies. "We didn't get to do half of our daily itinerary."[68] When one is in the company of a good friend, time seems to pass quickly. Even if particular moments are filled with frustration, or even all-out throttling, the net result of the day is one of enjoyment that leaves both Calvin and Hobbes longing for more time to do things together.

The desire for a kindred spirit as the bond of friendship explains why Calvin and Hobbes are so close. Moreover, their similarities indicate why Calvin does not have more friends. After yet another confrontation with Moe, Calvin explains to Hobbes that his sense of value precludes more friendships of consequence. The root of the problem for Calvin is that "people are such jerks."[69] In other circumstances, this comment might be ironic, given Calvin's own ability to descend into selfish acts such as the one Moe perpetuated, but in this case the complaint is sincere. There are a lot of people like Moe around who have no ability to find value in life other than through feeding selfish desires at the cost of others' interests. As a result, Calvin would rather be left alone than try to make more friends, because, he states, "If you can find even one person you really like, you're lucky."[70] It is not that Calvin does not want friends; his problem is that based on the criteria for true friendship there are very few eligible options.

By returning to the standard that Plato articulates in *Lyses*, one can recognize that Calvin understands what constitutes a true friendship. There must be a deep bond that unites two people despite any differences. As Calvin explains to Hobbes later in this conversation, "...And if that person can stand *you*, you're *really* lucky."[71] There are usually more than enough reasons for people not to be friends, a difference that aggravates an already difficult search for truly common ground between individuals. It is not simply that Moe is a jerk, then, that precludes more friendships; Calvin is aware that he, too, has qualities that make friendship difficult. To find a person in whom there can be no difference when there are strong differences between oneself and another is a task that Calvin accepts is nearly impossible. Importantly, when one does find such a person, the bond prompts the erasure of the reasons not to be friends. Hobbes listens patiently to Calvin's thoughts before offering a welcoming response: "What if you find someone you can talk to while you eat apples on a bright fall morning?"[72] The ability to share a simple moment is exactly what Calvin needs to hear, and the timing reveals that both Calvin and Hobbes have found the commonality that Plato cites as the basis of friendship. Calvin thus concludes that even one friend is more than enough, given the various ways in which individuals cannot relate to one another. With a smile, he agrees with Hobbes in a way that shows the depth of appreciation he has for Hobbes: "There's no point in getting greedy."[73]

When sharing a quiet experience with a friend, there is little need for anything else because the relationship brackets the friction that opens this scene. Moe's attitude is a problem, but not simply because it infringes on Calvin's well-being. The common ground that Plato describes thus includes not only the value Calvin and Hobbes find in sitting under a tree and eating an apple, but also the decision to accommodate the other person's interests that clash with one's own (something Moe obviously is unwilling to do). There are frequent examples of this corollary point throughout *Calvin and Hobbes*. For all the positive experiences the two friends share, their similarities are manifest when they can look past one another's deficiencies as well. Hobbes is decidedly patient with Calvin, while Calvin is able to move past Hobbes' aggression. Moreover, when both friends bend rules to serve their own interests, such behavior does not ruin the experience they share. Their ability to remain friends despite the mutual cheating that often occurs during a game indicates that they perceive a similarity in what they value and the benefit their friendship provides.[74] This recognition ultimately smooths out the conflicts that occur when, on occasion, their shared quality is a willingness to seek gain at the other's expense.

A further manifestation of this point is that when the two friends are apart, they anticipate a reunion. In the strip from October 3, 1993, Calvin has breakfast with Hobbes and then walks through a heavy rain to the bus stop. Hobbes waves goodbye as Calvin looks through the bus window. By the time Calvin gets to school, Calvin already looks anxious without Hobbes; the clock on the wall shows the time to be about 8:09, so the two friends have not been apart for long. In the final panel the reader sees Hobbes at the window looking out with a similar longing. Though there is no dialogue in this strip, the reader encounters the full weight of the friends' mutual absence. As a result, the deep affection they have for one another emerges without the need to vocalize as much. Plato's point, then, extends beyond activity; separated friends cannot do things together, which causes a measure of anxiety until they meet again.

It is often at the end of the day that the reader gets to see what Calvin and Hobbes think about their activities. Despite the emphasis on visual discourse, there is little doubt that both benefit from their shared experiences. In other strips, when Calvin and Hobbes do comment on what they are doing, the strength of their friendship becomes more readily apparent. As they stand outside watching a bug fly around in circles, Calvin shares a seemingly innocuous comment: "Bugs fly in such crazy loops and zigzags. I wonder why they don't get dizzy and barf."[75] Hobbes immediately shares Calvin's enthusiasm: "Maybe they do!"[76] By affirming the topic of discussion, Calvin continues to reflect on something that is of little consequence. Still, in good company, his imagination is able to extend his initial thought: "Eww, gross! Ha, ha, ha! But then why would they keep flying that way?"[77] Hobbes, in turn, ratchets up the excitement by linking Calvin's two ideas in his answer: "Maybe bugs *like* to barf!"[78] In this shared activity Calvin and Hobbes' friendship transforms an inconsequential moment into a strangely tender experience. The bug provides a stepping off point for their conversation, and then it is no longer part of the exchange. The inquisitive back-and-forth conversation between Calvin and Hobbes reveals the depth of the bond that they share. Calvin echoes this point in the strip's final frame as he and Hobbes walk on. Calvin remarks, "I tell you, Hobbes, it's great to have a friend who appreciates an earnest discussion of ideas."[79] The ideas, of course, are inane, but the willingness of both Calvin and Hobbes to respond enthusiastically to the other person underscores the extent to which shared interests provide the basis for, and then affirm, the friendship that the two have.

While talking about bug barf reveals the importance of Calvin and Hobbes' shared experiences, the examples from the strip that offer the most insight into friendship occur in the narratives wherein the two friends are separated. In an early strip, a dog attacks Calvin, who in a panic drops Hobbes while running away. As he runs into his house, Calvin is visibly upset and yelling to his mom about what happened: "Mom! Mom! A big dog knocked me down and he stole Hobbes!"[80] In the next frame, Calvin is hugging his mom's legs tightly, tears are streaming down his face, and he lets down his guard. "I tried to catch him, but I couldn't, and now I've lost my best friend!"[81] Calvin's mom chides him for taking Hobbes everywhere, but Calvin peers beyond the practical wisdom his mom offers. He can only feel worse that he managed to lose Hobbes.

The situation becomes so dire that Calvin will even turn to Susie for help.[82] After initially rejecting Susie's invitation to a tea party, Calvin decides to ask Susie to keep an eye out for Hobbes. Unbeknownst to Calvin, Susie has already found Hobbes. When Calvin peers over a brick wall and sees Hobbes sitting at the tea party table, Calvin offers an even rarer glimpse into his feelings for his best friend. When Calvin sees that Susie has found Hobbes, he gushes his appreciation in a string of thank yous.[83] Calvin is so grateful for Susie's help that he kisses her hand. Thus, Calvin does the unthinkable, at least by G.R.O.S.S. standards: he kisses a girl. This act is so out of character for Calvin that it warrants a brief excursus. In a meeting of G.R.O.S.S. that happens in the May 24, 1992, strip, Calvin and Hobbes make a list of things that girls are good for. After Calvin mentions that "girls are good for colonizing Pluto,"[84] Hobbes chuckles and adds to the list that "they're good for smooching! Hoo hoo!"[85] Calvin almost misses the comment but soon loses his temper in disbelief. The very notion of kissing girls is, according to Calvin, "treasonous."[86] There is, then, no mistake in how a G.R.O.S.S. member should interpret the act of kissing Susie Derkins (though Calvin and Hobbes agree to make an exception for the times when Calvin's mom kisses them goodnight, which once again speaks to the nuanced relationship that Calvin has with his mom as compared to other secondary characters). Given that Calvin kisses Susie's hand — an act which runs against Calvin's professed standards as Dictator for Life of G.R.O.S.S. — the importance of Hobbes' friendship is strikingly clear. Over thousands of strips, Calvin is nice to Susie maybe a handful of times. His outright affection is therefore unique in this instance, which emphasizes his joy at reuniting with his best friend. If it means getting Hobbes back, Calvin will bend just about any belief he otherwise considers to be non-negotiable.

Aristotle argues that true friendship exhibits a lasting commitment rather than a moment-to-moment affection for another person.[87] In addition to "spending time together," true friends exhibit "mutual affection."[88] Aristotle then qualifies this standard by stating that true friendship exhibits a reciprocal quality that requires sincerity: "For when a good man becomes a friend to another he becomes that other's good; so each loves his own good, and repays what he receives by wishing the good of the other and giving him pleasure."[89] Several examples illustrate how Calvin and Hobbes meet these criteria. When Calvin has to go to a funeral with his parents, he leaves in such a rush that he forgets to bring Hobbes. When they return, they realize that someone has broken into the home and stolen the valuables. Calvin searches frantically for Hobbes while thinking about his mom's reassurance: "Mom says Hobbes wouldn't have been stolen because he's not valuable."[90] The final frame pulls back and shows Calvin sitting alone, with tears streaming down his face. He mutters, "Well, *I* think he's valuable."[91] By an outsider's standard, Hobbes is nothing more than a stuffed tiger, but Calvin makes clear that he and Hobbes have become one another's standard of what is good in life.[92] Calvin could care less about the supposed valuable things because the one thing he treasures, the one thing that is truly a part of his identity, is his invaluable stuffed tiger and best friend. When Calvin's mom finds Hobbes in Calvin's bed, Calvin rushes to give Hobbes a big hug. His words convey the extent to which their friendship defines their individual well-being: "Hobbes, I'm so glad to see you!! You're safe and sound! And now I am too!"[93] This reunion calls to mind the discussion in Chapter Five concerning the narrative self.[94] Through his friendship with Hobbes, Calvin is able to conceptualize a particular self that, importantly, finds enduring value.

Hobbes' presence enables Calvin to find satisfaction and security amidst a narrative context that is deeply unsettling. They mutually provide the other with satisfaction and security, a mixture of affect that captures what Aristotle means by true friendship. Moreover, the need to embrace one another comes in one of the more challenging circumstances that are portrayed in *Calvin and Hobbes*. The fractured sense of security is so palpable that the reader encounters one of the few circumstances wherein Calvin's parents reveal an emotive range that is not filtered through Calvin's perspective. The embrace his mom and dad share in the May 10, 1989, strip mirrors the importance of Calvin and Hobbes' relationship, and speaks, therefore, to the power of friendship to generate stabilizing meaning in the throes of life's instability. Even when their house is no longer secure,[95] mutual affection enables Calvin's mom and dad to endure the narrative dislocation that threatens to collapse every last bit of meaning.

By Platonic and Aristotelian standards, Calvin and Hobbes are meaningful friends. In fact, immediately preceding the above example is a Sunday strip wherein Calvin is wide awake while Hobbes is asleep. Calvin reflects on the dislocation that characterizes life: "At nighttime, the world always seems so big and scary, and I always seem so small."[96] Calvin's wide eyes accent the loneliness he exudes as the strip focuses only on him. After a deep sigh, the strip pulls back to show Hobbes sleeping soundly next to Calvin, a presence that ultimately provides comfort. Calvin touches Hobbes' face lightly and says, "Good ol' Hobbes. What a friend."[97] In the next frame Calvin is finally able to lay his head on the pillow. His final words before falling asleep reveal the way in which the two have become one another's good: "Things are never quite as scary when you've got a best friend."[98] Here one finds a further value in friendship beyond the ability to conceptualize a self. A friend's presence enables the self to endure when otherwise it might not be able to withstand life's pressures. This is a common theme throughout *Calvin and Hobbes*; these two friends share their trials, travails, and triumphs with this note sounding constantly in the background. As a result, they experience a mutual affection because with one another, the world seems a little less scary. In the end, their friendship allows both of them to sleep peaceably.

The ways in which Calvin and Hobbes' friendship filters their individual identities as developed in *Calvin and Hobbes* reflects a concern that Watterson identifies as primary in his approach to the strip. In his preface to *The Complete Calvin and Hobbes*, Watterson describes how he feels that through the strip he was able to "hit some truth, and in doing so get to know myself better."[99] Among the lessons cited in this context, "deep friendship"[100] stands out as something developed through the way in which Calvin and Hobbes interact. Watterson echoes this point in *The Calvin and Hobbes Tenth Anniversary Book*. He writes, "My strip is about private realities, the magic of imagination, and the specialness of certain friendships."[101] As the primary source of meaning throughout the strip, Calvin and Hobbes' friendship clearly embodies this special bond. Aristotle describes such friendships as "rare,"[102] because "the wish for friendship develops rapidly, but friendship does not."[103] Calvin and Hobbes spend many a waking moment with one another, and their friendship is so deep that they even hope to spill into one another's dreams. Their bond, then, extends the text indefinitely, but in a way that ensures the continued possibility of finding meaning. Hobbes explains this point as they prepare to sleep and thus captures the essence of their friendship: "I think we dream so we don't have to be apart so long. If we're in each other's dreams, we can play together all night!"[104] The final panel for this strip shows both Calvin and Hobbes sleeping soundly, with content smiles on their faces. Deep friendship, the kind of rare bond that Aristotle describes, emerges forcefully in those soft smiles. Calvin and Hobbes truly incorporate one another's experience as formative for their own identities. The result may, on occasion, lead to scratches and bruises, but at the end of the day, neither Calvin nor Hobbes regrets these moments of conflict. Rather, they reinforce mutually the happiness that comes when each provides the other with genuine contentment.

John Caputo captures what is at stake for Calvin and Hobbes in the infinitely extended chance that dreams offer to enjoy their friendship. He explains that "the friend is always *more* than my fellow, which effectively means that friendship is caught up in the infinite disproportion of gift without exchange, in which the other, appearing without appearing, comes from a place of structural superiority and invisible immanence."[105] Textually, then, friendship supports the meanings that emerge through the strip's narrative and stresses how the bond between Calvin and Hobbes gives rise to the some of the strip's deepest meanings. The gift of friendship marks the beginning of *Calvin and Hobbes* and lasts until its end. Even in the strip's final moment, such qualities of friendship are unmistakably clear. With the same affectionate term that he uses elsewhere to describe Hobbes — "Ol' buddy"[106] — Calvin closes down ten years of adventure by setting off into a new world. The final moments of *Calvin and Hobbes* thus reinforce the foundational nature of Calvin and Hobbes' friendship. As they zip towards the edge of the page, Calvin and Hobbes once again set out to write their own story, which consistently exhibits a deep and abiding friendship.

CHAPTER SEVEN

What If God Is a Chicken?
Exploring Life's Big Questions

Calvin's friendship with Hobbes reflects a continued choice that, as has been discussed, can relapse. In this sense, friendship is not a constant feature of the strip in the sense that it can wax and wane as the self asserts on occasion values that must be released to enter into a meaningful friendship. In stressing the choice to engage another as a friend, the argument in the previous chapter circles around to the topic of consideration in this final chapter: finding value in the other who remains beyond both the real context from which the imagination departs and the contexts that the imagination generates. Stated differently, the importance of choice leads to a consideration of a possible divine presence that transcends both the real and imaginary horizons that occur in *Calvin and Hobbes*. Speaking broadly, then, the theme for this final chapter falls within the broad label of the metaphysical. Considerations under this umbrella term include: the possibility of a god (or gods), how that divine being/presence relates to human life, and the implications of this possibility and relationship for finding value in life when making choices.[1]

To clarify how the transition from a commitment to friendship to the possibility of a divine presence comes about, it will be helpful to return to the existential stress on an individual's choice. By condensing Plato's Allegory of the Cave and Kierkegaard's tripartite structure of possible ways to define value, the previous two chapters located the search for meaning within the individual's human condition and the consequent choices that an individual makes in order to understand this reality. Recalling the strip wherein Calvin loses Hobbes to a dog,[2] one can recognize how the commitment to a friend can plateau in its ability to endure life's unexpected and unsettling circumstances. As Calvin laments Hobbes' absence, he wonders, "What did I ever do to deserve this?"[3] After a pause in the third panel for

Calvin to look out his bedroom window and reflect on the question, in the fourth panel he yells outside, "Whatever it was, I'm *sorry* already!"[4] This strip thus opens into a deeply felt consequence of choice, the pain of losing what one chooses to value, and a broader human question in response to such pain: How can a person make sense of life's inevitable challenges?

With respect to the first point, Hobbes' absence captures the risk that choice brings to this particular friendship (as is the case with any friendship). When Calvin explains what happened to his mom, she points to his choice as the underlying factor in what happened: "Well Calvin, if you wouldn't drag that tiger everywhere, things like this wouldn't happen."[5] Though Calvin's mom offers sympathy in the panel that precedes this comment, her choice of words demarcates the real context to which her words speak and the wound that Calvin experiences. She does not call Hobbes by name, and her tone discounts the reason that Calvin takes Hobbes everywhere. Thus, she does not affirm the capacity in which Hobbes' friendship affects Calvin, even though the risk of Calvin's friendship with Hobbes is manifest in the choice that underlies the pain he feels. Had he chosen not to spend this time with Hobbes, then Hobbes would not be lost. Calvin must therefore confront the downside of the choice he makes to enrich his life through this friendship. As Allen and Springstead explain, this risk can ultimately collapse the motivation for friendship in the first place because it is so burdensome: "The difficulties an individual encounters in trying to fulfill ethical obligations may motivate him or her to become religious."[6] The reason for this friendship is to find meaning in life, but as this narrative illustrates, any meaning that emerges cannot overcome the latent risk that affects all friendships. Burdened by guilt for his responsibility in losing Hobbes, Calvin reflects, with a tear running down his cheek, "There's no problem so awful that you can't add some guilt to it and make it even worse."[7]

Alone in his bedroom, Calvin must reconcile the disruption he feels corporeally without Hobbes at his side. As a result, Calvin must look for meaning in a different guise, which he does by turning towards a religious possibility. The religious overtones in this particular strip are clear enough. The weight of his loss overwhelms Calvin and generates his question to the night sky. In perceiving that he is responsible for taking Hobbes out and thus exposing Hobbes to the risk that ends with their separation, Calvin compares his choice, the guilt he feels as a result, and the seemingly disproportionate consequences that he must now endure. The formula does not square, and thus he seeks clarity from a source outside of both his actual experience and his imagination. The question he asks opens the strip into a very common question that the religious person seeks to answer — namely, how a supposedly good divine reality can permit the disproportionate suffering that Calvin experiences when he loses Hobbes. His supposed fault — choosing to spend time with his friend — should not lead to the guilt and despair he feels as he yells into the night.

In asking this question, Calvin reveals the underlying search for value that a divine reality should provide. While this reality is only implied in Calvin's question, the logic at work is characteristic of theodicy. Broadly defined, a theodicy is an explanation that attempts to reconcile the disjunction Calvin experiences. Because the divine presence (in whatever form) is assumed to be good in some capacity, then this goodness should not permit suffering if the person in question does not deserve as much. Several assumptions are at work in this line of thought. The first, of course, is that the judgment of what constitutes a fair distribution arises from the individual. The choice and the result reflect Calvin's specific experience, which contrasts sharply with the appeal to some higher standard for clarification on what occurs. There exists, then, a tension in a theodicy between the immediate context of the person who asks this kind of question and an implied universal standard that ensures all specific experiences are considered the same. The fact that an individual is the source who perceives whether fairness has been achieved immediately compromises the second value: fairness should require that people experience consequences that equate with their actions. Calvin does not deny that he chose to take Hobbes with him this day; his complaint is that the choice does not warrant the pain he is feeling.

Because Western thought is heavily indebted to the Judeo-Christian creation narrative,[8] theodicy is a relevant consideration when examining this strip. In seeking to understand how life coheres with the value system that this God underwrites, Western theodicies have developed several important responses to the question that Calvin voices. One of the particular explanations for evil's presence in an otherwise good world comes from Augustine, who located the responsibility for bad things in an individual's actions.[9] God created a good world that remains good; through their free will humans incorporate evil into the world when they eat from the Tree of Knowledge.[10] This legacy can be seen in the context of a discussion that associates the question of value with the individual's ability to choose. After Augustine, the issue of God's goodness and human choice become tangled, which in turn frames responses to the question Calvin asks. Importantly, this answer does not scrub away the feelings that prompt searching questions. While Augustine's theodicy is reasonable, it does not assuage the feeling that prompts Calvin to wonder why he deserves to experience such a loss.

One of the strongest responses to the continuing disjunction between a good God and evil in the world that Augustine cannot erase fully is Determinism. In this approach, humans have no free will because there exists some causal effect for their actions, which counters the claims of free will.[11] Determinism, however, also exhibits shortcomings in resolving the question of theodicy, which demands the kind of alternative Gottfried Wilhelm Leibniz posits in *Theodicy: Essays on the Goodness of God, the Freedom of Man, and the Origin of Evil*.[12] Leibniz suggests that evil's presence in the world is part of creation insofar as it is part of the best possible world. The argument goes that God could have created a world without evil, but for whatever reason God determined that the world is better with evil around. Not surprisingly, Leibniz's theodicy suffers shortcomings, just as other classic answers to this problem do. In the end, such abstract arguments fail to provide a satisfying answer to the visceral examples of evil that have characterized the modern world. Voltaire makes this much clear in the character of Dr. Pangloss, whose blind adherence to Leibniz's idea leads to increasingly absurd experiences.[13]

In his well known book *When Bad Things Happen to Good People*,[14] Harold S. Kushner offers a difficult, if perhaps more honest, answer to the kind of question Calvin asks: Sometimes there can be no satisfying explanation for evil's presence. If true, this theodicy captures an essential point in the discussion at hand. When condensing God, human choice, and the instability of life, figuring out how to pursue what is good can prove overwhelming. Often times one is left to do as Calvin does: shout the frustration one feels when one experiences difficult circumstances.

The final value at work in this process is, then, the most important with respect to finding meaning in response to this experience of loss. Kushner captures the difficultly that an individual faces in understanding when things go awry: "I would find it easier to believe that I experienced tragedy and suffering in order to 'repair' that which is faulty in my personality if there were some clear connection between the fault and the punishment."[15] The notion that one's choices somehow correlate to specific occurrences that happen in the world is, for Kushner, an untenable thesis. Such thinking posits a cause and effect relationship that serves only to make sense of the question Calvin raises. Implicit in this thinking, of course, is the notion that someone or something directs this cause-effect relationship. While suggesting these links can temporarily explain a difficult circumstance — even if there is no soothing effect of the consequences that one is suffering — Kushner's point is well taken. If one examines what happens to Calvin, the chain of events that follows his initial choice to take Hobbes out to play is tenuous at best. Though one can understand Calvin's frustrations, the fact remains that there is little he could have done beyond what he did. Dogs are faster than people, and if the dog in question knocked Calvin over, then one could not realistically expect a six-year-old to do much to get his tiger back. There exists no agency with respect to the dog, and therefore there is no viable link between Calvin's choice to take Hobbes out of the house and the fact that Hobbes subsequently goes missing. To compensate for this disjunction, an understandable strategy is to manufacture a causal link where none exists. Thus, one finds a response similar to Calvin's: There is some force at work in life that brings about events in response to specific actions.

In voicing his question, Calvin effectively requests that the divine agent who/that oversees questions of universal fairness restore Hobbes because there is no satisfactory answer from Calvin's perspective as to why his choice to take Hobbes out produced the suffering he is still feeling. This implicit request shifts the equation slightly insofar as it transfers at least part of the responsibility for what is happening to someone/thing other than Calvin. On the one hand, this move can be attributed to a retreat into selfish interests, but there is a more nuanced dynamic at work. Granted, there are decidedly self-interested motivations behind Calvins's questions, but, in addition, there are two other concerns with respect to responsibility and value. First, Calvin's complaint includes Hobbes, who is still outside somewhere. Thus, Calvin is not wholly self-interested in making his appeal to a divine arbiter; presumably Hobbes is also suffering during this separation. Second, a willingness to plead his case to this assumed divine figure effectively relinquishes control of the right to choose. In demanding that the universe be restored to some kind of equilibrium, Calvin concedes that in this instance he cannot accomplish this end through his own choices.

Losing Hobbes exposes the limits of the individual's ability to structure her/his world to function only in accordance with her/his values. Choice allows a lot of freedom, but, as Allen and Springstead note, there are occasions wherein the power of choice no longer provides what the individual desires, either for her/himself or for her/his friend.

The disconnect between Calvin's experience and the guilt he feels after the fact exposes the shortcomings of stressing human choice as wholly determinative. Choice denotes weighing different circumstances, which in turn undermines any attempt to decode once and for all what the "best" choice of action is (or, in Calvin's case, would have been). Allen and Springstead explain the dilemma: "Were it possible for a theory or philosophy to tell an individual what he or she is — to determine completely the *kind* of person he or she is — then that person would cease to be an individual, that is a person who is responsible for what he or she becomes or does not become."[16] The individual's ability to make choices precludes the clarity of meaning that is at stake in understanding the world in general. Any attempt to conceptualize a self in total is, as Allen and Springstead argue, an endeavor that cannot be brought to a successful conclusion. There exists, always, the possibility that an individual can choose the other option with respect to who s/he wants to be. Moreover, the nature of choice is such that deciding one thing often prohibits a reversal that subsequently allows one to try the thing that one initially decides against. In linking this unknown element of choice to philosophy, Allen and Springstead thus call attention to the fact that no system can provide absolute clarity of meaning in life. If one could know in total every possible outcome, then one would cease to be an individual because the self becomes a self through choices. The corollary point is that the self is, in part, someone who carries with her/himself the unknown consequences of what could have been.

In conceptualizing life as a journey, this point emerges when employing the image of a crossroads. On occasion, individuals find themselves at a junction wherein a decision to do a particular thing opens up certain possibilities that come with going one direction, while simultaneously prohibiting access to the possibilities that lie in the other direction. In picking one direction or the other, the individual extends the journey, but in a way that necessarily produces an unknown remainder. This image is often used in conjunction with identifying the regrets of life; someone wishes s/he had "taken the other path." Regardless of how one characterizes the response to the choice that could have been made otherwise, the consequent feeling is similar to the guilt that Calvin admits in this narrative.

Calvin and Hobbes frequently find themselves at a crossroads when they are out with the sled. The narrative arc of several strips follows a recognizable pattern. Calvin introduces the hill, proclaims the danger of the journey ahead, and then pauses to consider some point of significance with respect to the choice of whether or not they should actually ride the sled down the hill. Often the two friends go ahead and take the plunge. In so doing, they necessarily choose a particular path that disallows the other possibility that Calvin cites in his dramatic introduction. In light of this framework, it is telling that in the strip from February 14, 1992, Calvin and Hobbes never begin the ride they set out to take. As they stand atop another horrendous hill, Calvin asks, "Do we turn around and retreat to the stupefying security of home and hearth? *Or* do we brave the descent, risk demise, and experience the flood of somatic sensation that screams we are alive, gloriously alive, however temporary?"[17] The choice is significant, given the values to which Calvin stakes this sled ride. The decision to risk bodily harm — a reminder that life is ultimately fragile — is one that can lead to a life-affirming experience. Similarly, the decision not to undertake the ride will enclose the friends in the safety of a home, which will preclude the chance to be viscerally aware of the rush life can bring in a moment. The immediate context, then, opens into a serious question about how a choice can provide or deny a sense that life is worth living despite its fragility.

When Calvin is done outlining what is at stake, he turns around to find that Hobbes is nowhere to be seen. In the final panel, Calvin has gone back to the house, where he finds Hobbes lying by the fire. He explains to Calvin that he interpreted the question of value as "rhetorical."[18] Based on this interpretation, Hobbes clearly decides that the risk of a moment's glory is not worth the possibility of a negative outcome. Thus, he takes the less thrilling but more accessible warmth of the fire. Calvin, who is still dressed in his snow clothes, responds in an interesting capacity: "The other way, though!"[19] Hobbes chooses a particular kind of value because the question is rhetorical, an outcome that Calvin similarly desires. There is, however, an important disjunction in their respective interpretations; they are mutually exclusive with respect to the choice that the rhetorical tone encourages. Though it reveals a difference of opinion on life's value, this strip does indicate how this specific decision draws out a broader conception of what matters in life. Hobbes prefers the less risky option, which speaks to his measured character. Calvin, on the other hand, embraces the immediate rush that follows from the choice that is decidedly more risky. The summary point, then, is that both interpret an either/or decision in a way that directs their life in a particular way. Moreover, the decisions that provide this guidance necessarily leave each with a way of understanding life that cannot incorporate fully the value that the other finds through his own choice. The difference lies in how Calvin and Hobbes understand the question, a fact evident in their respective positions while discussing what the question meant. Any answers that follow this question will, then, necessarily be different based on this initial interpretation.

With respect to the examples discussed so far, the ability to choose opens the text to particular values. At times the consequences of a choice indicate a general understanding of life (as they do in the February 14, 1992, strip), while at other times the outcomes produce unexpected results. In the May 26, 1986, strip, Calvin's experience opens into the guilt that often comes with a choice that turns out differently than one expects. The ramifications of Calvin's experience when he loses Hobbes call into question whether the choice was a good one. The ability to second-guess a specific choice points to a significant instability at the heart of what it means to be an individual. If choice is the conduit through which individuals construct their identities, then establishing a self requires that parts of the self remain subject to questioning.

When no answer is available to reconcile events with the self that an individual has created, two options are available. The first, as discussed above, is to project responsibility for the discord between the self and its experience onto some other force. Another example will capture how this dynamic functions in a different context and therefore speaks to the pervasiveness of this problem. The strip from February 12, 1995, shows Calvin waiting behind a tree with a snowball he made. His anticipation of hitting someone is apparent in his mischievous grin, yet for six panels he waits for a target (probably Susie) to materialize. Eventually he gives up and throws his snowball into the tree. As he walks away in frustration, a snowball hits him squarely in the face and he falls to the ground. Susie then appears and laughs at her success. The final panel shows Calvin still outside at night, shaking his fist into the air in protest of how this chain of events is not fair. His complaint, though implicit, is clear: he waited but did not get the opportunity to use his snowball that Susie got. The subtext to this frustration is the choice he made to throw the snowball against the tree. Had he chosen otherwise, he presumably would have seen Susie and could have used the snowball to satisfy the desire he expresses when he makes the snowball in the first place. If he were just to show frustration, then one could gloss over what happened as bad luck, but this explanation would obviously not satisfy Calvin's disappointment.

Much like his outburst when he loses Hobbes, this appeal to the night sky points towards the unnamed agent who is somehow responsible for what happened. In most examples wherein Calvin vents to this agent, one can attach the general label of god (or, perhaps, Santa) to the supposed recipient of these complaints. This claim rests on the basis of the multiple contexts wherein he specifically uses the term god to describe the power he understands to be at work in questions of goodness, badness, and the distribution of consequences in response to one's actions. In these different circumstances, one finds the same appeal to some divine agent to explain how specific events that are perceived as unfair (or unequal, or generally not in keeping with the individual's expectations) came about. The unspoken assumption in making these claims is, of course, that this divine agent will bring things back into equilibrium by satisfying some future desire.

This thought process sets aside the individual's responsibility for her/his choice, as well as the seeming fact that sometimes things just do not work out as people plan. The appeal to some other force to assuage the disappointment that follows such instances points to the existentialist idea that life is absurd because of an individual's endless ability to choose. Sartre is a prominent figure in this respect. In *Being and Nothingness*, Sartre explains the parameters that frame human existence: "Man is condemned to be free; because once thrown into the world, he is responsible for everything he does."[20] Sartre's word choice is precise; it captures the trap into which Calvin walks in shaking his fist in the air. The freedom to choose condemns the individual both to the regret that emerges when a choice goes wrong and the bracketing of any possible appeal. If choice lies at the heart of the human condition, then no individual can look to any other factor in explaining how particular consequences follow a specific choice. Allen and Springstead summarize well the point that Sartre makes: "Because of [our] inescapable freedom ... we have no essence to be completed or fulfilled. We have then contradictory features: the desire to be complete (*en soi*) and the inability ever to become complete. Our freedom condemns the passion for completeness to futility, yet we can never give up that passion."[21] In other words, Allen and Springstead note, "human beings are abusrd."[22] The paradox is relatively straightforward in this conception. The choice that allows an individual to seek meaning in response to her/his experiences is the very thing that ensures no meaning can be found. To recall Plato's leaky jar,[23] there is no way to keep the self "full" of meaning because there exists an inherent quality that precludes the fulfillment of one's desires.

The freedom to choose is therefore a paradoxical imprisonment. There is no way to evade the responsibility for one's actions, even if the events that follow a particular choice unfold contrary to one's expectations. By situating responsibility squarely — and only — within an individual's choice, Sartre prohibits other sources of meaning, particularly the kind of appeal that Calvin voices to a perceived divine power. Individuals can shakes their fists as much as they like (it is their choice, after all), but Sartre is clear that this is a dead end with respect to the implicit meaning the individual seeks in acting this way. In discrediting the existence of a divine being, Sartre thus points to the second way of reconciling life's challenges: accepting that at its core life is absurd because the individual's ability to choose can never provide clarity of meaning. His advice is simple in its total disruption: "It is up to you to give it a meaning, and value is nothing but the meaning that you choose."[24] While some would construe this remark as a positive reflection on freedom, to perceive Sartre's words as an encouragement is to miss the absurdity that frames human choice. He explains the paradox as follows:

> Each human reality is at the same time a direct project to metamorphose its own For-itself into an In-itself-For-itself, a project of the appropriation of the world as a totality of being-in-itself, in the form of a fundamental quality. Every human reality is a passion in that it projects losing itself so as to found being and by the same stroke to constitute the In-itself[25].

As discussed above, choices cannot bring about stable meaning because all choices necessarily remain open to regret — as one sees when Calvin loses Hobbes to the dog — or to realization that choices do not guarantee satisfaction, a reality Calvin experiences when he throws his snowball away only to encounter the very thing he decided could no longer occur.

The emphasis on choice accomplishes many things for the individual, but it cannot, in the end, override the fundamental dislocation that characterizes humanity.[26] The absurdity of existence threatens any attempt to find meaning, yet other thinkers stress that even when events remain out of an individual's control, the freedom to choose can still provide direction in how to travel through one's life. A measure of self-awareness is necessary to make the best possible choices. Pascal summarizes the point well: "Let us then realize our limitations. We are something and we are not everything."[27] Identifying (and accepting) this balance prevents the aesthete's self-excess and resists the descent into absurdity. Pascal explains, "Such is our true state. That is what makes us incapable of certain knowledge or absolute ignorance."[28] Unlike Plato or Sartre, Pascal thus suspends the human condition between the extremes that have been discussed. Pascal continues, "We burn with desire to find a firm footing, an ultimate, lasting base on which to build a tower rising up to infinity, but our whole foundation cracks and the earth opens up into the depth of the abyss."[29] Choice matters, of course, but it cannot alter the dual realities that he associates with the human condition. Humans are capable of great things, but they cannot transcend fully the limits that prohibit clarity of meaning. Humans can, however, accept their predicament and seek to find meaning in a capacity that avoids extreme ways of conceptualizing different concerns in life.

One of the specific questions about life that Pascal addresses is whether or not God exists.[30] In his famous Wager, Pascal approaches this question by determining whether or not it is reasonable to believe in God. To frame this discussion, Pascal identifies the characteristics of the God that exists if, in fact, God does exist. He writes, "If there is a God, he is infinitely beyond our comprehension, since being indivisible and without limits he bears no relation to us. We are therefore incapable of knowing either what he is or whether he is."[31] The specifics of God's character are not important because if God exists, this God is beyond the limits of what humans can know. Moreover, attempts to anthropomorphize God in order to structure the question of whether God exists is a false move, Pascal explains, because God is wholly other. To address the question of whether God exists, then, one must jettison preconceived notions about God in order to arrive at a reasonable answer. The question of God's existence is thus framed only in terms of the human experience.

Having established these initial parameters, Pascal then explains that there exists two possibilities: either God exists or God does not exist.[32]

The important point to remember, Pascal notes, is that human reason cannot deduce which is the case: "Reason cannot make you choose either, reason cannot prove either wrong."[33] This is a crucial point. Human reason cannot affirm or deny God's existence with definitive proof because meeting such a standard is beyond reason's capacity. As such, when considering whether God exists, an individual must answer the question in full recognition that there can be no proof one way or the other.

The result of this limitation is to construct a grid that outlines the possible outcomes the individual can expect. The grid in Figure One contains the various outcomes of this question:

Figure 1

	God Exists	God Does Not Exist
	Payout A	**Payout B**
Choose to Believe	A life of unmitigated pleasure is lost, but an eternal reward is gained.	A life of unmitigated pleasure is lost, but no eternal reward is gained.
	Payout C	**Payout D**
Choose Not to Believe	A life of unmitigated pleasure is gained, but an eternal reward is lost.	A life of unmitigated pleasure is gained and no eternal reward is gained.

Pascal describes the choice in starker terms, which in turn clarifies what is at stake in the choice about whether or not an individual should believe in God. Pascal writes:

> Here there is an infinity of infinitely happy life to be won, one chance of winning against a finite number of chances of losing, and what you are staking is finite. That leaves no choice; wherever there is infinity, and where there are not infinite chances of losing against that of winning, there is no room for hesitation, you must give everything. And thus, since you are obliged to play, you must be renouncing reason if you hoard your life rather than risk it for an infinite gain, just as likely to occur as a loss amounting to nothing.[34]

Given the density of this passage, a brief explanation of how Pascal sets up this matrix will be helpful. When discussing Pascal's Wager, what is to be won and what is to be lost should be thought of in terms that echo the previous discussion of the aesthete's values — and, moreover, look ahead to specific examples from *Calvin and Hobbes*. Thus, Pascal characterizes the loss of a life of pleasure as indicating that in choosing to believe in God one accepts that one must live by a certain moral code that precludes the kind of endless gratification that an aesthete values. Similarly, the notion of eternal rewards indicates that choosing to believe in God means living a moral life, and, should God exist, this life will gain entrance into a paradisiacal afterlife. Likewise, a decision not to believe in God permits the individual to behave however s/he wants, which can produce maximally a life of unmitigated pleasure. It is possible to bracket a specific notion of punishment if one chooses not to believe in God but it turns out that God actually exists (and thus punishes those who do not live in accordance with this God's moral expectations). In merely characterizing the question of an eternal payout in terms of what reward is gained, the discussion at hand avoids a specific notion of God beyond the framework that Pascal uses to introduce this idea (as will be discussed shortly, Calvin specifically understands the question of whether God exists in terms that do result in eternal punishment, i.e. Hell).

If a person chooses to believe in God, then one effectively agrees to live one's life in conjunction with a set of moral principles that one ascribes to God. Keeping in mind that no one knows for sure whether God ultimately expects such things, the wager is that by following a moral code, one hedges one's bets that God will reward such behavior with admission into an eternal paradise (Payout A in Figure One). If it turns out that God does not exist, one loses the pleasure one could have had by not following a moral code, but one does not through one's choice lose out on something of eternal value (Payout B in Figure One). The other wager is that God does not exist, in which case one can live unbound by any moral code. Such a decision allows a life of pleasure, but if God does exist and requires that individuals follow moral standards, then the decision not to believe costs the individual an eternal reward (Payout C in Figure One). Finally, if the individual chooses not to believe and thus to live independently of a moral code, and God does not exist, then one has gained significant pleasure and lost nothing (Payout D in Figure One).

What remains undetermined — and ultimately unknowable — in making this decision is whether or not God actually exists. Because of the unknowability that frames this matrix, Pascal's point is that whichever column turns out to be true is entirely beyond human comprehension. As such, the decision to believe or not to believe in God should focus only on the payouts that the individual can anticipate based on her/his decision. Consequently, an individual can only use her/his reason to weigh the different possible payouts in order to choose whether or not to believe. The strategy one should take then, is to ignore which of the vertical columns is more likely because this has no bearing on the relative value of each potential payout. If one is reasonable, the choice should be clear: one should believe. The reason is that such a decision minimizes potential losses while maximizing potential gains. Similarly, a decision not to believe minimizes potential gains while maximizing potential losses. Thus, according to the setup that Pascal provides, the less risky option and therefore reasonable choice is to believe in God.

An additional point from this example will tie Pascal, imagination, and meaning together with *Calvin and Hobbes*. First, Pascal is clear that the wager must be made because God's existence is independent of human choice. Thus, it would be irrational not to consider this question because one of the four payouts will occur, and, moreover, there is a clear risk for not choosing to believe. The reasonable step to take, then, is to assume that God does exist and frames decisions concerning value in conjunction with the expectation that God will reward certain behavior while punishing the opposite.

Despite the narrowness of some of his concerns, Calvin understands the subtlety at work in Pascal's argument. More specifically, Calvin can trace the notion of consequences from his choices to the possible outcomes that are beyond his control. As a result, he recognizes the need to evaluate a decision based on potential payouts that at the time of the decision remain unknown and beyond his control. An excellent example of this awareness occurs in the strip from July 15, 1992. The first panel shows a close-up of Calvin's face as he undertakes a passionate metaphysical explanation: "What if we die and it turns out that God is a big *chicken*?? What then?"[35] This panel provides no context for Calvin's question, but it does hint at the logic at work in Pascal's Wager. There exists an unknown possibility that may come to bear on a specific circumstance, which, the reader can intuit, elicits this remark. The next panel offers the context for the question and ties Calvin's point thematically to Pascal's Wager. The impetus for Calvin is to avoid having to eat his dinner. Despite his mom's detached response for Calvin to get on with the meal, he continues the argument: *"Eternal consequences, that's what!"*[36] A second matrix will capture the overlap this strip has with Pascal's Wager:

Figure 2

	God Is a Chicken Payout A	God Is Not a Chicken Payout B
Eat Dinner	Suffer through a meal and invite eternal consequences for eating God's likeness.	Suffer through dinner with no eternal repercussions.
	Payout C	Payout D
Do Not Eat Dinner	Avoid suffering through a meal and earn eternal reward for not eating God's likeness.	Avoid suffering through a meal with no eternal consequences.

As with Pascal's Wager, the matrix Calvin suggests makes clear the choice that he (and his parents) should make. Regardless of whether God is, in fact, a chicken, there is little to gain in either payout A or payout B. In both cases the choice to eat the dinner in question produces immediate suffering and risks eternal consequences. On the other hand, a decision not to eat the dinner avoids any immediate suffering and opens the possibility of some divine reward. Payout C or payout D is thus preferable, even if one cannot know ahead of time if God is actually a chicken. Calvin thus upholds Pascal's argument. When evaluating how to make a choice with implications that stretch into the afterlife, the safe bet is to minimize eternal consequences that are bad and maximize the chances for eternal rewards. If there is a decision that also avoids the need to suffer acutely, then the choice is even easier. There is, then, a good reason Calvin is so passionate in making his point in the first panel of this strip; there is (potentially) a lot at stake in not eating dinner.

While the above example is a bit of a ham, Calvin frames the particular context in a way that emerges elsewhere with significantly more depth. While sitting under a tree with Hobbes, Calvin asks, "What if there's no afterlife? Suppose this is all we get."[37] As one who is not prone to be greedy,[38] Hobbes reflects on his experience in the second panel before responding in the third panel, "Oh, what the heck. I'll take it anyway."[39] The comment slides past Calvin, who says sternly that if there is not an afterlife to reward good behavior, "I'd sure like to know *now*."[40] The response, of course, is deeply ironic insofar as it reveals precisely the point that emerges in Pascal's Wager. The fact remains that Calvin cannot know whether an afterlife exists and thus must decide whether behaving as though there is an afterlife is a worthwhile pursuit. He thus indicates that he is aware of the implications of an afterlife, both with respect to his immediate choices and the consequences that may not materialize until it is too late to change anything. The gap between what Calvin wants to know and what he can know thus refuses to close. As a result, Calvin reveals the burden that choice can be for someone whose conception of value resists extremes. Calvin speaks honestly; he is, as Pascal says, suspended between the extremes of Sartre's absurdity and Plato's freedom outside the cave. The challenge, then, is how to find an appropriate way to live life, given that there are no guarantees about an afterlife (or a god). This unknowability complicates the individual's freedom because without knowledge about what may be, the stakes for choosing well increase without providing any reprieve from the yawning question Calvin asks. It thus makes sense why he wants to know immediately. There is still a long time to live in the uncertainty that results from this question's unanswerability.

Calvin does seem inclined to bet that God exists when he faces the consequences of his actions. He both wonders whether he will be able to "plea bargain"[41] with God after trashing the house, and reflects on the seeming imbalance in the universe that allows some people not to suffer the presumed negative consequences of their selfish actions.[42] Elsewhere, Calvin's encounters with Moe echo the larger question of how to behave given that there is no way to know whether one will be held accountable in the afterlife. When Moe bullies Calvin, he sets the stage of asking whether the world is fair if consequences for actions in life do not warrant punishment (which is a derivative concern of theodicy). When Calvin is the one who must endure an act that warrants punishment but receives none, he presents another side of this question. If others are not held accountable for their actions, then why should the individual behave in accordance with some moral guideline?[43] Given that the question of whether to act morally is ultimately a choice, the fact that people like Moe choose to behave as they do and appear not to suffer consequences lends support to the absurdity that Sartre discusses. When discussing a character like Moe, one can understand not only Sartre's point about the absurdity of existence, but also his claim that Hell is other people.[44]

In this context, God's existence is important for determining whether there is sufficient motivation to be good. The question that Pascal poses thus filters through the human condition in a way that is manifest through specific choices in morally complex circumstances. In such instances, Calvin's struggles with the question of God's existence emerge forcefully. As is often the case at Christmas, Calvin reflects on several related issues concerning the judgment of his character and the mystery that infuses the entire structure in which he tries to make good decisions. In one instance he tells Hobbes, "This whole Santa Claus thing just doesn't make sense. Why all the secrecy.... If the guy even exists, why doesn't he ever show himself and prove it? And if he *doesn't* exist, whats the meaning of all this?"[45] These are tough — and fair — questions to ask, given what is at stake. With respect to Santa, the inability to verify the supposed judge (and jury[46]) casts into doubt the supposed rewards for being good.

Given what is at stake with Santa and the demands that the possibility of Santa's existence make on the individual, Calvin asks questions that uncover the gap between what is perceived from within the human condition and the possible existence of an arbiter beyond this condition. If Santa exists and if Santa really does apportion presents based on whether a child has been good, then it is fair for the child in question to wonder why such a powerful figure would choose to remain hidden. Because Calvin knows (or at least thinks he knows) that his choices influence directly whether he gets a reward, the desire for Santa to be held accountable for the choice to remain mysterious is, seemingly, a legitimate line of inquiry. The result of Santa not showing himself is problematic, as it casts into doubt the certainty with which Calvin can make a decision to be good. This specific example, then, highlights the initial terms that govern Pascal's Wager. In questioning Santa's role in the question of whether to be good, Calvin voices religious doubt because, as he explains to Hobbes in this strip, "I've got the same questions about God."[47] While his choice is important, the crucial element is the fundamental unknowability of the divine other. Herein one finds the limits of the Wager; the logic that suggests clearly to believe in God does not take into account the doubt that the terms generate. One can say logically that a choice to believe makes the most sense, but as Calvin reveals in his question, such a decision ignores the agency that God (or Santa) has in meting out rewards — or withholding them or, worse, punishing — which gives rise to the very question Calvin poses. If this figure has the power that is supposed, is there no responsibility in that figure's choice to offer some assurance? The question is important in part because the ability to verify God's existence normalizes good behavior. Otherwise, the spectrum of what constitutes good behavior slides into a question of relative value, which in turn complicates the decisions that individuals must make with respect to a normative standard of value.[48]

An implicit dichotomy adds a complicating layer to the question of whether God exists. On the one hand, there exists the ability to choose good behavior; at the very least, Calvin is capable of such things. On the other hand, the question of motivation ultimately reveals the ability — if not the tendency — to behave badly. Plato's analogy of the charioteer provides a helpful image to capture the tension that Calvin thus exhibits. In the *Phaedras*, Socrates describes the soul as a charioteer who must control two different horses. Each horse has a different nature: "The charioteer of the human soul drives a pair, and secondly one of the horses is noble and of noble breed, but the other quite the opposite in breed and character."[49] Because the two horses are not in step, the charioteer's task "is necessarily difficult and troublesome."[50] As the soul attempts to behave in accordance with goodness appropriate to its immortal destination,[51] it must wrestle to control the discord between its good inclinations and its unruly tendencies. Plato writes, "The horses and charioteers of the gods are all good and of good descent, but those of other races are mixed."[52] Because it is contained in a mortal body, the human soul's goodness is not wholly good, as it is among the gods. That being said, the human soul has the ability to encounter the good if it is committed to seeking this knowledge. The image is designed to emphasize how these divergent concerns disrupt the attempt to traverse the ridge between what is good and what is not. If the horses do not keep the same pace as they gallop, then the chariot runs the risk of crashing. The image, then, speaks to the dual possibilities with which Calvin struggles in trying to determine how to behave. Each of the inclinations can disrupt the other; just as the bad horse can counter the good horse, so too can the good horse upset the bad horse. As a result, there exists, always, the difficulty of staking one's choice to a particular standard.

Plato does not discuss in depth each horse's specific characters. Rather, he structures the example to stress the journey at hand and the difficulties the individual encounters during this process. As Allen and Springstead note, Plato accepts that whichever horse the charioteer favors will determine whether the individual acts in search of goodness or not: "For Plato, everyone gets what one loves or desires the most: sensual life in the world again and again ... or continuous knowledge of the true reality that gives never ending joy."[53] Yet again, the individual's choices boil down to what is perceived as valuable and therefore the motivations for one's decisions. Those who are committed to the pursuit of the world's pleasure can do so (even though the leaky jar analogy still holds); there is nothing inherent in the human character that prevents this course of action. The counter to this freedom is, for Plato, similar to the argument that Pascal makes. The choice to pursue good things ultimately offers lasting value.

Even though thinkers from Plato to Kierkegaard to Pascal indicate why choosing good over bad is beneficial for the individual, the fact remains that the latent tendency towards what is not good (in a metaphysical sense) can still hold sway over the individual. This remainder complicates the decision to pursue the good, especially when the possibility of choosing bad is conceptualized in terms that mirror arguments for choosing the good. The possibility of the Devil's existence similarly demands consideration. One can construct a wager table with the Devil's existence in place of God's existence. A crucial difference is that the possibility of eternal rewards is no longer a factor in weighing one's decisions. As such, the calculations are altered, as the ratio of risk and reward is substantially different. On a related point, the possibility of a Devil undermines the simplicity of Pascal's Wager insofar as deciding whether or not God exists assumes that there are no other relevant factors at play. The possibility that a Devil also exists thus expands the matrix significantly and complicates further how an individual must weigh potential payouts when making choices about the afterlife, and therefore how to act.

The outdoors frequently provides the setting for Calvin's questions about this metaphysical concern. As he hops from rock to rock to cross a creek, Calvin asks Hobbe, "Do you believe in the devil? You know, a supreme evil being dedicated to the temptation, corruption, and destruction of man?"[54] This speculation steps back from the question of individual choice, but the implications of the question are clear in Hobbes' response: "I'm not sure man needs the help."[55] Hobbes is perhaps more aware than most of just how many bad decisions a person can make, which prompts him to tether the issue of a Devil to the results of human choices.[56] The result is a twofold development with respect to the question of whether the Devil exists. The first point that one can distill from Hobbes' remark is that there are enough examples of devil-influenced behavior to take the question seriously, which legitimizes Calvin's inquiry. The second point to arise from this comment is the extent to which humans are capable of giving into devilish impulses (regardless of whether the Devil exists or not). The end result of this exchange is to stress that issues involving human choice should not be simplified into the kind of matrix Pascal suggests. While his Wager offers an important stepping off point in considering the implications of human choice beyond immediate circumstances, ultimately he leaves out several important qualifications and, moreover, fails to explain why so many people make what is an unreasonable choice.

The conception of the Devil that Calvin offers approximates a foundational narrative in Western thought: humanity's Fall from the Garden of Eden.[57] The specific issue of temptation affects a discussion of choice, because the kind of choice Pascal describes brackets such nuances. If, however, there exists some "higher" power that interacts with humanity specifically to direct choices away from some good, then a framework designed to help an individual determine what to choose should take this into account. Kevin Hart links the narrative of the Fall with the difficulty that subsequently affects how humans are to understand their world. If one brackets a specific theological reading, his comments converge on the question that Calvin asks. Hart writes, "The Fall may establish the human need to interpret yet it simultaneously sets firm limits to interpretation. No longer in harmony with God, this world becomes a chiaroscuro of presence and absence; everywhere one looks, there are signs of a divine presence that has withdrawn and that reveals itself only in those signs."[58] If the result of the Fall is to be ground in language (which is, of course, always ungrounded), then the role of the imagination in understanding the new realities that confront the human condition become apparent. As Kearney explains:

> [The] loss of paradise in turn signalled [sic] the birth of time. It corresponded to the specifically human experience of temporal transcendence as an imaginative capacity to recollect a past and project a future — that is, the capacity to convert the given confines of the here and now in an open horizon of possibilities. Once east of Eden, imagination was free to spread its wings beyond the timeless now into the nether regions of no-longer and not-yet.[59]

In this reading, the fall into language becomes a paradoxical liberation. While paradise is preferable to an indefinite state of exile, Kearney highlights that humans retain the ability to imagine what was lost in the Fall and therefore anticipate what might become again. The ability to transcend time through the imagination gives voice to claims that there are reasons to act in accordance with what is good. If an afterlife can be imagined, then there is some motivation to avoid a descent into absurdity.

The particular benefit that follows from exploring the imagination in a context that not only recognizes death but also links this point in life with the possibility of an afterlife is this temporal release. Much recent discussion of the imagination's role in anticipating the future is to reduce such possibilities to what did not happen in the past. Ruth M.J. Byrne opens her treatment of the imagination in this capacity: "My interest is in how people think about what might have been."[60] Despite the limitations that Byrne's project exhibits in this respect, her work is recommended in its capacity to approach the issues discussed in this book from a different perspective. It is important to note that while this reading draws specifically on a Judeo-Christian narrative, this is not the only conception of human responsibility with respect to good and/or evil.[61]

Calvin reveals, then, a nonspecific yet theologically-informed understanding of human nature. Though they can be prone to goodness at times, there is frequently a struggle between the kind of immediate desires that are often associated with what is bad and the willingness to do what is good. An extended narrative thread reveals both sides of this binary. When Calvin adds an ethicator to his duplicator,[62] he is able to clone a manifestation of his good side only. The duplicate goes about Calvin's day with diligencey. The chores get done,[63] he participates actively in school,[64] and he is nice to Susie.[65] This last act proves to be too much for the real Calvin, which leads to a confrontation. Angry that the duplicate would even talk to Susie, much less send her a valentine, Calvin wrestles with the manifestation of his good side.[66] The good side defends his actions to the point that he is willing to "tear [Calvin] limb from...."[67] As Calvin readies for the punch-out, his good side evaporates before he can finish his sentence because he "had an evil thought!"[68] Calvin and Hobbes are then left to consider the implications when a person's good side is prone to evil thoughts.

This example highlights the imagination's ability to understand life's important questions. Calvin recognizes immediately what implications follow the evaporation that takes place: "He could only be perfectly good as an abstraction. In his human manifestation, he wanted to throttle me."[69] Though Hobbes suggests that this paradox is only typical of Calvin, the point that Calvin makes resonates deeply with the difficulties that emerge when considering specifically whether God and the Devil exist, and, more broadly, questions of whether human nature is good, evil, or both. Such questions speak to a condition that easily bends towards self-interest. Even a purely good abstraction cannot resist the pull that the world can have on the individual when s/he must act in accordance with her/his virtues. The irony is thick in this instance, and it reveals the fragile nature of claims that humans are capable of good (and thus following through on the reasonable choice concerning God's existence). The point is not that Calvin turns out to be a genius because he built a machine with "a built-in moral compromise spectral release phantasmatron"[70]; when it comes to questions of God and good, all humans are capable of good and evil.

The ethicator's failure reiterates the importance of choice for the individual. When someone's good side cannot be fully good, the challenge of living in accordance with what is considered good thus constitutes a problem for which there is no clear solution. As such, ways to conceptualize goodness in relative terms will prove helpful in this discussion. Calvin's struggles open into two of the primary ethical concepts in Western thought: virtue ethics and deontological ethics. An example from *Calvin and Hobbes* will clarify each of these topics while simultaneously offering guidance in teasing out meaning within a context that does not offer space for a definitive answer to the important issues at hand in this chapter.

In examining virtue ethics, Hobbes provides a helpful example. In the now familiar context of being out in the woods, Calvin raises another question concerning value and how this idea relates to human choice. He asks Hobbes, "Do you think our morality is defined by our actions, or by what's in our hearts?"[71] The question demarcates virtue ethics from a purely consequentialist way of determining what counts as a good act. Calvin poses the question in a way that assumes some kind of moral standard. Insofar as his question seeks clarity about this broad notion, he reveals that more often than not his self-interested decisions only submerge his awareness of a more resilient and rewarding standard of value. At the very least, then, he does remain trapped in the absurdity that Sartre ascribes to the freedom of choice.

Virtue ethics stresses a person's character as the crucial influence on whether or not a person will choose in accordance with what is good. To clarify, in Pascal's Wager someone who viewed the decision through virtue ethics would opt to live the good life because this is the virtuous way to do so; the moral identity that precedes an act determines its moral value.[72]

As such, the consequences of the action thus become moot, as they are independent of the state of being that led to the action. Thus, rewards matter little because the virtue ethicist will live the good life simply because it is good.[73] A particular advantage to this approach is that it brackets the considerations that Pascal does not address. If an individual's state of being is the constitutive element in that person's moral identity, then gods and devils ultimately do not affect the specific circumstances that affect what is good or evil.

Aristotle's *Ethics* is one of the foundational texts in the field of virtue ethics. While accepting that happiness is a component of what is good, Aristotle distances himself from a simplistic understanding of what it means to be happy: "To say that happiness is the chief good seems a platitude, and a clearer account of what it is still desired. This might perhaps be given, if we could first ascertain the function of man."[74] To understand happiness, one must identify in a person's function (i.e. what makes her/him distinctly human) what happiness achieves. Aristotle dismisses survival and perception as the definitive human functions and settles on rationality as the constituent element of humanity that relates to happiness. Having made this claim, Aristotle then articulates a classic summary of virtue ethics:

> Now if the function of man is an activity of soul which follows or implies a rational principle, and if we say "so-and-so" and "a good so-and-so" have a function which is the same in kind ... if this is the case, and we state the function of man to be a certain kind of life, and this to be an activity or actions of the soul implying a rational principle, and the function of a good man to be the good and noble performance of these, and if any action is well performed when it is performed in accordance with the appropriate excellence: if this is the case, human good turns out to be activity of soul in accordance with virtue, and if there are more than one virtue, in accordance with the best and most complete.[75]

Because rationality is a uniquely human function, then using rationality well will lead to happiness. To use rationality well means to act in accordance with the virtue that reason can identify. To be happy, then, is to act in accordance with the good because an individual's humanity is characterized by the ability to identify the good through her/his rational capabilities.

In addition to the link between rationality, virtue, and happiness, it is helpful to note that Aristotle understands virtue to be a contextual value. That is, one cannot prescribe virtue in the abstract; to identify what is good and act accordingly requires the ability to understand and act in accordance with this good as it emerges in a specific experiential context. Thus, Aristotle explains about the individuals who are able to use their reason well or those who possess practical wisdom: "Now it is thought to be the mark of a man of practical wisdom to be able to deliberate well about what is good and expedient for himself, not in some particular respect, e.g. about what sorts of thing conduce to health or to strength, but about what sorts of thing conduce to the good life in general."[76] Moreover, the ability to use one's practical wisdom to identify the good in a given circumstance is a specifically rational act ("wisdom is a virtue and not an art"[77]) and thus an important element in seeking what is good.

Virtue ethics, then, seems to offer some clarity with respect to what is good. However, Hobbes answers Calvin in a way that complicates the issue: "I think our actions *show* what's in our hearts."[78] Viewed this way, choices derived solely from a person's character will produce consequences that reflect this antecedent quality. In his response, then, Hobbes muddies the capacity of virtue ethics to stabilize decisions about moral value. If consequences are taken to indicate someone's relative virtue, then decisions can ultimately be made based on utility, which can plunge decisions straight back into the realm of self-interest. The perceived causal link that Hobbes suggests can, moreover, fragment an otherwise clear sense of what constitutes good. If negative consequences follow from a virtuous act, then the supposed clarity that virtue ethics provides disappears rather quickly. A further problem emerges when one considers that this kind of thinking can gloss over someone's lack of virtue if her/his choices ultimately produce something that is considered good. In this instance, one lands dangerously close to a Machiavellian conception of value that justifies any action in pursuit of some good.[79]

There are, then, limits to the guidance virtue ethics can provide, which is one reason that deontological ethics seems at times to be a better guide in making moral decisions. The moral accent in deontology falls on duty, which indicates that an individual is obligated to uphold a particular duty regardless of consequences. An exchange between Calvin and his mom about his chores captures how deontological ethics can help an individual decide how to act. In the February 2, 1993 strip, Calvin walks in the door and throws his jacket on the ground. His mom explains that he should have done otherwise in a way that captures the essence of deontology: "Hang it up where it belongs! I'm not looking for extra work around here."[80] Calvin's mom thus responds in a way that recalls Immanuel Kant's categorical imperative.[81] An important point to highlight is Kant's stress on reason as the basis for a deontological understanding of ethics; therefore, the motivation to act morally cannot be reduced to an individual's happiness. Kant states, "We may fairly wonder how, after all previous explanations of the principles of duty, so far as it is derived from pure reason, it was still possible to reduce it again to a doctrine of happiness."[82] Thus, Kant claims, the "reward of virtue [comes] only from the consciousness of having done [one's] duty."[83]

The emphasis on duty and rationality thus produce one of Kant's famous maxims concerning ethics; the guide to acting morally is to act in accordance with the categorical imperative. Kant articulates the imperative that anchors moral actions: "Act only according to that maxim by which you can at the same time will that it should become a universal law."[84] An individual's duty to uphold this standard results from the capacity in which it affects her/him. One should act towards others in a way that one would welcome if one were the recipient of the same action. In following this principle, the individual thus acts morally independently of the consequences for one's actions. Thus, one finds the two distinctive features of deontological ethics. First, a person's character does not factor into her/his moral actions beyond her/his commitment to act in accordance with the categorical imperative.[85] Moreover, deontological ethics counters directly any consequentialist frameworks insofar as deontological ethics does not weigh consequences; the act is what matters. Calvin's mom does not threaten Calvin with punishment. Rather, she makes a claim that extends the categorical imperative's logic in a way that counters Calvin's reason for not picking up his jacket. The important point is that Calvin is obligated to behave in accordance with the categorical imperative as it relates to the specific task at hand. If Calvin does not want to do chores, then he should not act in a way that will require others to do the same.

While this example introduces the role of the categorical imperative in a deontological understanding of ethics, a further example will show that Calvin is not the only one who fails to act in way that could be construed as a universal moral law. When Calvin is about to eat worms for money, Calvin's mom shows up in the nick of time to save him from doing something he does not want to do.[86] She reprimands Susie for egging Calvin on: "And Susie, it's mean to take advantage of kids with no common sense."[87] If Susie were to apply Kant's dictum to this situation, she would realize (as

Calvin's mom does) that her actions are not bound by a duty. She presumably would not welcome a similarly selfish act, and therefore she should encourage Calvin in the capacity that she does. In this instance, as with the example above, the point is how one conceptualizes one's obligation to a normative ethic. This way of determining what actions are meaningful in a moral capacity offers a different way of making individual choices, particularly when others will be affected by these decisions. The point, again, is not what results a specific act will produce, but rather whether those actions can be construed as good regardless of what consequences might occur.

In the case of either virtue ethics or deontological ethics, two salient points emerge with respect to the broader issue at hand in this chapter. The first common denominator is to conceptualize goodness — and, therefore, how to find meaning in life in a way that exercises an individual's power to choose responsibly — in a capacity that does not look to an action's consequences to find value.[88] The stress in both cases remains with the fact that the individual is responsible for determining what s/he will do based on a standard that is independent of how an action will play out. The second point follows on directly from this independence from consequences. Both virtue ethics and deontological ethics attempt to define goodness in a context that cannot be reduced to simple terms (such as those that characterize Pascal's Wager). Choice is a difficult thing, and the very notion of trying to determine what is good carries the implicit possibility that an individual can choose to do what is not good. A system that attempts to identify standards of value, then, must take into account the nuances that characterize the human condition.

As Calvin shows repeatedly, the complicated nature of choice thus opens into the broader difficulty of finding meaning in life. The individual must contend with any number of challenging circumstances (often involving even more challenging individuals). To make sense of these experiences, the difficulties surrounding choice can be addressed by invoking some higher power. There are numerous examples of how Calvin attempts to find clarity by imagining how this divine agent/presence/power/god intersects his life. At times this figure seems to provide meaning; yet at other times, calling upon this metaphysical help serves to undermine the meaning that appears to materialize in response to this divine other. In Calvin's various experiences, such a figure cannot assuage fully the responsibility for making choices and then trying to reconcile those choices with the circumstances that follow.

Conclusion

For the most part, Calvin does not seem like the kind of person who prays, but his experience with a forgotten homework assignment indicates that at times he can turn towards the idea of the divine, even if such moments of panic do not sustain a broader pattern of behavior. Thus, when Calvin brings up the content of his prayers, Hobbes is understandably caught off guard. Calvin informs Hobbes that his prayers ask for "the strength to change what I can, the inability to accept what I can't, and the incapacity to know the difference."[1] This is a jarring prayer, one that mirrors Reinhold Niebuhr's famous Serenity Prayer: "God, grant me the serenity to accept the things I cannot change, courage to change the things I can, and wisdom to know the difference." That Calvin would know the Serenity Prayer is not necessarily a shock; it is a common thing to utter in a variety of difficult circumstances.[2] What is interesting, however, is the change that Calvin makes in making the prayer his own. On the one hand, he retains the basic tenor of Niebuhr's prayer. At the heart of this meditation is the recognition that humans are responsible for choices, and that there are occasions wherein the freedom to choose cannot always bring about what one desires. On the other hand, however, Calvin fundamentally alters how the prayer seeks guidance in navigating the difference between the two kinds of circumstances. Whereas Niebuhr's prayer begins by acknowledging a limit to what human choice can accomplish, Calvin stresses that his choices can bring about excitement in life. The humility that characterizes the Serenity Prayer thus transforms into a confidence that asks for ignorance in order to continue the pursuit of personal gratification.

Calvin's version of the Serenity Prayer is, then, hardly a calming litany. The tripartite focus of what he prays for strongly reflects the way that an aesthete lives her/his life. Unbridled choice allows endless possibilities to satisfy desires, a confidence that ultimately requires some willing ignorance to be sustained. Just as Plato's prisoners would rather limit their life to the shadows that they take for reality, Calvin wants to extend his capacity to mold the world to fit his needs. The result is a desire to gloss over the fact that this approach to life is no different than a leaky jar; sometimes there are things that no choice will change. Calvin ultimately knows this, an awareness that is evident in his prayer to retain the ability to reject any limiting factor in his choices.

This scene provides a helpful beginning to this book's conclusion because it returns to several themes that have been discussed in the previous chapters. This prayer is about understanding life (albeit in a way that refuses to account for the fragility of the human condition). Calvin's willful ignorance thus reveals knowledge of life's character that he seeks to avoid by finding value in the presumptive desire to change whatever he likes. The irony, then, is that he nurtures this attitude in a way that is contrary to the medium through which he seeks this meaning. While prayer does not preclude asking for self-interested things, the specific prayer that Calvin mirrors is antithetical to the values he expresses in telling Hobbes what he wants in life. There is a further irony insofar as Calvin implicitly acknowledges some divine presence listening to his prayer, and so recognizes that value is not contained wholly within the material world to which his prayer speaks. The message is ironic in its content and in its inversion of Niebuhr's Serenity Prayer. In this double irony one finds the richness of Calvin's particular understanding of life, which, despite a frequent emphasis on immediate gratification, does not preclude a recognition that value also lies beyond the self.

This example offers a symptomatic look at how *Calvin and Hobbes* opens into new meanings in unexpected ways. The irony at work in Calvin's prayer undercuts particular expectations, which in turn seeks to recalibrate meaning in Calvin's terms. While the discord between Calvin's version of the Serenity Prayer and the original is striking, it also reveals the power of the imagination to configure how the self understands life, and therefore presents to the reader the ability to reconfigure one's experiences to find new meanings. The questions that Calvin struggles with throughout the strip are still present in his skewed prayer; they simply take shape in a way that undermines the preconceptions that follow naturally from the way the topic is introduced. When one thinks about Calvin and prayer, the narrative suggestion is essentially the opposite of what occurs. This surprise certainly invites questions about the self-determined values that underwrite this prayer, but to focus on this issue only is to miss the meaning that emerges through the prayer's conflicting content.

Irony reveals that Calvin's prayer is deeply problematic and therefore indicative of the tenuous nature of any search for meaning. There exists a serious risk that irony's disruption opens the text not only to new meanings but also to despair. Sartre lingers, then, in his claim that an approach to life that privileges the individual's choice ultimately leads to despair. James W. Fernandez and Mary Taylor Huber capture this risk, which irony always brings to the text: "It is a potential consequence of all practice, arising as it does in the space between the world as planned or promised and the world as achieved or received."[3] The basic problem remains that choice does not guarantee the desired outcome that (presumably) drives this choice.[4] Hernandez and Huber call attention to the trapdoor that misplaced expectations, or even bad luck,[5] can undermine even the most diligent choices. The reason, of course, is that the world remains a different place to dwell, and there are forces at work — be they natural or something metaphysical — that can frustrate even the most conscientious decision makers.[6]

Calvin frequently encounters the reality that life can be frustrating (or worse) regardless of the factors that produce a specific decision. For example, in the strip from February 19, 1993, Calvin fashions the "biggest snowball in the world,"[7] which is nearly as big as he is. As he anticipates how he will use the snowball against someone, Hobbes points out a minor problem: "How are you going to pick it up?"[8] Calvin says nothing as he stares at his snowball with a crestfallen look on his face. In the strip's final panel, Calvin is lying on the ground, his hand over his eyes as he laments, "Reality continues to ruin my life."[9] The ruin he experiences in this particular context is the limit that reasonable considerations place on imaginative ideas. The joy he anticipates about using this snowball (perhaps against Susie) collapses immediately when Hobbes makes a very practical observation. The extreme swing in emotion that Calvin feels indicates how reason can frustrate attempts to transcend the world's limits in search of some imaginative experience.

While Calvin cannot throw a snowball that is as big as he is, there is an important footnote to this example. Reason can fence in some ideas, but it does not always have the final say on where meaning can be found. As Pascal explains, reason eventually reaches a limit in its ability to constrain the imagination: "Reason's last step is the recognition that there are an infinite number of things beyond it. It is merely feeble if it does not go as far as to realize that."[10] For Pascal, part of reason's identity is to acknowledge where it cannot affect one's life. A good example of this dynamic occurs when Calvin eats multiple boxes of Chocolate Frosted Sugar Bombs in order to send away for a beanie.[11] After multiple weeks of waiting for the beanie to arrive, and dealing with a broken battery case, Calvin finally puts on his beanie, only to realize that his vision of being able to fly with the beanie was misleading. The beanie does nothing but spin, which causes Calvin to curse the reality that reason would have made clear earlier if he were not letting his imagination wander to the lengths it did. He exclaims, "What is the point of a propeller beanie if you can't even fly when you wear it?!"[12] As he gets angrier, Calvin kicks the beanie and shouts, "What a rip-off!"[13] At this point the reader might expect Calvin to continue yelling, but the final panel in this narrative turns the table on reason's ability to disappoint. Calvin takes the box that the beanie arrived in and says with a smile, "At least it's not a *total* loss. It came in this great cardboard box."[14] Reason becomes irrelevant when something that reason cannot speak to materializes. The cardboard box has nothing to do with the failed experience Calvin has while wearing his beanie. The imagination, however, can transform a cardboard box into a variety of things that reason cannot constrain, a freedom that throughout *Calvin and Hobbes* produces some of the more significant experiences from which Calvin draws value.

A further example will expand on these summary points and convey in more depth the different layers of meaning that emerge in *Calvin and Hobbes*. In one of the last strips, Calvin and Hobbes are walking through the snow and discussing Christmas. Calvin explains why this is a good time to reflect on one's life: "Too often we don't examine our lives. This is a time to take stock and think about what's important."[15] Such introspection is slightly out of character. Just as Calvin's willingness to pray comes as a bit of a shock, here Calvin implies that he realizes his understanding of value can be skewed. However, when he elaborates on the reasons for reflecting on life, one encounters an ironic twist that offers a similar inversion to that of the prayer: "It's a time to rededicate oneself to frenzied acquisition ... a time to spread the joy of material wealth ... a time to glorify personal excess of every kind!"[16] There is a common lament around the holidays: Christmas has lost its meaning in the heavy-handed commercial interests that take over after Thanksgiving. Such worries stem, in part, from those who would no doubt agree with Calvin's monologue. The ability to maximize his material gain during Christmas is the impetus to recenter his life. The focus would make any aesthete proud; meaning can be found in the personal excess that precludes one from recognizing the inability of such things to last.

The shift that occurs in this conversation offers another example of the discord between expectation and actuality, though, as with the prayer, this conversation reveals this disjunction through a double irony. The first and more obvious irony is the way that Calvin's reflection only strengthens his self-serving resolve. Hobbes emphasizes the point when he comments on the result of Calvin's reflection: "Earthly rewards make consumerism a popular religion."[17] Calvin's renewed interest in material things thus supplants the salvific narrative that Christmas initiates. This point is subtle but important. Calvin specifically undermines the Christmas narrative's arc by claiming that the season allows one to "atone"[18] for not retaining one's material resolve. Without descending into a lengthy theological discussion, it is helpful to note the theological structure of the Christmas narrative. The biblical accounts of the story initiate a much different kind of atonement wherein Jesus' birth marks God's entrance into the world in order to redeem humanity.[19] This exchange thus rejects the transition out of a life defined by material interest into religious values and posits instead a life characterized by limited sources of meaning.

While this ironic shift is jarring, there exists a second irony in Hobbes' remark. Specifically, he summarizes the inversion that Calvin suggests in a way that exposes the unsustainable meaning that Calvin claims as normative. A religion based only on material things is hardly a religion that will speak to life's vicissitudes. Calvin's rededication is absurd in this respect. The material world that will provide meaning is the context that demands new meanings. Hernandez and Huber speak to the further shift that occurs with this inversion: "The problematic of unrequitement in which irony flourishes has a positive as well as negative pole. Belief may be lost for good as well as bad reasons. And the loss, whether justified or not, may excite the moral imagination to explore routes to a better way of life."[20] Though it cuts deeply into the importance of Christmas, this strip exhibits, then, two crucial features of the analysis that this book offers. Irony calls into question the expectations that structure how Calvin finds meaning, which in turn creates space within the text for the imagination to seek other, richer meanings beyond the limited (and limiting) context of Calvin's life. There is little doubt that Calvin loses a measure of belief in this strip, yet by doing so he allows Hobbes to pull aside the curtain that hides the instability of what Calvin proposes. In this capacity, Calvin's new, consumer-driven religion functions just as his skewed prayer does. By fashioning a religious element into a materially-driven search for meaning, he tacitly admits that his reconfiguration will falter, which in turn leaves his experience open to imagining new meanings once he fails to find what he wants in the world's material offerings.

Through his imagination, Calvin is able to transform expectations (be they Hobbes' or the reader's), and thus find both a strong conception of the self and a reality beyond the self. This process echoes the importance that Kearney ascribes to the imagination. In Kearney's words, the examples discussed thus far "designate our ability to transform the time and space of our world into a specifically human mode of existence (*Dasein*). This is the miracle of imagining."[21] Several important points materialize in Kearney's description of how the imagination functions. First, he frames this ability in the exilic terms that destabilize life.[22] Ringed by terms that emphasize mortality, humans must understand life in a way that finds meaning despite the displacing presence of death. This is the specific task that an individual must undertake in conceptualizing a self through narrative, which, as discussed,[23] only occurs in a context that undermines any identity that emerges through this process. Paradoxically — and this is the key role that imagination plays — meaning is still possible because the imagination is not bound by the realities to which it must respond. As the opening example illustrates, prayer can be something other than supplication, just as Spaceman Spiff can confront and conquer through the imagination circumstances that spatially and temporally overwhelm Calvin.

The miracle that Kearney describes is indeed paradoxical in this respect. The imagination often accomplishes what reason cannot do: "rethink the question"[24] of life. The realities that structure life often preclude meaning, which is precisely why the imagination can provide the miraculous escape that Calvin so often seeks. The specific dynamic at work is, according to Kearney, "the human power to convert absence into presence, actuality into possibility, what-is into something-other-than-it-is."[25] Though the content of Calvin's prayer is surprising, its effect is to convert an absent stability into a divine presence that will listen to an admittedly selfish request. The point, then, is not necessarily the distractions that Calvin seeks, but rather the ability to reconfigure the actual limits of life into a possibility that provides affirmation through those limits. Deep down, Calvin seems to know that his choice is ultimately helpless in the face of life's unexpected challenges; consequently, he transforms his fragility into a measure of strength. This is the transition that Kearney describes, which is a hallmark of the imagination. Boundaries become permeable and therefore allow responses to life's conditions that would otherwise not be possible.

Thus, the discussion has circled around to Calvin's ability to construct a self through his imagination. He rewrites the story of his life when he encounters circumstances wherein meaning cannot be found. He exhibits, then, the lingering ability to respond to his fragile condition, which Kearney cites as an invaluable counterweight to life's difficulty. Kearney claims, "For all our sentiments of disorientation, however, we have not forfeited the capacity to narrate."[26] As he identifies this ability to imagine the journey through an unstable space, Kearney does not restrict what kinds of stories are possible; he only states that humans retain the ability to narrate. Consequently, they always have the ability to structure their search for meaning through the imagination's freedom. Calvin frequently retreats to this safe house. He may struggle to endure boredom, loss, or even Susie, but through these travails he captures the depth to which narrative constitutes the self. As Kearney explains, "In this sense I argue that our very existence is narrative, for the task of every finite being is to make some sense of what surpasses its limits — this strange, transcendent otherness which haunts and obsesses us, from without and from within."[27] The imagination's strength is not just its ability to find meaning amid life's challenges; it also reaches and transcends the ultimate border that can paralyze even the most imaginative individuals.[28] The ability to narrate provides direction in finding meaning when humanity confronts the horizon of mortality. For Kearney, this is why the imagination matters: "It is precisely *because* we are beings who know that we will die that we keep on telling stories, struggling to represent something of the unpresentable, to hazard interpretations of the puzzles and aporias that surround us."[29] The imagination can descend into the absurdity of life and find meaning at the point meaning ceases to exist. The result, as Calvin shows when he is most vulnerable, is the faint awareness that there exists something beyond life. This flickering presence resists death's closure and ensures that the text is always open to an imaginative alternative.

In one of the last strips from *Calvin and Hobbes*, the reader finds an apprehensive Calvin awake in the middle of the night. The reason he cannot sleep is anxiety.[30] In an apparent soliloquy, he explains the root of this unsettled feeling: "In the dark, it's easier to imagine awful possibilities that you'd never be prepared for."[31] While it is difficult to label one particular strip the most revealing with respect to a particular concern in this project, Calvin's admission pulls off the various self-confident, self-interested masks that one routinely finds in the strip. Here, perhaps more so than at any other point, Calvin confesses that he is not immune to the uncertainty that defines life. The visual context intensifies the uneasiness that prevents him from sleeping. This is one of a few examples wherein Calvin is in bed and Hobbes is not visible beside him. When the strip does show Hobbes in the third panel, Calvin adds to his sense of vulnerability: "And it's hard to feel courageous in loose-fitting, drowsy bear jammies."[32] Even when Hobbes is next to him, there are times when Calvin speaks honestly about the fragility of being human. The bravado that Spaceman Spiff exhibits is gone as Calvin sits quietly apart from the kinds of circumstances that usually ignite his imaginative departures. In bed he has a temporary reprieve from the frustrations that Spiff can conquer through his fearlessness, but this pause exposes just how vulnerable he is. At the end of the day, his imagination cannot erase the weakness that characterizes all of humanity.[33]

When day breaks, however, the anxiety from the night's awful possibilities gives way to an energetic willingness to journey into whatever unexpected circumstances the day might bring. A good place to find Calvin's enthusiasm is a strip that takes place on a Saturday morning, or, even better, on a summer morning. In the August 7, 1995, strip, for example, Calvin's mom stands sleepily just outside the door, coffee in hand, and remarks, "Just once I'd like to see you manage this during the school year."[34] Calvin probably does not hear her, as he is running away with Hobbes, the flag the two friends use for any number of games, and the hat he often wears during his adventures. A smile fills his face as his excited yell follows him through this single-panel strip. As the sun rises, Calvin races out to meet the adventures that the summer morning provides. Unlike the anxiety he experiences during the night, at daybreak he can meet the world's challenges with his imagination and his best friend.

The world that Calvin sets out to explore is vast, a reality he admits both in bed when he feels his fragility in this space[35] and as he sets out to explore it. Whereas the night opens into dreams that cannot be controlled, during the day the imagination can search for meaning on its own terms. Bachelard captures the essence of what the day offers, which in turn helps to understand the confidence that Calvin exhibits as he bolts from his house:

One might say that immensity is a philosophical category of daydream. Daydream undoubtedly feeds on all kinds of sights, but through a sort of natural inclination, it contemplates grandeur. And this contemplation produces an attitude that is so special, an inner state that is so unlike any other, that the daydream transports the dreamer outside the immediate world to a world that bears the mark of infinity.[36]

At night, dreams can turn into nightmares. During the day, however, dreams explore the world without impediment because the imagination can respond to the helplessness that the night brings. What Bachelard recognizes — and what is important as this book moves towards its conclusion — is that the imagination's conquering spirit is a natural inclination. Whereas reason and experience must take into account the limits the world imposes as the individual makes her/his choices, the imagination can generate the eagerness to explore the world despite these boundaries. Calvin leaves his house early in the morning with no apparent agenda; he is prepared — with his friend, his flag, and his hat. This adventure is at its beginning the step towards transcendence that the imagination allows insofar as it can take the daydreamer beyond the real world.

As Pascal discusses the imagination, one finds a similar contrast between the realities of life and the freedom of the imagination to transcend these challenges. Whereas reason is considered the key resource humanity has at its disposal to find meaning, Pascal claims that the imagination provides a more reliable way to understand one's experiences: "[The imagination] is the dominant faculty in man, master of error and falsehood ... it would be an infallible criterion of truth if it were infallibly that of lies. Since, however, it is usually false, it gives no indication of its quality, setting the same mark on truth and false alike."[37] Irony returns to make yet another subtle but effective point. Whereas reason is bound by a latent commitment to some measure of objectivity, the imagination is free from such restrictions. Pascal grants that it is prone to falsehoods at times (Calvin makes this much clear), yet this is precisely its liberating quality. The imagination can respond to both what is true and what is false, an adaptability that serves individuals well when they are aware that life is not always reasonable.[38] The imagination makes no necessary claim to objectivity, which allows it to master error in a different capacity than reason. Rather than try to scrub away the errors that inevitably appear in life, the imagination can accommodate those unexpected moments and still find meaning.

One should not be surprised, Pascal notes, that those who cling to reason object to claiming that the imagination can travel beyond reason's limits. He notes dryly, "Reason may object in vain, it cannot fix the price of things."[39] Reason is a merchant that offers an inferior product in certain respects, which can be unsettling. The imagination's service can "satisfy its guests more fully and completely than reason ever could."[40] As a result, those who embrace the imagination as an alternative way to find meaning "are far more pleased with themselves than prudent men could reasonable be."[41] In the West's intellectual tradition, the contrast between reason and imagination favors the former, which is why Pascal's argument here can be fractious. However, the distinction he makes emerges clearly when one considers Calvin's imagination. He is decidedly unreasonable in many ways, but this is precisely the point. He may not satisfy the reasonable expectations of those around him, but he also extends an irresistible invitation to join him as he rushes out to explore the summer day. The result, as Pascal notes, is a kind of satisfaction with life that reason cannot provide.[42] The difficulties of finding (and keeping a hold of) meaning are easy enough to identify; the ability to enjoy life despite those challenges is a far more difficult task. As Calvin shows, however, the task can be met — even if it cannot be conquered — through the imagination's release.

While Pascal makes clear the imagination's value transcends a tradition that privileges reason, he does not reject altogether humanity's rational abilities. Rather, he stresses that reason alone cannot provide the meaning in life that individuals need. The wise person, he writes, is the one who "adopts those principles which human imagination has rashly introduced at every turn. Anyone who chose to follow reason alone would have proved himself a fool."[43] There exists in the imagination a wild energy that cannot be contained. Ideas sprout from the imagination's ability to transcend the world's limitations, which, Pascal notes, conflicts with reason's more staid nature. Even though the energy that drives the imagination is unwieldy, it does open into the adventures wherein the imaginative individual can tap into a way of life that reason alone cannot accommodate. Importantly for Pascal, the decision not to embrace the imagination's freedom is a foolish act; this constituent part of the human self enriches the different ways that individuals can inscribe their identities into life. Such meaning must be wary — as reason is — that life is still unpredictable and thus the human condition is unstable, but this caution does not preclude the adventurous spirit that Calvin exhibits as he runs into a day full of yet-to-be-determined experiences. The reasonable context of school that is absent from this day recedes as his imagination advances confidently towards whatever the day might bring.

Calvin, then, is a bit of a fool, but this label reveals the ability of *Calvin and Hobbes* to find meaning in and through a unique textual world. Characterized by Calvin's pervasive imagination, the strip finds meaning in contexts that threaten constantly to stifle Calvin's spirit. As a response to the latent instability that shadows the text as it unfolds, the imagination opens into different values, choices, consequences, and, perhaps most importantly, relationships that bubble with meaning. Pascal summarizes well what is at stake in the strip's context: "Imagination decides everything: it creates beauty, justice, and happiness, which is the world's supreme good."[44] Aristotle would certainly agree, particularly when one considers that the beauty, (occasional) justice, and happiness that Calvin experiences are largely the result of his friendship with Hobbes, which is conceptually and experientially built on the basis of his imagination.

For all his energy, though, Calvin never loses sight of the realities in life that require an imaginative response. He knows that even though he can develop varied narrative selves, he cannot escape who he is as a person. He must understand what is valuable and make choices based on the meanings he constructs. The primary locus for undertaking this challenge is his bond with Hobbes. In the midst of the world around him, Calvin trusts in the friendship that begins in the very first strip.[45] He, like Hobbes (and presumably all tigers), is a bit foolish, but in that shared condition the two friends find a warmth that resists even the night's cold, lonely setting.[46] The strip from January 7, 1989, summarizes this point well, and therefore provides a fitting coda to this book. As he warms his hands in front of the fire, Calvin reflects, "There's something magical about having a fire. The crackles and snaps, the warm, flickering light ... everything always seems safe and cozy if you're sitting in front of a fire."[47] These things are all true, of course, particularly in the midst of a winter night. Calvin's words, though, extend well beyond this context. The fire is a metaphor for his friendship with Hobbes, a point made in the final panel of this strip. The image rounds out Calvin's words. Hobbes is asleep as Calvin leans against his best friend's stomach. The fire is nice, but, as always, Hobbes' presence makes the meaning a little more significant: "And if you've got a hot tiger tummy to lie against ... *well!*"[48]

Chapter Notes

Introduction

1. Graham Allen, *Intertextuality, 2nd Edition* (London: Routledge, 2011), 1. Allen's book provides an excellent historical overview of how intertextuality developed as a critical concern.

2. Allen, *Intertextuality*, 1.

3. *Ibid.*

4. *Ibid.*

5. *Ibid.*, 2.

6. Hermeneutics are an important concern when examining any text. In one sense, this entire book will be an exercise in hermeneutics insofar as it discusses how a text gives rise to meaning. Moreover, the text in question is a bit of an unorthodox site for a critical exploration, which generates specific hermeneutical challenges (e.g., how to understand the visual element in *Calvin and Hobbes*). That being said, I have made a methodological decision not to engage in a technical hermeneutical discussion that draws heavily on current theoretical concerns in the field. There are numerous resources that can assist the reader who seeks a more structured hermeneutical analysis of *Calvin and Hobbes*. Hans-Georg Gadamer's *Truth and Method* (New York: Continuum, 2004) is a good starting point for this type of critical inquiry. In addition to Gadamer's seminal text, I recommend Anthony C. Thiselton's *Hermeneutics: An Introduction* (Grand Rapids: William B. Eerdmans Publishing Co., 2009) and Werner Jeanrond's *Theological Hermeneutics* (London: SCM Press, 1994).

Chapter One

1. John Campanelli, "'Calvin and Hobbes' Fans Still Pine 15 Years After Its Exit," *The Plain Dealer* (1 February 2010), available at: http://www.cleveland.com/living/index.ssf/2010/02/fans_still_pine_for_calvin_and.html (accessed 17 June 2011).

2. *Ibid.*

3. December 31, 1995. All references to *Calvin and Hobbes* will be by date and come from Bill Watterson, *The Complete Calvin and Hobbes* (Kansas City: Andrews McMeel Publishing, 2005).

4. *Ibid.*

5. *Ibid.*

6. Kevin Whitelaw's hope is symptomatic on this point: "There is, however, always hope that Calvin will return and, with his lucky stuffed tiger, take us exploring again" (quoted in Walter de Gruyter, "The Psychological Appeal of Bill Watterson's Calvin," available at: http://plos.deepdyve.com/lp/de-gruyter/the-psychological-appeal-of-bill-watterson-s-calvin-3OAGYbZkGl (accessed 17 June 2011).

7. Jacques Derrida, "Living On," *Deconstruction and Criticism* (New York: Continuum, 2004), 64.

8. Jacques Derrida, *Of Grammatology*, trans. Gayatri Chakravorty Spivak (Baltimore: The Johns Hopkins University Press, 1997), 49.

9. "One could call *play* the absence of the transcendental signified as limitlessness of play, that is to say the destruction of onto-theology and the metaphysics of presence" (Derrida, *Of Grammatology*, 50).

10. Derrida, *Of Grammatology*, 61.

11. *Ibid.*

12. *Ibid.*, 65.

13. *Ibid.*

14. May 20, 1992.

15. *Ibid.*

16. *Ibid.*

17. See Bill Watterson, *The Calvin and Hobbes 10th Anniversary Book* (London: Warner Books, 1995), 152.

18. Julian Wolfreys, *Derrida: A Guide for the Perplexed* (New York: Continuum, 2007), 8.

19. Jacques Derrida, *Writing and Difference*, trans. Alan Bass (London: Routledge and Kegan Paul, 1978), 278.

20. Wolfreys, 31–32.

21. Sarah Wood, *Derrida's* Writing and Difference (New York: Continuum, 2009), 105.

22. See, for example, the strip dated May 20, 1992.

23. November 17, 1992.

24. *Ibid.*

25. *Ibid.*

26. *Ibid.*

27. Watterson, *The Complete Calvin and Hobbes, Book One*, 5.

28. Derrida, *Margins of Philosophy*, 5–6.

29. *Ibid.*, 6.

30. *Ibid.*, 7.

31. Valentine Cunningham, *Reading After Theory* (Oxford: Blackwell Publishers, 2002), 50.

32. *Ibid.*, 125.

33. *Ibid.*, 69.

34. There are multiple layers of irony at work in *Calvin and Hobbes*, and, therefore, this book. See Chapter Four for more on this point.

35. Cunningham, 69–70.

36. See my discussion in Chapter One for more on this point.

37. April 20, 1990.

38. *Ibid.*

39. April 28, 1990.

40. The narrative arc in this particular strip reflects not only what Calvin likes but also Hobbes' preference, as explained in the April 20, 1990, strip. There, Hobbes interjects that his favorite part of baseball is that "mostly we just argue over the rule we make up! That's the part *I* like!" (April 20, 1990).

41. May 2, 1990. This strip offers the first of many examples of irony, which I discuss thoroughly in Chapter Four. Despite the emphasis on rules, the players who are mad at Calvin ignore the fact that the umpire would not have let the pitcher commence if a player on the batting team were still in the field.

42. May 3, 1990.

43. April 30, 1990.

44. May 3, 1990.

45. May 5, 1990.
46. *Ibid.*
47. *Ibid.*
48. May 27, 1990.
49. Derrida, *Margins of Philosophy*, 65.
50. *Ibid.*, 66.
51. *Ibid.*
52. November 18, 1985.
53. November 20, 1985.
54. Discussion of how Calvin and Hobbes relate can add little to the current project. For readers who are interested in what Calvin's relationship to Hobbes might reveal about the human psyche, there exist a range of studies. Walter de Gruyter offers some introductory comments in "The Psychological Appeal of Bill Watterson's Calvin." More in-depth analyses can be found in Ellen Handler Spitz's *The Brightening Glance: Imagination and Childhood* (New York: Anchor Books, 2007) and Philip Sandifer, "When Real Things Happen to Imaginary Tigers," *Interdisciplinary Comic Studies* 3.3 (2007), available at: http://www. english.ufl.edu/imagetext/archives/v3_3/sandifer/ (accessed 17 June 2011). While it would be easy to ascribe a particular psychoanalysis to *Calvin and Hobbes*, the approach in this study accepts that the strip constitutes a text that should be read on its own terms.
55. Derrida, *Margins of Philosophy*, 268.
56. "An Interview with Bill Watterson."
57. David Jasper, *The Study of Literature and Religion: An Introduction* (London: MacMillan Academic and Professional, Ltd., 1992), xvi.
58. Linguistic theory posits an absence at the heart of metaphor (see Paul Ricoeur, *The Rule of Metaphor: The Creation of Meaning in Language*, trans. Robert Czerny, Kathleen McLaughlin, and John Costello [New York: Routledge, 2009]). In a purely textual sense, this is, of course, true. However, in the context of this study — and this is the important point at hand — Hobbes is not *merely* a metaphor. Rather, he functions metaphorically in his ability to accommodate a paradoxical duality within the construct of *Calvin and Hobbes*. See also Derrida, *Margins of Philosophy*, 269–271.
59. Derrida, *Margins of Philosophy*, 310.
60. *Ibid.*, 313.
61. *Ibid.*, 314.
62. September 24, 1987.
63. September 26, 1987.
64. September 28, 1987. This is one of two instances when the line between Hobbes' two identities blurs; the other occurs when Calvin's mom stays with Hobbes while Calvin goes to get some things to take care of an injured raccoon; see the strip from March 10, 1987.
65. September 30, 1987.
66. *Ibid.*
67. Timothy Clark, *Derrida, Heidegger, Blanchot: Sources of Derrida's Notion and Practice of Literature* (Cambridge, UK: Cambridge University Press, 1992), 129. In this passage, Clark is quoting Maurice Blanchot, who I discuss in Chapter Three.
68. See Watterson, *10th Anniversary Book*, 152.
69. Watterson, *10th Anniversary Book*, 21.
70. *Ibid.*
71. Campanelli, "Bill Watterson, Creator of 'Calvin and Hobbes,' Looks Back with No Regrets."
72. Cunningham, 132.
73. Cunningham echoes this point: "A classic keep[s] yielding meaning but also seems to keep withholding it" (40).

74. Watterson, *10th Anniversary Book*, 22.

75. For an in-depth discussion of Watterson's life, Nevin Martell's *Looking for Calvin and Hobbes: The Unconventional Story of Bill Watterson and His Revolutionary Comic Strip* (New York: Continuum, 2010) is particularly helpful.

76. The strip from August 15, 1990, offers one of the more obvious examples of Watterson's familiarity with philosophy. Insofar as Watterson rarely quotes another source directly, the fact that Calvin's dad does as much stresses the relevance of Thoreau to the narrative context.

77. Watterson, *10th Anniversary Book*, 21.

78. See, for example, the strip from January 21, 1993.

79. See John Calvin, *The Institutes of the Christian Religion*, trans. Henry Beveridge (Peabody, MA: Hendrickson Publishers, Inc., 2009), Book 3, Chapter 22.

80. Watterson, *The Complete Calvin and Hobbes, Book One*, 211.

81. Matthew 26:40; see also Mark 14:37 and Luke 22:45–46. All biblical references in this book come from *The Holy Bible: Containing the Old and New Testaments*, New Revised Standard Version, Oxford World Classics (Oxford: Oxford University Press, 1995).

82. This narrative thread runs from April 6 through April 11, 1987.

83. April 7, 1987.

84. April 9, 1987.

85. The motivations at work in this particular strip anticipate a larger discussion both about how an individual determines value and the contexts in which such value is often location. For more on the former point, see Chapter Five, and for more on the latter point, see Chapter Seven.

86. For another example of this point, see the March 7–19, 1994, strips.

87. April 9, 1987.

88. See Watterson, *10th Anniversary Book*, 20.

89. Calvin, *The Institutes*, 3.20.2. Even a cursory glance at how Calvin understands God (see, for example, *The Institutes* 2.4.6) will reveal the divergence between the reformer's faith and the motivations that Calvin has in praying not to do a problem at the chalkboard.

90. Richard Beck, "The Theology of Calvin and Hobbes' Part I, Chapter I: '*Virtue Needs Some Cheaper Thrills*,'" available at: http://experimentaltheology.blogspot.com/2008/08/theology-of-calvin-and-hobbes-part-1.html (accessed 1 July 2011).

91. Watterson, *10th Anniversary Book*, 20.

92. *Ibid.*

93. This narrative occurs in the March 18–April 3, 1991, strips.

94. Richard Beck, "The Theology of *Calvin and Hobbes*, Part I, Chapter 2: The Democracy of Sinners," available at: http://experimentaltheology.blogspot.com/2008/09/theology-of-calvin-and-hobbes-part-1.html (accessed 1 July 2011).

95. See William Shakespeare. *Hamlet*, Norton Critical Editions, ed. Robert S. Miola (New York: W.W. Norton & Company, 2010), 3.i.58–92. Watterson also incorporates Shakespeare into the text in the July 18, 1992, strip.

96. March 6, 1994. See *Hamlet*, 3.i.68–70.

97. March 6, 1994.

98. Richard Kearney, "Deconstruction, God, and the Possible," *Derrida and Religion*, eds. Yvonne Sherwood and Kevin Hart (New York: Routledge, 2004), 298–299.

99. Jacques Derrida, *The Post Card*, trans. Allan Bass (Chicago: University of Chicago Press, 1987), 4.

100. Wood, 12–13.

101. Richard Kearney, *On Paul Ricoeur: The Owl of Minerva* (Farnham, UK: Ashgate, 2004), 34. This link between the imagination and how meaning emerges from the text is

an important development of Deconstruction. Kearney explains: "What is indisputable is that Heidegger's rereading of the Kantian concept of imagination blazed the trail for the subsequent hermeneutic acknowledgment of imagination as a pathway leading to, rather than away from, the truth of being" (*On Paul Ricoeur*, 37).

Chapter Two

1. Timothy Schroeder and Carl Matheson, *The Architecture of the Imagination: New Essays on Pretence, Possibility, and Fiction*, ed. Shaun Nichols (Oxford: Clarendon Press, 2006), 19.

2. *Ibid.*

3. *Ibid.*, 22.

4. For more on this point, see Chapter Seven.

5. Mark Knight and Louise Lee, "Introduction," *Religion, Literature and the Imagination: Sacred Worlds*, ed. Mark Knight and Louise Lee (New York: Continuum, 2010), 1.

6. Quoted in Richard Kearney, *Poetics of Imagining: Modern to Post-Modern* (Edinburgh: Edinburgh University Press, 1998), 1.

7. Richard Kearney, *The Wake of the Imagination: Toward a Postmodern Culture* (London: Routledge, 1998), 359.

8. Kant is important in his examination of imagination. For example, Kant affirms the imagination as a means for the individual to comprehend her/his world; it "connects *all* representations by a free act of volition" (quoted in Rudolf A. Makkreel, *Imagination and Interpretation in Kant: The Hermeneutical Import of* The Critique of Judgment (Chicago: University of Chicago Press, 1990), 15; my emphasis). However, an extended discussion of Kant's conception of the imagination would create friction with this project's methodological outline. I cite this passage from Makkreel not only to recommend his work as an accessible overview of what is at stake in how Kant understands the imagination (not to mention that his German translation is far better than what I can offer), but also to depart from the abstract discussion Kant undertakes in *Critique of the Power of Judgment*, trans. Paul Geyer and Eric Matthews (Cambridge: Cambridge University Press, 2000). For a more recent discussion of this topic, see Jane Kneller, *Kant and the Power of Imagination* (Cambridge: Cambridge University Press, 2007).

9. Samuel Taylor Coleridge, *Biographia Literaria*, available at http://www.gutenb erg.org/cache/epub/6081/pg6081.html (accessed 24 July 2011), Chapter XIV.

10. *Ibid.*

11. January 1, 1995.

12. *Ibid.*

13. *Ibid.*

14. Gaston Bachelard, *The Poetics of Space: The Classic Look at How We Experience Intimate Places*, trans. Maria Jolas (Boston: Beacon Press, 1994), 145.

15. *Ibid.*

16. In a related narrative thread, Calvin gets in trouble at school for drawing a series of pictures that show dinosaurs flying rocketships. Though Ms. Wormwood does not understand, Hobbes gets the point right away (see the strips from October 31, 1990 through November 3, 1990). Hobbes' receptivity here suggests that he understands what is at stake in combining incongruent things and, therefore, indicates why he is willing to play the T-Rex/F-14 game with Calvin. The imagination cannot be bound by reasonable standards.

17. See the strips from October 31, 1990 through November 3, 1990.

18. Bachelard, 145.

19. Contrary to Kant, then, Coleridge does not merely distinguish between formation (*Einbildung*) and creation (*Bildungskraft*). Coleridge suggests a qualitative distinction that

sanctions the combination of ideas (however stupid it might seem). For more on the Kantian distinction, see Makkreel, 12–14.

20. Coleridge, Chapter XVIII.

21. Timothy Clark, *The Poetics of Singularity: The Counter-Culturalist Turn in Heidegger, Derrida, Blanchot and the Later Gadamer* (Edinburgh: Edinburgh University Press, 2005), 4.

22. Coleridge, Chapter XIII.

23. July 6, 1992.

24. July 7, 1992.

25. *Ibid.*

26. *Ibid.*

27. *Ibid.*

28. *Ibid.*

29. In this respect, the visual element in this strip is striking in its addition to the narrative context. The fact that the snowman's expression conveys a strong sense of contemplation speaks to how the visual element of the strip enhances its imaginative possibilities. I discuss this point in depth in Chapter Three.

30. January 22, 1993.

31. *Ibid.*

32. *Ibid.*

33. The other can be found in the November 23, 1990, strip.

34. Carl A. Raschke, *Theological Thinking: An Inquiry*, AAR Studies in Religion (Atlanta: Scholars Press, 1988), vii.

35. See my discussion of mortality in Chapter Three.

36. Issues surrounding choice are discussed at length in the second part of this book. With respect to this specific point, see my discussion of Plato's Allegory of the Cave in Chapter Five.

37. Martin Heidegger, *Hölderlin's Hymn "The Ister,"* trans. William McNeill and Julia Davis (Bloomington, IN: Indiana University Press, 1984), 29–30.

38. I discuss another example of how the melting of snow provides a metaphor for the human condition in Chapter Three.

39. Genesis 3:19.

40. Cunningham, 29.

41. Campanelli, "Bill Watterson, Creator of 'Calvin and Hobbes,' Looks Back with No Regrets." Clark echoes this point: "One condition for such freedom is the duty of using the thinking and writing of others to 'particularise' oneself, to become aware of the limits of one's own arguments and opinions" (*The Poetics of Singularity*, 64).

42. Derrida, *Margins of Philosophy*, 322.

43. Roland Barthes, *The Death of the Author*, trans. Richard Howard, available at: http://evans-experientialism.freewebspace.com/barthes06.htm (accessed 5 July 2011).

44. *Ibid.* Derrida echoes this point in *Margins of Philosophy*: "Writing is read … and does not give rise to a hermeneutic deciphering, to the decoding of a meaning or truth" (329).

45. Barthes, *The Death of the Author*.

46. *Ibid.*

47. Clark, *The Poetics of Singularity*, 46.

48. May 28, 1995.

49. *Ibid.*

50. *Ibid.*

51. *Ibid.*

52. *Ibid.*

53. *Ibid.*

54. *Ibid.*

55. "An Interview with Bill Watterson," available at: http://bob.bigw.org/ch/interview. html (accessed 17 June 2011).

56. Jacques Derrida, "Deconstruction and the Other: An Interview with Richard Kearney," *"Debates in Continental Philosophy: Conversations with Contemporary Thinkers,* ed. Richard Kearney (New York: Fordham University Press, 2004), 155.

57. "An Interview with Bill Watterson."

58. June 16, 1993.

59. *Ibid.*

60. March 27, 1994.

61. *Ibid.*

62. *Ibid.*

63. *Ibid.*

64. *Ibid.*

65. September 26, 1993.

66. February 18, 1990.

67. *Ibid.*

68. *Ibid.*

69. Derrida, *Of Grammatology,* 91.

70. *Ibid.,* 92.

71. February 18, 1990.

72. *Ibid.*

73. January 20, 1991.

74. *Ibid.*

75. *Ibid.*

76. *Ibid.*

77. December 31, 1990.

78. January 2, 1991.

79. January 3, 1992.

80. January 7, 1991.

81. Calvin's dad enters the narrative to make precisely this point. See the January 5, 1991, strip.

82. January 8, 1991.

83. January 10, 1991.

84. *Ibid.*

85. *Ibid.*

86. January 15, 1991.

87. January 18, 1991.

88. *Ibid.*

Chapter Three

1. Paul Ricoeur, *From Text to Action: Essays in Hermeneutics, II,* trans. Kathleen Blamey and John B. Thompson (London: The Althone Press, 1991), 106.

2. Kearney, *On Paul Ricoeur,* 41.

3. Watterson, *10th Anniversary Book,* 104.

4. *Ibid.*

5. *Ibid.*

6. August 8, 1989.

7. One never wants to say never when reading the text, but a direct correlation between the visual and the verbal discourse seems unlikely in this particular strip.

8. August 8, 1989.

9. *Ibid.*

10. July 23, 1995.

11. January 6, 1993.

12. Martell, 111.

13. October 6, 1992.

14. *Ibid.*

15. See Watterson, *10th Anniversary Book*, 200.

16. October 6, 1992.

17. Roland Barthes, *The Pleasure of the Text*, trans. Richard Miller (New York: Hill and Wang, 1975), 32.

18. Paul Ricoeur, *Hermeneutics & the Human Sciences*, trans. John B. Thompson (Cambridge: Cambridge University Press, 1981), 162.

19. *Ibid.*, 148. Ricoeur echoes here the salient features that Derrida identifies and, moreover, which underpin the exploratory contours of *Calvin and Hobbes*. See my discussion of Derrida in Chapter One.

20. See Ricoeur, *Hermeneutics & the Human Sciences*, pp. 148–149; and Timothy Clark, *Derrida, Heidegger, Blanchot: Sources of Derrida's Notion and Practice of Literature* (Cambridge: Cambridge University Press, 1992), 1–3.

21. I discuss this point in more depth as it relates specifically to Calvin's character in Chapter Five. Derivative concerns are then addressed in Chapters Six and Seven.

22. An extended discussion of this metaphysical component can be found in Chapter Seven. While this component of humanity's identity is important, I bracket such considerations in the current discussion.

23. Carl G. Vaught, *Metaphor, Analogy, and the Place of Places: Where Religion and Philosophy Meet* (Waco, TX: Baylor University Press, 2004), 6.

24. *Ibid.*

25. October 7, 1990.

26. *Ibid.*

27. *Ibid.*

28. Vaught, 7.

29. *Ibid.*

30. *Ibid.*

31. *Ibid.*, 131.

32. *Ibid.*

33. *Ibid.*, 10.

34. "In contrast to both time and eternity, the mystery of space is its capacity to bind things together and to hold hem apart, not only metrically, but also physically as parts of a spatial continuum" (Vaught, 10).

35. Vaught, 11.

36. December 28, 1986.

37. *Ibid.*

38. Vaught, 11.

39. *Ibid.*

40. December 28, 1986.

41. *Ibid.*

42. See Vaught, 136.

43. See Vaught, 137.

44. Vaught, 137.

45. See Vaught, 133.

46. Gianni Vattimo, *The Adventure of Difference: Philosophy After Nietzsche and Hei-*

degger, trans. Cyprian Blamires with the assistance of Thomas Harrison (Cambridge, UK: Polity Press, 1993), 14.

47. Vattimo advances this thematic freedom to an ontological inquiry: "Lived in this way, the infinity of interpretation, and the perpetual repetition of the dialectic/dialogic of question and answer as the very marrow of history, has the feel of wandering or exile. And the term 'wandering' is of course often favoured by Heidegger as a way of describing the condition of thought *in the epoch of metaphysics*: but in fact it does not at all define the essence of man" (31). Kearney echoes this point: "This power, to transform given meanings into new ones, enables one to construe the future as the possible theatre of one's liberty, as a horizon of hope" (*On Paul Ricoeur*, 39).

48. April 16, 1991. Another example of the weighty portrayal of life's fragility occurs in the strip from April 26, 1988.

49. Jean-Yves Lacoste's recent book, *Experience and the Absolute: Disputed Questions on the Humanity of Man*, Perspectives in Continental Philosophy, trans. Mark Raftery-Skehan (New York: Fordham University Press, 2004), examines questions concerning human experience as refracted through death's reality. As he provides his analysis, Lacoste offers a personalized narrative that intersects with the broader hermeneutical and phenomenological concerns that I am discussing in this chapter. In this capacity, he mirrors the exploration that Calvin undertakes frequently, albeit in a significantly different context. For more on this point, see especially Lacoste, 30–70.

50. This narrative arc occurs in the strips from March 9, 1987, through March 18, 1987.

51. See the March 12, 1987, strip.

52. March 16, 1987.

53. See the March 17, 1987, strip.

54. I discuss the challenging nature of metaphysical questions for Calvin in Chapter Six.

55. March 18, 1987.

56. Richard Kearney, *Strangers, Gods, and Monsters* (London: Routledge, 2003), 231. Martin Heidegger's influence is apparent in how Kearney and others discussed in this chapter characterize death's influence on the human condition. Specifically, Heidegger's notion of "being-thrown" emphasizes the release from an originary stability, and therefore that humans have been released into a context where, without such an anchor, are left to make sense of their continually disjointed condition. See Martin Heidegger, *Being and Time*, trans. John Macquarrie and Edward Robinson (London: SCM Press, 1962), I.6.118–189, ¶ 40; and Martin Heidegger, "Building Dwelling Thinking," *Poetry, Language, Thought*, trans. Albert Hofstadter (New York: Perennial Library, 1971), 145–161.

57. February 20, 1991.

58. I discuss a different example wherein Calvin uses snow as a metaphor for humanity in Chapter Five, when I discuss the strip wherein Calvin brings a snowflake into class.

59. Calvin echoes this form of expression in the strip from December 5, 1993.

60. February 21, 1990.

61. *Ibid.*

62. *Ibid.*

63. I examine specific values that follow from this reflective scene in the second part of this book.

64. See my discussion of Kierkegaard in Chapters Five and Six.

65. Maurice Blanchot, *The Space of Literature*, trans. Ann Smock (Lincoln, NE: University of Nebraska Press, 1989), 33.

66. I use the term eternal to signal a conception of the afterlife that does not reflect any particular faith tradition. There exist throughout *Calvin and Hobbes* multiple references and reflections on whether there is an afterlife and, moreover, the implications of that pos-

sibility for how one should live life. I discuss these specific instances in more depth in Chapter Seven.

67. Blanchot, 33.

68. *Ibid.*, 31.

69. *Ibid.*, 62.

70. One of the few exceptions to this statement can be found in the strip from September 26, 1993. Despite the different conclusion in this strip, the emphasis on an imaginative departure remains the same.

71. For a more detailed analysis on this point, see also Blanchot, 46–48.

72. See Chapter One for my discussion on Derrida.

73. Blanchot, 22.

74. *Ibid.*, 237.

75. See Bachelard, 71.

76. See Watterson, *10th Anniversary Book*, 19–20.

77. "Release ... The Complete Calvin and Hobbes: Fans from Around the World Interview Bill Watterson."

78. Bachelard, 71.

79. Blanchot, 237.

80. *Ibid.*

81. Clark stresses this thematic link with Derrida's work: "This is the side of Blanchot's work that Derrida often engages. A word is neither totally absent, nor present, it *lives on* as a kind of life-in-death" (Timothy Clark, *Derrida, Heidegger, Blanchot*, 74). Moreover, the suspension that occurs within a text highlights how the text constitutes a space between the author and the reader.

82. See the discussion of Paul Gauguin in Chapter Five.

83. Blanchot, 238.

84. Clark, *Derrida, Heidegger, Blanchot*, 82.

85. *Ibid.*, 84.

86. See discussion of the T-rex flying an F-14 in Chapter Two. As discussed, despite the admittedly stupid nature of the strip, a crucial dynamic emerges in this example.

87. Bachelard, 4.

88. March 4, 1991.

89. *Ibid.*

90. *Ibid.*

91. Bachelard, 5.

92. *Ibid.*, 7.

93. January 5, 1990.

94. *Ibid.*

95. *Ibid.*

96. *Ibid.*

97. Bachelard, 31.

98. *Ibid.*, 32. "When we are lost in darkness and see a distant glimmer of light, who does not dream of a thatched cottage?" (Bachelard, 32).

99. Bachelard, 34.

100. January 17, 1988.

101. Bachelard, 40.

102. January 17, 1988.

103. See especially the strip from September 22, 1987.

104. January 17, 1988.

105. December 26, 1988.

106. *Ibid.*

Chapter Four

1. June 27, 1986.
2. *Ibid.*
3. *Ibid.*
4. *Ibid.*
5. Wayne C. Booth, *A Rhetoric of Irony* (Chicago: The University of Chicago Press, 1974), 10.
6. *Ibid.*, 11.
7. *Ibid.*
8. *Ibid.*, 12.
9. There exists extensive literature on different types of irony, but there is little to be gained in distinguishing between categories such as narrative or cosmic irony. In the context of this chapter's discussion, it will suffice to say that irony is announced within *Calvin and Hobbes* through the text's visual and verbal discourses.
10. Booth, 27.
11. *Ibid.*, 28.
12. I use the term to follow Booth's critical logic, not to make claims about the gender roles and consequent dynamics between Calvin and Susie. While I think an analysis of Susie as embodying feminist principles would be worthwhile, in this particular example, to broaden the implications of victimhood beyond irony's function would be a stretch. To the reader who would argue that victimhood is *always* implicit when examining feminist concerns, I would counter that, if anything, Susie's ability to reverse the roles of victimizer and victim constitutes a transcendence of the normative concerns that victimhood bring to a text.
13. Booth, 48.
14. While I dismiss the critical trajectory that Booth follows, I do not entirely discount his work. *A Rhetoric of Irony* remains an important fixture in the academy's irony-related landscape. Of particular importance is Booth's stress on irony's subtle character (see 60–61 and 80–82).
15. D.J. Enright, *The Alluring Problem: An Essay on Irony* (Oxford: Oxford University Press, 1986), 16.
16. Booth, 242.
17. Enright, 16.
18. *Ibid.*, 35.
19. October 1, 1987.
20. *Ibid.*
21. *Ibid.*
22. *Ibid.*
23. For a good example, see the narrative thread in the August 20 through September 8, 1990, strips.
24. David Jasper, *Rhetoric, Power and Community: An Exercise in Reserve* (London: MacMillan, 1993), 128.
25. *Ibid.*
26. *Ibid.*, 128–129.
27. July 27, 1989.
28. *Ibid.*
29. *Ibid.*
30. *Ibid.*
31. Enright, 87.
32. June 15, 1986.

33. *Ibid.*

34. *Ibid.*

35. *Ibid.*

36. *Ibid.*

37. There is a broader thematic concern in Calvin's approach — namely, the question of how the egoist determines what is valuable. I discuss this point in more depth in Chapter Five.

38. June 15, 1986.

39. I discuss how Socrates relates to *Calvin and Hobbes* in more depth in Chapter Five.

40. Plato, *Plato in Twelve Volumes*, Vols. 5 & 6, trans. Paul Shorey (Cambridge, MA: Harvard University Press, 1969), 414a–417b. I list the book reference for Plato's work, but for those interested in Plato's work, Tufts' Perseus Digital Library is an invaluable resource. All quotations from Plato in this project come from and are available at: www.perseus. tufts.edu (all Plato citations accessed 25 July 2011).

41. Gregory Currie, *Narratives and Narrators: A Philosophy of Stories* (Oxford: Oxford University Press, 2010), 148.

42. *Ibid.*

43. *Ibid.*, 152. In his book *Skepticism and Literature: An Essay on Pope, Hume, Sterne, and Johnson* (Oxford: Oxford University Press, 2003), Fred Parker provides helpful analysis of irony's development through early modern English literature. In discussing how irony functions specifically in this literary epoch, Parker does well to stress that irony has not simply re-emerged as a postmodern concern. The result is to avoid the jump to a heavy-handed postmodern reading of irony (see, for example, Albert Cook, "The Meta-Irony of Marcel Duchamp," *The Journal of Aesthetics and Art Criticism* 44 [Spring 1986]: 263–70).

44. See Watterson, *10th Anniversary Book*, 184.

45. See Chapter Four, note 43.

46. September 24, 1992.

47. *Ibid.*

48. Currie, 150.

49. *Ibid.*, 154.

50. Though I only offer a couple of examples from Calvin's snowmaking career that are ironic, it is worth noting that this is one of the recurring contexts in which irony is strongly present. Importantly, Calvin admits as much (see the February 20, 1992, strip).

51. February 9, 1995.

52. There is an interesting echo between this scene and the strip I discuss in Chapter Two when considering the snowman who thinks about evolution while looking at a snowball.

53. Currie, 154.

54. While not an overly common theme, there are other examples wherein Calvin's assertions of power over the natural world suffer irony's effects in this capacity. See, for example, the May 3, 1992, strip.

55. January 3, 1993.

56. *Ibid.*

57. *Ibid.*

58. Currie, 164.

59. See Chapter One for more on this point.

60. Plato, *The Republic, Plato in Twelve Volumes*, Vol. 3, trans. W.R.M. Lamb. (Cambridge, MA: Harvard University Press, 1967), 419a–445e.

61. *Ibid.*, 444e–445a.

62. *Ibid.*, 445a.

63. Søren Kierkegaard, *The Concept of Irony: With Continual Reference to Socrates*, eds.

and trans. Howard V. Hong and Edna H. Hong (Princeton: Princeton University Press, 1992).

64. Brad Frazier, "Kierkegaard on the Problems of Pure Irony," *The Journal of Religious Ethics* 32, no. 3 (Winter 2004), 418.

65. *Ibid.*, 419.

66. *Ibid.*

67. Søren Kierkegaard, *Concluding Unscientific Postscript*, trans. David F. Swenson (Princeton: Princeton University Press, 1941), 448.

68. *Ibid.*

69. I discuss the implications of Kierkegaard's aesthete when discussing Calvin's egoism in Chapter Five.

70. Kierkegaard, *Concluding Unscientific Postscript*, 448.

71. *Ibid.*

72. *Ibid.*, 449; my emphasis.

73. See the narrative thread that begins on August 2, 1991, and ends August 21, 1993.

74. See Chapter Two for a lengthy analysis of the imagination.

75. Kierkegaard, *Concluding Unscientific Postscript*, 450.

76. *Ibid.*

77. *Ibid.*, 451.

78. December 20, 1987.

79. *Ibid.*

80. There is, of course, no shortage of examples of Calvin's dad proclaiming how much character he has and, moreover, how these values clash with Calvin's own norms for determining what is meaningful in life (see the February 18, 1995, strip for a particularly striking example of this contrast). It is important to note with respect to the December 20, 1987, strip, that the comic balances Calvin's dad's principles ironically by responding to Calvin's own struggle to find meaning in weighing values. By destabilizing an aesthete perched near an ethicist's values, the irony in the December 20, 1987, strip thus functions in a dual capacity insofar as it speaks both to the difference between the ethicist's desire to cling to specific values and the uncertainty regarding values that separates the aesthete from the ethicist.

81. Robert C. Roberts, "Sense of Humor as a Christian Virtue," *Faith and Philosophy* 7, no. 2 (1990), 181.

82. Will Williams stresses that the disjunction is contradictory, but with specific reference to the norm that one carries into an ironic or comic situation. Will Williams, "The Legitimacy of the Comic: Kierkegaard and the Importance of the Comic for His Ethics and Theology," PhD dissertation, Baylor University, 2011.

83. Kierkegaard, *Concluding Unscientific Postscript*, 459.

84. *Ibid.*

85. Williams.

86. *Ibid.*

87. April 17, 1991.

88. *Ibid.*

89. *Ibid.*

90. Calvin does not always subvert his mom when it comes to confronting one another's expectations about his behavior. Elsewhere, Calvin's mom is very much the subversive voice in the exchange. See, for example, the strip from February 26, 1990.

91. November 8, 1993.

92. *Ibid.*

93. Enright, 163.

94. *Ibid.*

Chapter Five

1. August 28, 1995.
2. One sees a similar reaction from Calvin when his dad decides to give him an allowance in the February 26, 1986, strip.
3. See, for example, the August 17, 1989, strip.
4. August 28, 1995.
5. March 11, 1986.
6. See the July 16, 1988, strip.
7. See the July 20, 1992, strip.
8. Kierkegaard, *Concluding Unscientific Postscript*, 378.
9. *Ibid.*
10. *Ibid.*
11. Diogenes Allen and Eric O. Springstead, *Philosophy for Understanding Theology*, 2nd *Edition* (Louisville: Westminster John Knox, 2007), 190.
12. *Ibid.*
13. It is important to stress once again that I make no claim over Watterson's religious identity in discussing such points.
14. *Ibid.*
15. Allen and Springstead, *Philosophy for Understanding Theology*, 190.
16. *Ibid.*, 191.
17. See the December 8, 1988, strip.
18. See the March 14, 1993, strip.
19. Allen and Springstead, *Philosophy for Understanding Theology*, 191.
20. Blaise Pascal, *Pensées*, trans. A.J. Krailsheimer (New York: Penguin Books, 1995), 36. I discuss Pascal in more depth in Chapter Seven and the Conclusion.
21. Kierkegaard, *Concluding Unscientific Postscript*, 378. I discuss issues pertaining to the religious sphere in Chapter Six.
22. I speak here of the various alter egos he adopts; see, for example, the November 27, 1993, strip.
23. November 27, 1993.
24. See the October 10–11, 1993, strips.
25. May 2, 1991.
26. See the point I raise in Chapter Two about literalists.
27. One of the more biting examples of this point can be found in Calvin's engagement with *Chewing Magazine*. The content that provides meaning in this magazine is decidedly less revealing that the smell of roses, but Calvin does not seem to notice. See the narrative thread from May 5 to 8, 1992, to consider this point in more depth.
28. May 2, 1991.
29. *Ibid.*
30. A further example of this point can be found in the April 23, 1995, strip.
31. Particularly good examples of this point occur in the October 13, 1990, and June 19, 1992, strips.
32. Anticipating an observation I will make in Chapter Five, I cite a point Derrida makes concerning Plato's dialogues: "it is often the Foreigner (*xenos*) who questions" (Jacques Derrida, *Of Hospitality: Anne Dufourmantelle Invites Jacques Derrida to Respond*, Cultural Memory in the Present, trans. Rachel Bowlby [Stanford: Stanford University Press, 2000], 5). At the core of Plato's exploration, then, one finds a tension between the individual and the other. This mutuality enables the individual to reconcile the other's presence as part of her/his own search for meaning.
33. Plato, *The Republic*, 359d–360b.

34. *Ibid.*, 360b–360c.

35. *Ibid.*, 360c.

36. Michel Foucault, *Discipline and Punish: The Birth of the Prison, 2nd Edition*, trans. Alan Sheridan (New York: Vintage Books, 1995), 11.

37. *Ibid.*

38. *Ibid.*, 57.

39. August 28, 1986.

40. August 29, 1986.

41. On this point, see James E. Miller, *The Passion of Michel Foucault* (Cambridge, MA: Harvard University Press, 2000), 372–374.

42. Plato, *Gorgias, Plato in Twelve Volumes*, Vol. 3, trans. W.R.M. Lamb (Cambridge, MA: Harvard University Press, 1967), 493e.

43. *Ibid.*

44. *Ibid.*, 493e–494a.

45. Of course, a Platonic reading of value does not cohere with the Deconstructive readings that I offered earlier in this book. I draw on Plato in full recognition of this point in order to discuss the specific image he provides to explain the impossible task someone of the aesthete's mindset undertakes in defining value in immediate terms.

46. Plato, *The Republic*, 514a–520a.

47. *Ibid.*, 514a–514b.

48. *Ibid.*, 515c.

49. *Ibid.*, 516a–516c.

50. *Ibid.*, 516c.

51. *Ibid.*, 517a.

52. January 5, 1993.

53. *Ibid.*

54. Though related tangentially, the strip from September 13, 1992, offers an interesting mirror to this particular strip.

55. March 25, 1992.

56. *Ibid.*

57. Aristotle, *The Ethics of Aristotle: The Nicomachean Ethics*, Penguin Classics, trans. J.A.K. Thomson (New York: Penguin, 1976), I.13. I discuss Aristotle in more depth in Chapter Six.

58. August 4, 1989.

59. October 15, 1986.

60. January 5, 1993. A more nuanced example of the dynamic at work in this strip can be found in the November 27, 1992, strip. At times, then, Calvin remains committed to ignorance, which provides a strange counter-argument to a claim that ignorance is vacuous as a way of living. On the other hand, the fact remains that he could transform the energy he spends on ignorance into pursuits that at the very least fulfill some of his immediate desires.

61. The Greek word λύσιν that Plato uses to describe the event that initiates the prisoner's release (Plato, *The Republic*, 515c) is the noun form of a first-person action. The implication, then, is that the prisoner plays a role in the act that results in his freedom. I am grateful to Dr. AKM Adam at Glasgow University for clarity on this point.

62. January 5, 1993.

63. April 9, 1989.

64. *Ibid.*

65. *Ibid.*

66. *Ibid.*

67. Thomas Hobbes, *Leviathan, in the English Works of Thomas Hobbes of Malmesbury;*

Now First Collected and Edited by Sir William Molesworth, Bart (London: Bohn, 1839–1845), Chapter XIII, available at: http://oll.libertyfund.org/index.php?option=com_staticxt&staticfile=show.php%3Ftitle=585&layout=html#chapter_89842 (accessed 26 July 2011).

68. July 10, 1987.

69. *Ibid.*

70. *Ibid.*

71. *Ibid.*

72. February 10, 1993.

73. *Ibid.*

74. Calvin O. Schrag, *The Self After Postmodernity* (New Haven: Yale University Press, 1997), 1.

75. *Ibid.*, 8.

76. *Ibid.*

77. See my discussion of what constitutes a text in Chapter Three.

78. Schrag, 19.

79. *Ibid.*

80. See Chapter One for a relevant discussion of this point.

81. Schrag, 22.

82. *Ibid.*, 26.

83. See Chapter One for more on this point.

84. See my discussion of the sidewalk and mortality in Chapter Three.

85. Schrag, 37.

86. *Ibid.*

87. Paul Ricoeur's *Time and Narrative* offers a significant discussion of both historical and literary conceptions of how these two themes intersect (and interact). While an extended analysis of any one volume, much less all three, is beyond the scope of this project, it is helpful to point out how Ricoeur relates time to the search for meaning. He writes: "The direction in which to search for the solution is in the enigma itself, just as the enigma is in the solution" (Paul Ricoeur, *Time and Narrative, Volume II*, trans. Kathleen McLaughlin and David Pellaeur [Chicago: University Press of Chicago, 1984], 17). Ricoeur captures the incomplete nature of any narrative context. While certain meanings can be posited and examined, the properties that give rise to these meanings simultaneously deny their longevity. There remains, always, an unknown element within the text (much like Derrida's trace); moreover, this latent presence-as-absence ensures that any solution remains untenable.

88. Schrag, 37.

89. June 8, 1986.

90. *Ibid.* For a good example of how different conceptions of time can be imagined as the basis for different realities, see Alan Lightman, *Einstein's Dreams* (London: Bloomsbury, 1993).

91. Watterson admits that he still enjoys this particular strip (see Watterson, *10th Anniversary Book*, 163).

92. May 1, 1992. Though Watterson is critical of some abstractions that accompany academic discourse (see Watterson, *10th Anniversary Book*, 184), the reference to Gauguin dovetails rather well with the themes that Gauguin explores in his painting. The disjunction that Schrag identifies and Calvin echoes in this strip emerge frequently in Gauguin's work. Rudolf Arnheim could well be summarizing discourse when explaining Gauguin: "If one looks further through Gauguin's oeuvre, one comes across other aspects of a similar conception. There are groups of figures randomly aligned randomly in bunches and held apart by gaps" (Rudolf Arnheim, "Gauguin's Homage to Honesty," *Leonardo* 25, no. 2 [1992]: 177).

Chapter Six

1. May 1, 1992. See Chapter Five, Note One.

2. Textually, there is much at stake in reconfiguring how one individual relates to another. The movement towards an ethicist's value structure is not simply the recognition that others can have value in their own right as opposed to an individual's desires. Hans Georg Gadamer's later work examines this issue specifically. Friendship is, for Gadamer, a complex exchange that engages the other but cannot be reduced to a simple dichotomy of interests: "There is brought in a change in the state of the I and Thou. Every Other is at the same time the Other of an Other" (Hans Georg Gadamer, "Subjectivity and Inter-subjectivity; Subject and Person" *Continental Philosophy Review* 33, no. 3 [July 2000]: 282). As David Vessey explains, in this essay Gadamer affirms and departs from Martin Buber's famous I/Thou relationship as normative for an authentic relationship between people and finds in Aristotle an alternative construct for balancing the various factors of friendship (David Vessey, "Gadamer's Account of Friendship as an Alternative to an Account of Intersubjectivity," *Philosophy Today* 49, no. 5 (2005): 61–67; see also Martin Buber, *I and Thou*, trans. Walter Kaufmann (New York: Touchstone, 1970). Darren R. Walhof highlights that for Gadamer, "solidarity, friendship, and otherness" constellate the examination of this topic (Darren R. Walhof, "Friendship, Otherness and Gadamer's Politics of Solidarity," *Political Theory* 34, no. 5 [October 2006]: 571). In this capacity, I recommend Gadamer insofar as I discuss Aristotle's conception of friendship as illuminating how Calvin and Hobbes relate to one another. See also Hans Georg Gadamer, *Hermeneutics, Ethics, and Religion*, Yale Studies in Hermeneutics, trans. Joel Weinsheimer (New Haven: Yale University Press, 1999).

3. October 25, 1993.

4. October 26, 1993.

5. October 27, 1993.

6. October 28, 1993.

7. Kearney, *Strangers, Gods, and Monsters*, 3.

8. *Ibid.*, 101.

9. *Ibid.*, 4.

10. For a particularly good example of the issues from this short discussion, see the strip from March 22, 1989.

11. Kearney, *Strangers, Gods, and Monsters*, 8.

12. Such characters, Kearney explains, "serve, I am suggesting, as imaginary personifications of our inner alienation, reminding us that we are not at home with ourselves, even at home" (*Strangers, Gods, and Monsters*, 50).

13. See, for example, the strip from July 9, 1992, which exposes this absurdity.

14. Jean-Paul Sartre, *No Exit*, available at: http://www.sartre.org/Writings/NoExit.htm (accessed 26 July, 2011).

15. *Ibid.*

16. Kearney, *Strangers, Gods, and Monsters*, 9.

17. I use the term not to suggest any connotation beyond the fact that Rosalyn is able to unsettle Calvin in a way that others cannot.

18. September 7, 1995.

19. Jacques Derrida, quoted in Michael Nass, "'Alors, qui êtes-vous?' Jacques Derrida and the Question of Hospitality," *SubStance* 34, no. 1 (2005): 8.

20. *Ibid.*, 9.

21. Watterson, *10th Anniversary Book*, 27.

22. Jacques Derrida, "The Principle of Hospitality," *Parallax* 11, no. 1 (2005): 6.

23. September 5, 1995

24. September 7, 1995.

25. October 29, 1993.

26. *Ibid.*

27. *Ibid.*

28. April 22, 1990.

29. *Ibid.*

30. *Ibid.*

31. *Ethics*, VIII.1.

32. *Ibid.*

33. Jason A. Scorza contrasts Aristotle's notion of friendship with Ralph Waldo Emerson's. Specifically, Scorza notes that for Emerson, "there is no obvious justification *as such* to model their conduct towards one another on the norms of friendship" (Jason A. Scorza, "Liberal Citizenship and Civic Friendship," *Political Theory* 23, no. 1 [February 2004]: 85). This contrast buttresses the link between an Aristotelian understanding of friendship and the role of choice at work in committing resources to the development and maintenance of friendship. In light of Emerson's understanding, there is no obvious reason to have friends insofar as virtue — and thus a good life — is filtered through the individual's relationship to her/his broader social context. Consequently, there must be a conscious decision to find meaning outside of this normative context. In Calvin's case, this decision is frequently the basis for his friendship with Hobbes, who helps Calvin find meaning *despite* the contexts in which Calvin finds himself.

34. This arc appears in the strips from September 11 through September 21, 1989.

35. September 21, 1989.

36. *Ibid.*

37. *Ibid.*

38. See my discussion of the home in Chapter Seven.

39. As mentioned elsewhere, it is important to note that Hobbes is, on occasion, the cause of friction in his friendship with Calvin.

40. Aristotle, *Ethics*, VIII.ii.

41. *Ibid.*, VIII.iii.

42. See Chapter Four.

43. October 18, 1986.

44. December 3, 1989.

45. *Ibid.*

46. *Ibid.*

47. *Ibid.*

48. Robert Axelrod, *The Evolution of Cooperation: Revised Edition* (New York: Basic Books, 2006).

49. See Aristotle, *Ethics*, VIII.iii.

50. Aristotle, *Ethics*, VIII.iii.

51. *Ibid.*, VIII.iv.

52. January 8, 1989.

53. "Their chief interest is in their own pleasure and the opportunity of the moment" (Aristotle, *Ethics*, XIII.iii).

54. January 8, 1989.

55. *Ibid.*

56. See November 20, 1985.

57. See December 13, 1989.

58. This narrative occurs from August 20 to September 8, 1990.

59. Aristotle, *Ethics*, VIII.iii.

60. *Ibid.*

61. December 25, 1985.
62. *Ibid.*
63. *Ibid.*
64. Aristotle, *Ethics*, VIII.iii.
65. Plato, *Plato in Twelve Volumes*, Volume 8, trans. W.R.M. Lamb (Cambridge, MA: Harvard University Press, 1955), 207c. Naomi Reshotko offers an engaging analysis of Plato's *Lysis* in "The Good, the Bad, and the Neither Good nor Bad in Plato's Lysis," *Southern Journal of Philosophy* 38, no. 2 (2000): 251–262.
66. August 15, 1993.
67. *Ibid.*
68. *Ibid.*
69. October 8, 1989.
70. *Ibid.*
71. *Ibid.*
72. *Ibid.*
73. *Ibid.*
74. See the strip from February 28, 1990.
75. July 14, 1992.
76. *Ibid.*
77. *Ibid.*
78. *Ibid.*
79. *Ibid.*
80. May 26, 1986.
81. *Ibid.*
82. May 31, 1986.
83. *Ibid.*
84. May 24, 1992.
85. *Ibid.*
86. *Ibid.*
87. Again, Aristotle's notion of true friendship as distinct from a friendship of utility parallels the difference between Kierkegaard's notion of the aesthete as compared to the ethicist. The crucial distinction lies in a willingness to let go of immediate gratification in service of the self in order to engage the other at the cost of one's own desire.
88. Aristotle, *Ethics*, VIII.v.
89. *Ibid.*
90. May 3, 1989.
91. *Ibid.*
92. While I will mostly stick to my earlier claim not to dwell on the imaginative construct that allows Calvin and Hobbes to be friends, it is worth noting in this strip the depth of meaning that this imagined relationship contains. This is, after all, one of the rare occasions when Calvin cries.
93. May 3, 1989.
94. See my discussion of the narrative self in Chapter Five.
95. See my discussion of Blanchot in Chapter Three.
96. April 23, 1989.
97. *Ibid.*
98. *Ibid.*
99. Watterson, *The Complete Calvin and Hobbes, Book One*, 18.
100. *Ibid.*
101. Watterson, *The 10th Anniversary Book*, 11.
102. Aristotle, *Ethics*, VIII.iv.

103. *Ibid.*
104. January 13, 1991.
105. John Caputo, *More Radical Hermeneutics: On Not Knowing Who We Are*, Studies in Continental Thought (Bloomington, IN: Indiana University Press, 2000), 71.
106. December 31, 1995.
107. *Ibid.*
108. Schrag, 26.
109. Blanchot, 77.

Chapter Seven

1. At the outset, I reiterate the point that in examining these concerns I make no claim over Watterson's personal understanding of these issues. Any parallels with a particular faith tradition that emerge in the analysis that follows indicate only my own particular readings and consequent associations.
2. See Chapter Six.
3. May 27, 1986.
4. *Ibid.*
5. May 26, 1986.
6. Allen and Springstead, *Philosophy for Understanding Theology*, 189.
7. May 26, 1986.
8. See Genesis 1–2.
9. See Augustine, *On the Free Choice of the Will, on Grace and Free Choice, and Other Writings*, ed. Peter King (Cambridge, UK: Cambridge University Press, 2010), 3–126.
10. See Genesis 3.
11. This point is of particular interest for those who would align Calvin with his name-sake insofar as the emphasis on an individual's choice generates friction when read alongside *The Institutes*.
12. Gottfried Wilhelm Leibniz, *Theodicy: Essays on the Goodness of God, the Freedom of Man, and the Origin of Evil*, ed. Austin Farrer (New Haven: Yale University Press, 1952).
13. See Voltaire, *Candide*, Norton Critical Editions, ed. and trans. Robert M. Adams (New York: W.W. Norton & Company, 1991).
14. Harold S. Kushner, *When Bad Things Happen to Good People* (New York: Anchor Books, 2004).
15. Kushner, 28.
16. Allen and Springstead, *Philosophy for Understanding Theology*, 188.
17. February 14, 1992.
18. *Ibid.*
19. *Ibid.*
20. Jean-Paul Sartre, *Being and Nothingness, Jean-Paul Sartre: Basic Writings* (Taylor and Francis, Amazon Kindle Edition, 2002), 4,2,iii.
21. Allen and Springstead, *Philosophy for Understanding Theology*, 192.
22. *Ibid.*
23. See my discussion of Plato's leaky jar in Chapter Five.
24. Sartre, *Being and Nothingness*, 4,2, iii.
25. *Ibid.*
26. As has been discussed elsewhere, both textually and ontologically, this displacement is a defining influence.
27. Pascal, 199.
28. *Ibid.*
29. *Ibid.* Pascal thus anticipates the dislocation that characterizes 20th and early 21st

Century Continental Philosophy. Heidegger, for example, discusses the poet's (i.e. the writer's) role as hovering above and then descending into the uncertainty of life's abyss. The *Abgrund*—the void towards which things tend—must be experienced and endured to come to terms with life (see Martin Heidegger, "What Are Poets For?" in *Poetry, Language, Thought*, trans. Albert Hofstadter [New York: Perennial Classics, 2001], 87–140, with a particular emphasis on pp. 90–100).

30. It is important to note at the outset of this point that Pascal's Wager understands God in terms of the Judeo-Christian tradition. This has no necessary bearing on the examples from *Calvin and Hobbes* that I will discuss subsequently.

31. Pascal, 418.

32. *Ibid.*

33. *Ibid.*

34. *Ibid.*

35. July 15, 1992.

36. *Ibid.*

37. July 21, 1993. Elsewhere Calvin assumes that there is an afterlife (November 24, 1990), but he similarly questions the parameters of this existence.

38. Hobbes tends to respond to Calvin's speculation with a measured contentment. See, for example, the April 17, 1986, strip.

39. July 21, 1993.

40. *Ibid.*

41. December 2, 1988.

42. See, for example, the strip from September 20, 1989.

43. For a particularly strong example of this point, see the strip from November 8, 1990.

44. See my discussion of the exchange between Calvin and Hobbes when Calvin attempts to mail a letter to Santa in Chapter Six.

45. December 21, 1987.

46. See the December 18, 1987, strip.

47. December 21, 1987.

48. For a particularly helpful example of this point, see the strip from December 11, 1988.

49. Plato, *Phaedrus, Plato in Twelve Volumes,* Vol. 9, trans. Harold N. Fowler (Cambridge, MA: Harvard University Press, 1925), 246b.

50. *Ibid.*

51. See my discussion of the Allegory of the Cave in Chapter Five.

52. Plato, *Phaedrus*, 246a–b.

53. Allen and Springstead, *Philosophy for Understanding Theology*, 25.

54. April 6, 1992.

55. *Ibid.*

56. Elsewhere Calvin mentions the Devil directly in response to an action he knows not to be "good." See the strip from January 22, 1989.

57. See Genesis 3.

58. Kearney, *Poetics of Imagining*, 2.

59. Kevin Hart, *The Trespass of the Sign: Deconstruction, Theology and Philosophy* (Cambridge, UK: Cambridge University Press, 1989), 4.

60. Ruth M.J. Byrne, *The Rational Imagination: How People Create Alternatives to Reality* (Cambridge, MA: The MIT Press, 2005), 1.

61. Specifically, I point to the strip from October 8, 1993, as an example of a decidedly non–Judeo-Christian reference (though the message on the sign is often attributed to Jesus). In fact, Mahatma Gandhi coined the phrase.

62. This sequences runs from March 18 through April 3, 1991.

63. See the March 20, 1991, strip.

64. See the March 22, 1991, strip.

65. See the March 26, 1991, strip.

66. Hobbes' comment during this exchange links this particular example back to the issues discussed in the last three chapters: "How existential can you get?" (April 1, 1991).

67. April 2, 1991.

68. *Ibid.*

69. April 3, 1991.

70. April 2, 1991.

71. October 18, 1990.

72. There is, of course, an echo of Gyges' Ring in this point. See my discussion of Gyges Ring in Chapter Five.

73. It is interesting to note that, viewed through virtue ethics' prism, the choice in Pascal's Wager should be the same.

74. Aristotle, *Ethics*, I.7.

75. *Ibid.*

76. Aristotle, *Ethics*, VI.5.

77. *Ibid.*

78. October 18, 1990.

79. The reversal at work has the potential to skew understandings of what is good. People can justify a lot of things in pursuit of some good, a strategy that ignores altogether questions of whether the ends really do justify the means. It is fair to ask, for example, if Rosalyn is justified in threatening Calvin with a rat tail (a morally questionable act) if he does not get into the pool (the "good" end, in Rosalyn's calculation); see the July 23, 1986, strip.

80. February 2, 1993.

81. For more on Kant's ethics (and there are many books available that discuss this topic), see TK Seung, *Kant: A Guide for the Perplexed* (New York: Continuum, 2007), especially 90–130; and Gordon Graham, *Eight Theories of Ethics*, (London: Routledge, 2004), especially 98–127.

82. Immanuel Kant, *The Metaphysical Elements of Ethics*, trans. Thomas Kingsmill Abbott, available at http://www.forgottenbooks.org/info/9781605069869 (accessed 23 July, 2011), 3.

83. *Ibid.*, 4.

84. Immanuel Kant, *Foundations of the Metaphysics of Morals*, quoted in Gordon Graham, *Theories of Ethics: An Introduction to Moral Philosophy with a Selection of Classic Readings* (New York: Routledge, 2011), 308.

85. For simplicity's sake I bracket the claim that a commitment to uphold the imperative is a kind of virtue.

86. May 22, 1993.

87. *Ibid.* Susie is well aware of what she is doing, a point she concedes when she tells Calvin, "Usually, if you're calling any shots at all, you're not eating worms" (May 20, 1993).

88. Consequentialist ethics approach questions of a choice's value in these terms. Probably the most famous consequentialist system is Utilitarianism, which Jeremy Bentham in *An Introduction to the Principles of Moral Legislation (Collected Works of Jeremy Bentham*, eds. J.H. Burns, and H.L.A. Hart (Oxford: Oxford University Press, 1996) and John Stuart Mill made famous in *Utilitarianism*, 2nd Edition, ed. George Sher (Indianapolis: Hackett Publishing Co., 2002). The basic premise is that good decisions are those that bring the greatest amount of good to the greatest number of people, wherein good is defined in accordance with the pleasure principle.

Conclusion

1. August 28, 1992.

2. The prayer's ability to speak to a variety of contexts is apparent in numerous ways. It provides an important reflection for use in Alcoholics Anonymous, and it is the subject of numerous life improvement books (a quick search of amazon.com will yield more choices than anyone could realistically make). The spectrum of uses speaks to the prayer's embeddedness in contemporary culture, which in turn makes its emergence in *Calvin and Hobbes* slightly less surprising.

3. James W. Fernandez and Mary Taylor Huber, "Irony, Practice, and the Moral Imagination," *Irony in Action: Anthropology, Practice, and the Moral Imagination*, eds. James W. Fernandez and Mary Taylor Huber (Chicago: The University of Chicago Press, 2001), 261.

4. It is worth recalling Pascal's Wager, which encourages an individual to choose to believe in God precisely because there is no guarantee about God's existence.

5. How Calvin missed Susie from so close is a cautionary tale; even the best of plans can succumb to the kind of mysterious influence at work in this strip.

6. The Book of Job is a classic text in this regard. Though Job is upright and God-fearing, God is still willing to bet with the Devil on Job's loyalties. The result is a string of experiences that systematically break down the life Job builds through his good choices. The story of Job is, moreover, a classic touchstone for theodicy (see my discussion of this point in Chapter Seven), which emphasizes further the caution that irony suggests.

7. February 19, 1993.

8. *Ibid.*

9. *Ibid.*

10. Pascal, 188.

11. This narrative arc runs in the February 27 through March 18, 1989, strips.

12. March 18, 1989.

13. *Ibid.*

14. *Ibid.*

15. December 18, 1995.

16. *Ibid.*

17. *Ibid.*

18. *Ibid.*

19. See Matthew 1:18–2:12 and Luke 2:1–20.

20. Hernandez and Huber, 261.

21. Kearney, *Poetics of Imagining*, 3.

22. The reference to Heidegger's conception of humanity as *Dasein* is crucial in this respect. As thrown, humans must understand their condition while subject to spatial and temporal reminders that they lack the originary anchor to understand life apart from its dislocation. For more on this point, see Heidegger, *Being and Time*, 40. For a helpful overview of Heidegger's work, see David R. Cerbone, *Heidegger: A Guide for the Perplexed* (New York: Continuum, 2008); and William Blattner, *Heidegger's Being and Time: A Reader's Guide* (New York: Continuum, 2007).

23. See my discussion of Calvin Schrag in Chapter Five.

24. Kearney, *Poetics of Imagining*, 6.

25. *Ibid.*, 3.

26. Kearney, *Strangers, Gods and Monsters*, 230.

27. *Ibid.*, 231.

28. See my discussion of the sidewalk in Chapter Three.

29. Kearney, *Strangers, Gods and Monsters*, 231.

30. December 28, 1995.

31. *Ibid.*
32. *Ibid.*
33. Hobbes offers a contrast that furthers this point with his one comment in this strip. Whereas Calvin's jammies accent his vulnerability, Hobbes is brimming with confidence when he says, "That's why tigers sleep in the buff!" (December 28, 1995). The contrast extends Calvin's awareness of humanity's vulnerability by emphasizing that tigers — like other animals — do not have to endure the burden of constructing a self.
34. August 7, 1995.
35. See the October 14, 1993, strip.
36. Bachelard, 183.
37. Pascal, 44.
38. See the April 16, 1986 strip.
39. Pascal, 44.
40. *Ibid.*
41. *Ibid.*
42. "Imagination cannot make fools wise, but it makes them happy" (Pascal, 44).
43. Pascal, 44.
44. *Ibid.*
45. See the strip from November 18, 1985.
46. See my discussion of the home in Chapter Three.
47. January 7, 1989.
48. *Ibid.*

Bibliography

Allen, Diogenes, and Eric O. Springstead. *Philosophy for Understanding Theology, 2nd Edition*. Louisville: Westminster John Knox, 2007.

Allen, Graham. *Intertextuality, 2nd Edition*. London: Routledge, 2011.

Aristotle. *The Ethics of Aristotle: The Nicomachean Ethics*. Penguin Classics. Trans. J.A.K. Thomson. New York: Penguin, 1976.

Arnheim, Rudolf. "Gauguin's Homage to Honesty." *Leonardo* 25, no. 2 (1992): 175–177.

Augustine. *On the Free Choice of the Will, On Grace and Free Choice, and Other Writings*. Edited by Peter King. Cambridge, UK: Cambridge University Press, 2010.

Axelrod, Robert. *The Evolution of Cooperation: Revised Edition*. New York: Basic Books, 2006.

Bachelard, Gaston. *The Poetics of Space: The Classic Look at How We Experience Intimate Places*. Translated by Maria Jolas. Boston: Beacon Press, 1994.

Barthes, Roland. *The Death of the Author*. Translated by Richard Howard. Accessed July 5, 2011. Available at: http://evans-experientialism.freewebspace.com/barthes06.htm.

_____. *The Pleasure of the Text*. Translated by Richard Miller. New York: Hill and Wang, 1975.

Beck, Richard. "The Theology of Calvin and Hobbes' Part I, Chapter I: 'Virtue Needs Some Cheaper Thrills.'" Accessed July 1, 2011. Available at: http://experimentaltheology. blogspot.com/2008/08/theology-of-calvin-and-hobbes-part-1.html.

Bentham, Jeremy. *An Introduction to the Principles of Moral Legislation (Collected Works of Jeremy Bentham)*. Edited by J.H. Burns and H.L.A. Hart. Oxford: Oxford University Press, 1996.

Blanchot, Maurice. *The Space of Literature*. Translated by Ann Smock. Lincoln, NE: University of Nebraska Press, 1989.

Blattner, William. *Heidegger's Being and Time: A Reader's Guide*. New York: Continuum, 2007.

Booth, Wayne C. *A Rhetoric of Irony*. Chicago: The University of Chicago Press, 1974.

Buber, Martin. *I and Thou*. Translated by Walter Kaufmann. New York: Touchstone, 1970.

Byrne, Ruth M.J. *The Rational Imagination: How People Create Alternatives to Reality*. Cambridge, MA: The MIT Press, 2005.

Calvin, John. *The Institutes of the Christian Religion*. Translated by Henry Beveridge. Peabody, MA: Hendrickson Publishers, Inc., 2009.

Campanelli, John. "'Calvin and Hobbes' Fans Still Pine 15 Years After Its Exit." *The Plain Dealer*, 1 February 2010. Accessed June 17, 2011. Available at: http://www.cleveland.com/ living/index.ssf/2010/02/fans_still_pine_for_calvin_and.html.

Caputo, John. *More Radical Hermeneutics: On Not Knowing Who We Are*. Studies in Continental Thought. Bloomington, IN: Indiana University Press, 2000.

Cerbone, David R. *Heidegger: A Guide for the Perplexed*. New York: Continuum, 2008.

Clark, Timothy. *Derrida, Heidegger, Blanchot: Sources of Derrida's Notion and Practice of Literature*. Cambridge, UK: Cambridge University Press, 1992.

_____. *The Poetics of Singularity: The Counter-Culturalist Turn in Heidegger, Derrida, Blanchot and the Later Gadamer.* Edinburgh: Edinburgh University Press, 2005.

Coleridge, Samuel Taylor. *Biographia Literaria*, Accessed July 24, 2011. Available at: http://www.gutenberg.org/cache/epub/6081/pg6081.html.

Cook, Albert. "The Meta-Irony of Marcel Duchamp." *The Journal of Aesthetics and Art Criticism* 44 (Spring 1986): 263–70.

Cunningham, Valentine. *Reading After Theory.* Oxford: Blackwell Publishers, 2002.

Currie, Gregory. *Narratives and Narrators: A Philosophy of Stories.* Oxford: Oxford University Press, 2010.

De Gruyter, Walter. "The Psychological Appeal of Bill Watterson's Calvin." Accessed June 17, 2011. Available at: http://plos.deepdyve.com/lp/de-gruyter/the-psychological-appeal-of-bill-watterson-s-calvin-3OAGYbZkGl.

Derrida, Jacques. "Deconstruction and the Other: An Interview with Richard Kearney." *Debates in Continental Philosophy: Conversations with Contemporary Thinkers.* Edited by Richard Kearney. New York: Fordham University Press, 2004, 139–156.

_____. "Living On." *Deconstruction and Criticism.* New York: Continuum, 2004.

_____. *Of Grammatology.* Translated by Gayatri Chakravorty Spivak. Baltimore: The Johns Hopkins University Press, 1997.

_____. *Of Hospitality: Anne Dufourmantelle Invites Jacques Derrida to Respond.* Cultural Memory in the Present. Translated by Rachel Bowlby. Stanford: Stanford University Press, 2000.

_____. *The Post Card.* Translated by Allan Bass. Chicago: University of Chicago Press, 1987.

_____. "The Principle of Hospitality." *Parallax* 11, no. 1 (2005): 6–9.

_____. *Writing and Difference.* Translated by Alan Bass. London: Routledge and Kegan Paul, 1978.

Enright, D.J. *The Alluring Problem: An Essay on Irony.* Oxford: Oxford University Press, 1986.

Fernandez, James W., and Mary Taylor Huber. "Irony, Practice, and the Moral Imagination." In *Irony in Action: Anthropology, Practice, and the Moral Imagination*, edited by James W. Fernandez and Mary Taylor Huber, 261–264. Chicago: The University of Chicago Press, 2001.

Foucault, Michel. *Discipline and Punish: The Birth of the Prison.* 2d ed. Translated by Alan Sheridan. New York: Vintage Books, 1995.

Frazier, Brad. "Kierkegaard on the Problems of Pure Irony." *The Journal of Religious Ethics* 32, no. 3 (Winter 2004): 417–447.

Gadamer, Hans-Georg. *Hermeneutics, Ethics, and Religion*, Yale Studies in Hermeneutics. Translated by Joel Weinsheimer. New Haven, Yale University Press, 1999.

_____. "Subjectivity and Intersubjectivity; Subject and Person." *Continental Philosophy Review* 33, no. 3 (July 2000): 275–287.

_____. *Truth and Method.* Translated by Joel Weinsheimer and Donald G. Marshall. New York: Continuum, 2004.

Graham, Gordon. *Eight Theories of Ethics.* London: Routledge, 2004.

_____. *Theories of Ethics: An Introduction to Moral Philosophy with a Selection of Classic Readings.* New York: Routledge, 2011.

Hart, Kevin. *The Trespass of the Sign: Deconstruction, Theology and Philosophy.* Cambridge, UK: Cambridge University Press, 1989.

Heidegger, Martin. *Being and Time.* Translated by John Macquarrie and Edward Robinson. London: SCM Press, 1962.

_____. *Hölderlin's Hymn "The Ister."* Translated by William McNeill and Julia Davis. Bloomington, IN: Indiana University Press, 1984.

_____. *Poetry, Language, Thought.* Translated by Albert Hofstadter. New York: Perennial Library, 1971.

Hobbes, Thomas. *Leviathan, in The English Works of Thomas Hobbes of Malmesbury; Now First Collected and Edited by Sir William Molesworth, Bart.* London: Bohn, 1839–1845.

The Holy Bible: Containing the Old and New Testaments. New Revised Standard Version, Oxford World Classics. Oxford: Oxford University Press, 1995.

"An Interview with Bill Watterson." Accessed June 17, 2011. Available at: http://bob.bigw. org/ch/interview.html.

Jasper, David. *Rhetoric, Power and Community: An Exercise in Reserve.* London: MacMillan, 1993.

_____. *The Study of Literature and Religion: An Introduction.* London: MacMillan Academic and Professional, Ltd., 1992.

Jeanrond, Werner. *Theological Hermeneutics.* London: SCM Press, 1994.

Kant, Immanuel. *Critique of the Power of Judgment.* Translated by Paul Geyer and Eric Matthews. Cambridge, UK: Cambridge University Press, 2000.

_____. *The Metaphysical Elements of Ethics.* Translated by Thomas Kingsmill Abbott. Accessed July 23, 2011. Available at: http://www.forgottenbooks.org/info/978160506 9869.

Kearney, Richard. "Deconstruction, God, and the Possible." In *Derrida and Religion*, edited by Yvonne Sherwood and Kevin Hart, 297–308. New York: Routledge, 2004.

_____. *On Paul Ricoeur: The Owl of Minerva.* Farnham, UK: Ashgate, 2004.

_____. *Poetics of Imagining: Modern to Post-Modern.* Edinburgh: Edinburgh University Press, 1998.

_____. *Strangers, Gods and Monsters: Interpreting Otherness.* London: Routledge, 2003.

_____. *The Wake of the Imagination: Toward a Postmodern Culture.* London: Routledge, 1998.

Kierkegaard, Søren. *The Concept of Irony: With Continual Reference to Socrates.* Edited and Translated by Howard V. Hong and Edna H. Hong. Princeton: Princeton University Press, 1992.

_____. *Concluding Unscientific Postscript.* Translated by David F. Swenson. Princeton: Princeton University Press, 1941.

Kneller, Jane. *Kant and the Power of Imagination.* Cambridge, UK: Cambridge University Press, 2007.

Knight, Mark, and Louise Lee. "Introduction." In *Religion, Literature and the Imagination: Sacred Worlds*, edited by Mark Knight and Louise Lee, 1–7. New York: Continuum, 2010.

Kushner, Harold S. *When Bad Things Happen to Good People.* New York: Anchor Books, 2004.

Lacoste, Jean-Yves. *Experience and the Absolute: Disputed Questions on the Humanity of Man.* Perspectives in Continental Philosophy. Translated by Mark Raftery-Skehan. New York: Fordham University Press, 2004.

Leibniz, Gottfried Wilhelm. *Theodicy: Essays on the Goodness of God, the Freedom of Man, and the Origin of Evil.* Edited by Austin Farrer. New Haven: Yale University Press, 1952.

Lightman, Alan. *Einstein's Dreams.* London: Bloomsbury, 1993.

Makkreel, Rudolf A. *Imagination and Interpretation in Kant: The Hermeneutical Import of the Critique of Judgment.* Chicago: University of Chicago Press, 1990.

Martell, Nevin. *Looking for Calvin and Hobbes: The Unconventional Story of Bill Watterson and His Revolutionary Comic Strip.* New York: Continuum, 2010.

Mill, John Stuart. *Utilitarianism.* 2d ed. Edited by George Sher. Indianapolis: Hackett Publishing Co., 2002.

Miller, James E. *The Passion of Michel Foucault.* Cambridge, MA: Harvard University Press, 2000.

Nass, Micahel. "'Alors, qui êtes-vous?' Jacques Derrida and the Question of Hospitality." *SubStance* 34, no. 1 (2005), 8.

Parker, Fred. *Scepticism and Literature: An Essay on Pope, Hume, Sterne, and Johnson.* Oxford: Oxford University Press, 2003.

Pascal, Blaise. *Pensées.* Translated by A.J. Krailsheimer. New York: Penguin Books, 1995.

Plato, *Plato in Twelve Volumes.* Vol. 3. Translated by W.R.M. Lamb. Cambridge, MA, Harvard University Press, 1967.

_____. Vols. 5 & 6. Translated by Paul Shorey. Cambridge, MA: Harvard University Press, 1969.

_____. Vol. 8. Translated by W.R.M. Lamb. Cambridge, MA: Harvard University Press, 1955.

_____. Vol. 9. Translated by Harold N. Fowler. Cambridge, MA, Harvard University Press, 1925.

Raschke, Carl A. *Theological Thinking: An Inquiry.* AAR Studies in Religion. Atlanta: Scholars Press, 1988.

"Release ... The Complete Calvin and Hobbes: Fans from Around the World Interview Bill Watterson." Accessed July 1, 2011. Available at: http://www.andrewsmcmeel.com/calvinandhobbes/interview_text.html.

Reshotko, Naomi. "The Good, the Bad, and the Neither Good nor Bad in Plato's Lysis." *Southern Journal of Philosophy* 38, no. 2 (2000): 251–262.

Ricoeur, Paul. *From Text to Action: Essays in Hermeneutics, II.* Translated by Kathleen Blamey and John B. Thompson. London: The Althone Press, 1991.

_____. *Hermeneutics and the Human Sciences.* Translated by John B. Thompson. Cambridge, UK: Cambridge University Press, 1981.

_____. *The Rule of Metaphor: The Creation of Meaning in Language.* Translated by Robert Czerny, Kathleen McLaughlin, and John Costello. New York: Routledge, 2009.

_____. *Time and Narrative, Volume II.* Translated by Kathleen McLaughlin and David Pellaeur. Chicago: University Press of Chicago, 1984.

Roberts, Robert C. "Sense of Humor as a Christian Virtue." *Faith and Philosophy* 7, no. 2 (1990): 177–192.

Sandifer, Philip. "When Real Things Happen to Imaginary Tigers." *Interdisciplinary Comic Studies* 3, no. 3 (2007). Accessed June 17, 2011. Available at: http://www.english.ufl.edu/imagetext/archives/v3_3/sandifer/.

Sartre, Jean-Paul. *Being and Nothingness.* In *Jean-Paul Sartre: Basic Writings.* Taylor and Francis, Amazon Kindle Edition, 2002.

_____. *No Exit.* Accessed July 26, 2011. Available at: http://www.sartre.org/Writings/NoExit.htm.

Schrag, Calvin O. *The Self after Postmodernity.* New Haven: Yale University Press, 1997.

Schroeder, Timothy, and Carl Matheson. *The Architecture of the Imagination: New Essays on Pretence, Possibility, and Fiction.* Edited by Shaun Nichols. Oxford: Clarendon Press, 2006.

Scorza, Jason A. "Liberal Citizenship and Civic Friendship." *Political Theory* 23, no. 1 (February 2004): 85–108.

Seung, T.K. *Kant: A Guide for the Perplexed.* New York: Continuum, 2007.

Shakespeare, William. *Hamlet.* Norton Critical Editions. Edited by Robert S. Miola. New York: W.W. Norton & Company, 2010.

Spitz, Ellen Handler. *The Brightening Glance: Imagination and Childhood.* New York: Anchor Books, 2007.

Thisleton, Anthony C. *Hermeneutics: An Introduction.* Grand Rapids: William B. Eerdmans Publishing Co., 2009.

Vattimo, Gianni. *The Adventure of Difference: Philosophy after Nietzsche and Heidegger.*

Translated by Cyprian Blamires, with the assistance of Thomas Harrison. Cambridge, UK: Polity Press, 1993.

Vaught, Carl G. *Metaphor, Analogy, and the Place of Places: Where Religion and Philosophy Meet.* Waco, TX: Baylor University Press, 2004.

Vessey, David. "Gadamer's Account of Friendship as an Alternative to an Account of Inter-subjectivity." *Philosophy Today* 49, no. 5 (2005): 61–67.

Voltaire. *Candide,* Norton Critical Editions. Translated by Robert M. Adams. New York: W.W. Norton & Company, 1991.

Walhof, Darren R. "Friendship, Otherness and Gadamer's Politics of Solidarity." *Political Theory* 34, no. 5 (October 2006): 563–593.

Watterson, Bill. *The Calvin and Hobbes 10th Anniversary Book.* London: Warner Books, 1995.

_____. *The Complete Calvin and Hobbes.* Kansas City: Andrews McMeel Publishing, 2005.

Williams, Will. "The Legitimacy of the Comic: Kierkegaard and the Importance of the Comic for His Ethics and Theology." PhD Dissertation. Baylor University, 2011.

Wolfreys, Julian. *Derrida: A Guide for the Perplexed.* New York: Continuum, 2007.

Wood, Sarah. *Derrida's Writing and Difference.* New York: Continuum, 2009.

Index